Revised Edition

CONSTRUCTIVE PLAY

Applying Piaget in the Preschool

George E. Forman
University of Massachusetts

Fleet Hill
University of Massachusetts

Addison-Wesley Publishing Company

Menlo Park, California · Reading, Massachusetts
London · Amsterdam · Don Mills, Ontario · Sydney

This book is published by the Addison-Wesley Innovative Division.

ISBN-0-201-20084-8
11 12 13 14 15 - ML - 95 94 93

PREFACE

Teachers who would like a practical guide for applying Jean Piaget's insights to preschool education should read this book. *Constructive Play* contains over 100 simple games that have been deduced from Piaget's principles of child development. These open-ended activities allow children to design their own rules and play at their own pace. The objectives of these games range widely. Children can learn about the physical world, about the social world, and particularly about the role of the self in the construction of knowledge. Therein lies our title—*Constructive Play*.

This book is actually a sequel to an earlier, more theoretical book, *The Child's Construction of Knowledge: Piaget for Teaching Children*, by George Forman and David Kuschner, published by the National Association for the Education of Young Children. The current book can be used with or without the parent book, since we provide a sufficient rationale for the play activities for you to understand their significance from the perspective of child development. But for the person who wants a deeper insight we have cross-referenced this practical guide with the theoretical text.

If you find the chapter titles strange, it is because the activities are named after the principles that we used to invent them. We also think that our "deductive" approach of going from the Piagetian principles to classroom activities may make our suggestions conspicuously novel. For example, we suggest that children should have painting easels that spin, pencils that continuously leak, bowling pins that can be drained of sand, paint brushes that are bent, toy trains that cannot come off their tracks, holes in the middle of tables, and art paper attached flat to the ceilings. Once the rationale is understood, however, these activities are taken as obvious extensions of common sense.

The first chapter is an overview of the principles that generated the activities and of our basic approach to teaching young children. This chapter is divided into three parts. The first describes the *content* of the activities, the second the type of *progress* that teachers can expect to see in children, and the third the nature of the *process* that children use in constructive play.

The subsequent chapters contain three unique features: detailed descriptions of child behavior, so that you can become a better observer of your own pupils; examples of good and bad teaching; and a focus on developmental trends. Generally, we have divided the examples of the child at play into categories of younger and older children. In this way you can get a clearer understanding of how the child develops and not just of whether a child succeeds in some all-or-none fashion.

The activities are designed for children 2 to 5 years old. Given the high-action nature of these games, with the whole body used in many cases, they are appropriate to children even in the lower end of this age range. Most of the games can be played with inexpensive, recycled materials, and many are no more than new uses for what most preschools have in stock, such as blocks, sand tables, and pasteboard boxes.

Throughout the book, but mostly in Chapter Three, we highlight social interaction and social development, even though the activity may involve objects as well. For example, we use hospital stretchers that take two children to handle and Plexiglas easels with which two children can take part in a painting "dialogue." And we have a teacher bandage her arms to elicit help from the children. In the last chapter we discuss how often we educators make false distinctions between social and cognitive development and between people and objects. In that chapter we also explain our overarching goal: to help the child develop *interactive consciousness*, the awareness of how one's actions and attitudes create what one presumes is "out there" in the external world.

Our thanks begin with the first staff of teachers at the School for Constructive Play, where all of these activities were field tested. Clara Blum, George Fine, Tom Healy, Barbara Kay, and Lisa Pritcher, under the leadership of Fleet Hill, coalesced into a beautiful balance of talent, energy, and support that made innovation thrive in the cradle between the reasonable and the possible. We also thank Peter Oldziey, head teacher during the second year, for his compassionate disposition and consummate artistry as a mime and as a teacher of young children. The book itself would have lacked life without Arthur Mann's photography and would have lacked clarity without the artwork by Joan Green. We hope that the students at the University of Massachusetts who were at one time or another involved with the design of the curriculum for the School for Constructive Play will feel that this book is also a product of their blended, but not anonymous, effort. Our reviewers, Sandra Anselmo of the University of the Pacific and Carol Falender of the University of California at Los Angeles, offered many useful suggestions for improving the quality of this book.

When *Constructive Play* was originally published in 1980, its intended audience was primarily preschool teachers. In the meantime we have had many discussions with parents and providers of home programs for young children. In this revised edition of *Constructive Play* we have, therefore, decided to expand our activities for home use. The home offers many opportunities that might be difficult in a classroom, as well as vice versa. The home offers many opportunities for learning activities that require a close and intimate understanding of the individual child, your child. The home offers a greater chance to carry over an activity from one day to the next because there are fewer children using the same space and same materials. Parents have a greater chance to understand the meanings children attribute to experience, because parents are with the child more and bear witness to the important events in the young child's life. There are also certain social situations that are perfect for staging a learning encounter that could not happen at school, such as forms of social and physical knowledge that occur during bedtime rituals, bathing rituals, and family meals.

Yet we would like to caution the parent that we are not keen on the new push for parents to create the "superbaby." It is distressing to find so many books for parents and teachers that are based on a "training" model of education, a model that makes a false dichotomy between learning and play, a model that pushes children into school-type lessons for preschoolers. Our goal for young children's education should not be to speed up development nor to prepare the child for first grade, but rather to spread out development and to build on to the gains of infancy and toddlerhood.

We invite parents, as well as teachers, to see the value of play, at least a certain type we call constructive play, in fostering the young child's ability to solve problems in both the material world of science, math, art, and craft as well as the social world of language, social understanding, and justice. We believe the Piagetian perspective will foster competence, curiosity, and creativity through its respect for how the particular child, through play, constructs meaning for the events encountered. The thoughtful parent can do more than anyone to help the child develop at a natural pace from infancy to childhood if only we learn to emphasize what the child is, rather than what we want the child to be.

George Forman
Fleet Hill
1983

CONTENTS

Chapter One

An Introduction to Constructive Play

BACKGROUND

The child learns through play. In fact, Jean Piaget insists that meaningful learning requires a period of open-ended "playing around" with the alternative ways of doing something. Constructive play is a preliminary stage in the development of skill, and skill is preliminary to creativity. Play that does not increase skill may be pleasurable in a narrow sense but is not what we would call constructive. Constructive play, by definition, builds on itself to increase the competence of the child. This competence, in turn, increases the child's pleasure by making even more creative acts possible. The cycle repeats itself, with the new creative acts becoming yet another form of play at a higher level of understanding until they are mastered. Development, as Piaget phrases it, is a spiral of knowledge moving upward through alternating play and skill.

Another characteristic of constructive play, central to Piaget's theory of development, is that the player herself must do the constructing. Meaningful learning is more likely when the child herself invents the alternative ways of doing something. In fact, if the child is only imitating alternatives modeled by a teacher or a parent, we do not call it play; it becomes drill. But if the child herself invents some new way to do something, the chances are that she will also better understand how that new way relates to the other ways that she has performed the act in the past. Of course, things are not that simple. As you will see, modeling by a teacher or parent is sometimes just what is needed to prime the child to begin her own inventive play. The point remains, however, that invention by the child is essential to constructive play.

The occurrence of constructive play, as opposed to random play, requires the presence of a supportive environment and a sensitive teacher or parent. The teacher, in particular, prepares the classroom with specific objectives but does not hold a commitment to those objectives once the children enter the room. The teacher watches the children enter each prepared area and notes what goals they establish for themselves. To improve his or her sense of what the children are thinking, the teacher may parallel-play near them. At opportune times the teacher can ask a brief question or present a small problem by changing some part of the game, such as moving a target to a new position or changing the shape of a train track. Then, the teacher can take note of how the children solve the problem. He or she can learn a great deal at these times.

Many details for just how a teacher can learn from observing children and how a knowledge of child development can be applied in the classroom (or playroom) are presented in the parent book to this handbook, *The Child's Construction of Knowledge: Piaget for Teaching Children* (by George Forman and David Kuschner). We recommend that those of you who have not seen *The Child's Construction of Knowledge* refer to it for clarification of the more theoretical points of Piaget's theory and its application to education. The parent book also covers in detail teaching style in general, such as methods for entering children's play without distracting them from their self-set goals. We will from time to time cross-reference this handbook with the relevant sections in *The Child's Construction of Knowledge* (henceforth abbreviated CCK).[1]

The activities described in this book have all been field tested in an experimental preschool program called the School for Constructive Play. This school meets for 2½ hours on Monday, Wednesday, and Friday afternoons at the Human Development Laboratory School of the University of Massachusetts in Amherst. During our first year the program was directed by George Forman, with Fleet Hill as head teacher. During our second year Forman continued as director, with Peter

---

[1] Published in 1977 by Brooks/Cole Publishing Company, Monterey, California.

Oldziey as head teacher; Hill worked with us as a consultant. The program is based on Piaget in the sense that our activities are planned to maximize constructive play.

To this end, we emphasize three things. First, the content of the activities deals with areas of knowledge that Piaget has identified as critical for development. Second, the progress of each child is viewed from a Piagetian perspective. And third, the process of how a child learns and how a teacher or parent facilitates the child's learning also is discussed from a Piagetian perspective. The remainder of this chapter explores these three emphases on content, progress, and process.

CONTENT

The Learning Encounter Defined

Teachers and parents usually do not place young children, particularly 2- and 3-year-olds, at a table or in a circle and have an extended lesson on some single theme. Learning for the young child is more episodic. The theme changes frequently; the rhythm ebbs and flows. Within any single activity, such as digging in the sand table, the child may have numerous encounters with events that are educational. The child may discover, for example, that a spoon handle makes different marks in the sand than the bowl of the spoon does. He may also learn that his playmate Jenny cannot see an object on his side of the sand bucket, that he can dig to the bottom of the sand table, and that he enjoys his play more if he takes a few minutes to negotiate sharing the shovels with his playmates. All of these encounters are educational and add their value to his knowledge base.

At the School for Constructive Play we find it useful to think about learning encounters as occurring within general activities. The activity is the label adults attach to what takes place in an area of the room (block play, dramatic play) or the general objective for the area (such as cooperative play). The learning encounter is the particular aspect of the physical or social world that the child is dealing with at a moment in time. This distinction between adult objectives and child behavior emphasizes the child-centered approach to our teaching. We always ask what learning encounters occur within a particular activity. In this handbook we will maintain this distinction by giving you both the theoretical rationale for an activity and numerous examples of actual learning encounters that occur during the activity.

Two Aspects of All Learning Encounters:
Correspondences and Transformations

When a child encounters some potentially educational event, he must deal with one or both of the following aspects of a problem. First, he must figure out how something present is similar to or different from some more familiar event. Second, he must figure out how something that is similar to or different from a more familiar event got to be that way. The former aspect concerns *correspondences*, the latter concerns *transformations*.

Correspondences. Some problems call on the child to make correspondences between objects or events, to compare and contrast. For example, to place a piece from a jigsaw puzzle in the form board, the child has to establish the correspondence between the puzzle piece and the puzzle space. Or say the child leaves his cup of juice on the window sill while he takes a turn at a game. When he returns to the window sill, he sees that there are now two cups of juice there. He wonders which one is his. That is, he has to establish a correspondence between the cup he had before and one of the two cups he now sees. These are everyday examples of encounters with the need to establish correspondences.

Correspondences come in two types. The first, *identity*, involves a correspondence between two sightings of the same object. The second type, *equivalence*, involves a correspondence between two or more objects.

In identity, the child asks Is this the same one that I had before? The child looking for his own cup of juice on the window sill is facing a correspondence-of-identity problem. Here are two more examples:

> Jane rides a tricycle, leaves it for a moment, and returns, only to find another child on what she presumes to be her tricycle. Actually, this is a different tricycle. She argues with the suspected poacher that it is indeed the same tricycle that she had been riding before.

> Carmen is playing with a big glob of clay. She has worked hard to get it into the shape of a ball. She leaves the table for a moment to get a wooden spoon to make imprints in her ball of clay. Meanwhile, a nearby child pounds a fist mark into the big ball of clay. Upon returning to the table, Carmen sees the hole in her clay and grabs a quantity from her neighbor to fill up the hole. The neighbor complains, but Carmen explains that somebody took clay from her ball. She has failed to make a correspondence between the identity of the clay forming the rim of the fist mark and that same clay when it was in the form of a ball some minutes before. In fact, that possibility never occurs to her.

In equivalence, the child asks Is this one similar to or different from another one? There are two or more objects involved in the comparison, as in the case of the jigsaw-puzzle piece and the hole in the form board. It would be incorrect to say that the hole is identical to the piece. In the precise sense, only one and the same object can be identical to itself on different sightings. The hole is equivalent to the piece or corresponds to the piece. Events can also be equivalent. Pushing the right-side rope on a clothesline pulley is equivalent to pulling the left-side rope. Both actions make the basket on the left side come toward the person. Raising the top end of an incline is equivalent to lowering the bottom end. Both actions cause a ball to roll down the incline faster. Children can be found solving all sorts of equivalence correspondences. Here are some examples:

> Jessica sees seven plates around the table. She has been asked by the teacher to give each place a peanut butter spreader. She places one spreader for each plate, thereby making a correspondence between the number of plates and the number of peanut butter spreaders.

> David is digging a tunnel in the sand. He needs a long-handled spoon to break through to the other side of his mound. He reaches for the spoon, but another child picks it up and begins to play with it. David pauses, looks over to the kitchen corner, darts off, and returns with the arm of a broken doll that he remembers from the previous day. The doll's arm does the burrow job nicely.

> Chris sees a caterpillar on a bush outside the bay window of the classroom. He smiles broadly and runs over to the terrarium with rapt anticipation. "Wow, it's still here," he says when he sees the caterpillar behind the glass. "That must be another one!" he exclaims, pointing outside. Chris has solved the difference between an identity correspondence and an equivalence correspondence.

In general, correspondences are established either between two sightings of the same object or event (identity) or between different objects or events (equivalence). These terms are useful in understanding what a child encounters in her attempts to solve particular problems. Yet many problems involve more than a simple comparison or contrast between things as they are at some moment in time. Children are also called on to deal with how things change. This brings us to the notion of transformations.

Transformations. A transformation is something that the child (or adult) does to change things. (It could be, instead, an imaginary reconstruction of how something changed.) Each transformation implies a beginning state and an ending state; the transformation comes in between. Clear water (initial state) can be transformed into pink water (ending state) by adding red food coloring (the transformation).

If the child wants to reestablish the initial state, she must know something about how the pink water became pink. Say this child, for her own reasons, wants the pink water to be clear; that is, she wants to establish a correspondence between this water, currently pink, and her ideal image, the clear water. (A transformation that *undoes* a previous transformation is called a *reversal*.) Given that this water, previously clear, has been changed into a pink solution, we can say that the child wants to reverse the transformation clear-to-pink. There are two basically different ways for children to reverse a transformation, the *inverse* and the *reciprocal*.

Take the inverse reversal first. Suppose the child thinks that someone added color to the clear water. She may take a piece of cloth and pour the pink water through it. She is trying to do the direct reverse of what she assumes has been done to the clear water. Color has been added; she tries to subtract it. Piaget calls this direct form of reversal (subtracting what was added) the inverse reversal. In this particular case the inverse reversal fails, because the cloth does not strain out the color.

There is another type of reversal possible. The child can make the pink water clear again by adding large quantities of clear water. At least this action takes her in the direction that she prefers. Adding clear water is not the direct opposite to adding red food coloring; it is more indirect. But it has the same effect of reversing the initial change clear-to-pink. Piaget calls this type of reversal the reciprocal reversal. Note that both the terms *inverse*[2] and *reciprocal* apply only to those cases where the child attempts to undo an initial transformation. Inverse and reciprocal define the relation between two transformations, not between the beginning and ending states of a single transformation.

These terms will be used throughout the remainder of this handbook. The teacher who can see the structure of the child's learning encounter is a better prepared teacher. He can protect the child's work space when the child is engrossed in exploring different forms of correspondences and transformations. He can even, because of his understanding of the child's behavior, make unobtrusive yet very valuable entries into the child's play (see CCK pp. 107–114 and pp. 135–140).

Four General Types of Learning Encounters

The content of our curriculum is divided into four general types of learning encounters: establishing identity and equivalence, changing perspective, representing motion, and making functional relations. Talking about these types is more specific than saying that an encounter involves correspondences and transformations, because that can be said about any learning encounter. But the types are general enough to serve as topics for the next four chapters of this book. Each chapter heading—Chapter Two's is *Establishing Identity and Equivalence*—refers to a general problem or goal with which children frequently deal. The chapter itself is then further divided into general activities—for example, Sand Play or the Overhead Projector—which are then discussed in terms of the learning encounters germane to that chapter.

Remember that the learning encounter is not a game that a teacher or parent designs to teach a particular concept. Learning encounters occur within the game or activity and should always be defined from the child's point of view. The games and activities within each chapter could have been classified a hundred different ways. For example, sand play can be used to develop all four of the general types of learning encounters. But we feel that it is important to keep the theory central, so we have made some choices regarding the predominant learning encounter that a given activity will probably present to the child.

---

[2] In CCK we used the terms *negation* and *reciprocal action* (Chapter Nine). But it is clear in Piaget's recent work that *negation* is a more general term than applies here.

TABLE 1-1.   The Four Types of Learning Encounters

1. Establishing Identity and Equivalence
   A. Identity: Same object, different state
                     Same object, different use
   B. Equivalence: Different object, same state
                        Different object, same use
2. Changing Perspective
   A. Self-to-object perspective
   B. Self-to-other perspective
3. Representing Motion
   A. Freezing motion
   B. Unitizing motion
   C. Imagining motion
4. Making Functional Relations
   A. Changing direction
   B. Changing distance
   C. Changing limits

We do not want readers to come away from this book thinking of these activities as special-purpose, didactic exercises, as is true of most of Montessori's materials. To look at these activities as if they "exercised" some mental faculty, such as taking another child's point of view, would be completely antithetical to a Piagetian perspective. The child should invent her own problems, and the teacher or parent should pay close attention, without intervention, to the child's spontaneous play (see Chapter Six in CCK). We will try to cross-reference these activities as much as possible in order to break the mind set that each activity is designed for only one purpose. By cross-referencing, we mean that an activity introduced under one general category will be mentioned again in other general areas.

We have tried to strike a balance between a good use of theory and a good use of flexibility. Although there is a danger in designing activities too specifically, there is an equal danger in a mindless "let's see what the children do with these" approach to activities. Materials for painting and making collages, recycled materials, and jigsaw puzzles are often placed in the classroom with no more justification than that "they develop hand-eye coordination." Because every waking motion the child makes involves hand-eye coordination, this could not possibly be a good justification for these materials. We are not saying that painting and collages should be eliminated; we are saying that teachers and parents need to think more specifically about their educational value. We hope that the organization that we present in this book for thinking about early education will be somewhere between the overly general and the overly specific, somewhere between "hand-eye coordination" and "it teaches them the numeral 3."

Establishing Identity and Equivalence.   Learning encounters that establish identity and equivalence occur when the child confronts a question of the basic sameness of a person, object, or event.

The child may wonder if what he sees now is in some sense the same as what he saw earlier—that is, if it has the same identity. For example, in shadow play the child watches the teacher cast the shadow of an object hidden in a shadow box. If the teacher rotates a spoon in front of the light source, the shadow grows thin and straight as the spoon moves to its profile. The child, who has identified the object casting the shadow as a spoon, is perplexed. He now says "a knife" when the teacher asks "What do I have in my hand?" This child is confronting a problem of establishing identity.

Identity encounters have two variations. In the example above the object itself remained the same, but the states of the object changed. First it had one shape of shadow, then another shape of shadow. We will call this version *same object, different state.*

The other variation involves a change in the use, even though the object remains the same. For example, the child comes into the snack corner and finds that there is no chair for him. He spies a plastic bucket in the role-play corner, gets it, turns it upside down, and sits on its bottom. He has changed the use of the bucket from an object that holds things in (water, sand) to an object that holds things up (the child himself while sitting). He has not physically rearranged the parts of the object. The identity of the physical object has been conserved. We call this the *same-object, different-use* variation of transforming identity.

Note that in the example above the child did not change the identity. So it might seem inaccurate to call what happens in these encounters establishing identity. But the label makes sense if we think in terms of a range of ability across children of different ages. For a younger child the bucket has but one use: to hold things inside of it. For the older child the bucket's use is not confused with its identity of being "a bucket." Rather, its use is relative to its position, what the child needs it for, and so on. For the younger child changing the use is like changing the identity. That is, you can no longer call the bucket a bucket if you are sitting on the bottom of this plastic thing. So what we mean by the phrase *establishing identity* is simply that a child is faced with a situation in which he must figure out if the identity of something is the same in spite of certain changes.

The other half of this type of learning encounter deals with equivalence. Here the child must make some type of correspondence between two different objects or events. For example, at the School for Constructive Play we have a scaled-down, three-dimensional model of our outdoor playground. We put this in the bay window of the classroom, from where the child can also see the outside playground. We play games in which a staff member sits on a piece of outdoor equipment, such as the jungle gym, and the child tries to place a little wooden person in the scaled-down model at the same place. That is, the child has to make a mental transformation of the real person's position into a position in the model.

Establishing equivalence, like establishing identity, has two variations. They are *different object, same state* and *different object, same use*. The example of the playground model illustrates the first variation. The state (position) of the staff member outside is the same as the state of the wooden person, but the two objects that indicate these states are different. The child has to establish an equivalence between the real person and the wooden person.

Different-object, same-use encounters place the child in a situation in which one object needs to function as another object. At the risk of momentary confusion, let's go back to the inverted bucket. As we saw, using the bucket first to carry water and then to sit on is a case of same object, different use. The identity remains the same; the use changes. Looking at the bucket as if it were a chair would be a case of different object, same use. The child has established an equivalence between the bucket and the chair in terms of a common use. The fact that the same situation—the child's using a bucket to sit on—can be seen as two different types of learning encounters should be a reminder that these activities have many purposes. Within each activity there is always a vast variety of learning encounters going on simultaneously.

Encounters that call for thinking about equivalences often involve symbols. The playground model is a symbol of the outdoor playground. The child needs to understand the first as a stand-in for the latter in order to make the required correspondences between the two. Photographs are symbols of real events. If a child is trying to figure out where a particular photograph was taken (different object, same state), she must first understand that the photograph (one object) is equivalent to the real landscape (the other object).

Sometimes the symbol is not embodied in something tangible such as a three-dimensional model or a photograph. The child himself has to conjure up the mental image. For example, say a child darts off to the role-play corner to get a doll's arm to help him burrow a tunnel through his mound of sand. This child sees the long-handled spoon being used by another child and *imagines* the equivalence between that spoon and the doll's arm he saw the day before.

Because of the demands on representational thinking, encounters that deal with equivalences are generally more difficult than those dealing with identities. This is true only because the physical difference between two objects can be greater than the physical difference between two sightings of the same object. Therefore, the mental effort to establish a correspondence between two different objects is greater than the effort to establish a correspondence between the same object on two different occasions.

Changing Perspective.　As in all learning encounters there is a correspondence involved in changing perspective. Unlike identity and equivalence, however, this type of encounter entails a correspondence between two views of something. The child has to understand, for instance, that his view may or may not correspond to another child's view of the same thing. On occasion it is important for the child to transform her view into the other child's view so that she can better understand the other child's behavior.

For example, Trina sees Howie laughing while looking at a ball of modeling clay. At least it looks like a ball from where Trina is sitting. From Howie's perspective it is a silly clown's face. If Trina does not consider that Howie may be seeing something different than she, she may erroneously conclude that Howie, for some unexplainable reason, is laughing at a ball of clay. Trina pauses, thinks, and then changes her view into Howie's view by going around to his side of the table. Piaget would call Trina's behavior an act of *decentering* from her own view. Instead of exclusively centering on her own (egocentric) view, she takes Howie's view, at least in the physical sense of walking to his side of the table.

Not all transformations of perspective are physical; some are mental, as would be the case if Trina figured out what angles Howie was seeing of the object without walking around to stand next to him. We will save this fine distinction for our discussion of the activities themselves.

We will make one general distinction now between two types of perspectives. Some encounters require the child to think about the relation between himself and an object, a *self-to-object* perspective. The child must figure out where he should place himself in space to get a desired view of something or how he should place the object to get a desired perspective. The Gate Game, one of our activities at the School for Constructive Play, is a good example. The child is given a tennis ball, stands on one side of a waist-high table, and rolls the ball through archways cut into a cardboard partition in order to knock over a target on the other side. To successfully hit the target, the child has to place himself at a certain position along the back edge of the table so that his body, the archway, and the target are all aligned. He can roll the ball through the archway from most any position, but there is only a small range of positions from which he can hit the target. He must think about his perspective relative to the archway *and* the target.

In other learning encounters the child needs to think about another child—what that child sees and what that child is doing. We call this a *self-to-other* perspective, sometimes termed social decentration. Take the simple example of two children trying to carry a stretcher together. At least one of the children has to think about the other child. If they are both egocentric, they may not make much progress with the stretcher. The child who follows has to anticipate where the other child is heading and what that other child is about to do and then make adjustments in how he carries his end. Children who have difficulty in this sort of cooperative venture may be having trouble taking the other child's point of view.

We are using the word *perspective* here in more than just a visual sense. Sometimes the perspective is a matter of someone's intentions, feelings, or needs. Some activities place the children in situations where it becomes important for them to consider how another child is feeling. These situations can also be called self-to-other encounters with perspective.

Representing Motion. Many times a child has to deal with the path taken by a moving object. For example, to understand that a playground swing, when released, will not drop straight to the ground, the child has to think about the arc that the swing usually makes. Somehow he must represent, in his mind, the usual path of this particular object in motion, or else he might inadvertently hit a playmate with the swing. Yet motion itself is not something that the child can look at, as he would the color or shape of the swing. Motion is an occurrence and therefore has to be either reconstructed from memory or anticipated in advance. That is, the child has to represent the shape of the motion.

In the activities designed to maximize this type of encounter, we do many things to make it easier for the child to represent the shape of motion. One of our activities, called the Swinging Sand, consists of a plastic ketchup bottle, the kind with a nozzle, suspended upside down by a string hanging from the ceiling. As the bottle swings, it continuously drains fine, dry sand onto black construction paper on the table below. The sand leaves a physical trace of the motion. In other activities the child has to think about the shape of a motion without seeing a physical trace. But the general theme in all of these activities is our attempt to encourage the child to represent the shape of a motion, as opposed to representing the shape of a non-moving object. (See CCK, pp. 52–58, for more details on why knowing the shape of a motion is important from a Piagetian perspective.)

We have distinguished three types of learning encounters that involve the shape of motion. The first we call *freezing motion.* The Swinging Sand is a good example. The motion of the swinging ketchup bottle is "frozen" by the sand trace. If the bottle makes a circular motion and stops, the action of the bottle is forever gone; but that action has left behind a trace of its form. Other examples of freezing motion are painting with the fingers or with a brush, driving a tricycle through a water puddle and beyond onto dry cement, and making etches in the beach with a stick.

On other occasions the child encounters discontinuous motion, such as when he drags a stick along a picket fence. Here, the motion is broken up into parts by each slap of the stick against the next picket. At the School for Constructive Play we make deliberate attempts to pose these types of encounters. We call them *unitizing motion.*

In activities that unitize motion, the child breaks a continuous action into parts. A plastic spool rolls down an incline lined with "speed bumps," cardboard humps that make the spool bounce but do not stop its rolling altogether. The child can change the spacing of the speed bumps and thereby change the action of the rolling spool. This means that the same motion can be "unitized" in different ways. The continuity of the action has been conserved, but the "division" of that action changes with the spacing of the speed bumps. While we are using terms such as *unitizing* and *division* in a metaphorical sense, it is consonant with Piaget's theory of intellectual development to consider these action games as precursors to academic skills such as measurement and arithmetic. A precursor is an elementary form of a more advanced skill (see pp. 7–11 in CCK).

In the activities mentioned so far under representing motion, the motion has been perfectly visible to the child. Some of the activities that we designed encourage the child to imagine the form of a motion. We call this *imagining motion.* One of our best examples is a variation of the old shell game. The teacher or parent hides a tennis ball under one of three berry cartons turned upside down. In the middle of the table where the game is played is a hole bigger than the tennis ball but smaller than the perimeter of the carton. As the adult moves the carton hiding the ball, the child watches closely. The adult makes sure that this carton passes over the hole in the table. The teacher or parent stops moving the cartons and invites the child to find the tennis ball.

Two-and-a-half-year-olds will look under all three cartons, 3-year-olds will do the same and then look under the table, and 4-year-olds will dive under the table as soon as they see the carton hiding the ball pass over the hole. They have no difficulty imagining the motion of the ball, even though they do not actually see that motion (or hear it, because the adult has placed a pillow on the floor directly under the hole in the table).

These invisible motions, what Piaget calls invisible displacements, usually require some sort of inference. The child must relate different things he sees in order to conclude where the object has gone. In the shell game the child who successfully solves the problem reasons as follows: The ball is under that basket. When the basket moves, the ball moves with it. When the carton moves over the hole, the ball is over the hole. Holes are empty spaces. Empty spaces do not support objects that are smaller than they are. *Therefore*, the ball must have dropped through the hole.

Dealing with invisible displacements requires more, as you have just been told, than *seeing* a hole in the table. The 2½-year-olds can *see* the hole, but they cannot construct the relations between the motion of the basket, the motion of the ball, and so on in order to *understand* the hole. This is what Piaget means when he says that knowledge is not a copy of some external object, but rather the result of a constructive process of relating things that are seen. The seeing (copying, if you will) is no problem; the knowing (construction, if you will) is the problem (see pp. 50–52 in CCK).

Making Functional Relations.   The last general type of learning encounter, more than the preceding three types, deals with cause-and-effect relations. When a child makes a functional relation, she discovers how a change in one thing corresponds to a particular direction of change in something else. For example, if a child throws a ball to the floor harder than she did in her previous throw (an increase in force), she soon realizes that the ball will bounce higher than before. In this case, an increase in one thing (force of throw) corresponds to an increase in another thing (height of bounce). The functional relation, then, is direct.

In other cases the functional relation between two changes could be inverse. What if the child is holding a ball of play dough instead of a rubber ball? When she throws this ball harder to the floor, the height of the ball itself decreases. The relation between the force of the throw and the standing height of the ball of play dough is an inverse functional relation.

Understand that in functional relations the child is doing more than making a simple cause-and-effect association between two events, such as realizing that one throw leads to one bounce of the ball. The child is doing something more complicated. She is thinking about different forces of throwing (one variable) and relating that variable to another variable (different heights of bounce). That is, the child is relating one *change* with another *change*, not merely one instance with another instance. (See CCK, pp. 76–78, for a more complex discussion of where functional relations fit into the course of cognitive development as a whole.)

Two variables can have a variety of functional relations. A change in one variable might cause a change in the *distance* something else moves. Force of throw and height of bounce would be a good example of a functional relation in which the effect is a change of distance. Another example would be the relation between the change in the pitch of an incline and the distance that a ball rolls after the child releases it on that incline. The steeper the child makes the pitch, the farther the ball rolls across the floor.

Some functional relations create changes in the *direction* an object moves in space (not to be confused with the direction, direct or inverse, of the relation itself). For example, the child can change the direction of the ball's bounce by changing the angle at which the ball strikes the floor. Here the direction can be varied all the way from a bounce straight up to what is actually a roll across the floor.

The last variety of functional relations occurs when the very *limits* of the effect are changed. In certain special situations the child can experiment with the range of possible outcomes, the limits of the effect. Since this variety of functional relations is slightly more difficult to explain than distance and direction, let's look at a specific activity we designed at the School for Constructive Play, the Weighted Wheels.

The Weighted Wheels are actually sections of cardboard tube about 5 inches in diameter. Inside the cardboard ring we place a Tinker Toy dowel, like a spoke, that cuts a diameter. On the dowel we place a heavy bead that can be positioned anywhere along the dowel. The bead serves as a counterweight. If the child pushes the bead flush against the inside of the cardboard ring, the ring, when rolled and allowed to stop on its own, always stops in the same orientation. (The ring is painted half green and half brown to accentuate the orientation of the final resting position.) Alternatively, if the bead is placed in the center of the dowel, the ring can come to rest in any position. By changing the placement of the bead the child can vary the *limits* of the final resting position of the ring. Limits in most of these types of activities that we have designed range from the single possibility (a determined effect) to an unlimited number of possibilities (a random effect).

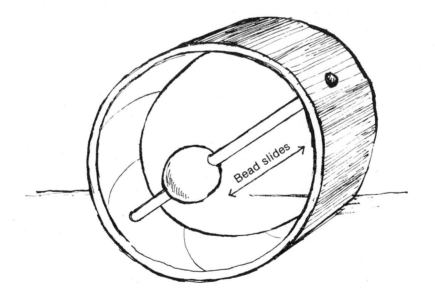

FIGURE 1.1.   The Weighted Wheel.

Summary.   These four general types of learning encounters define the content of all the activities that follow. The children, in spontaneous play with other children and with materials, are in the continual process of establishing identity and equivalence, changing perspectives, representing motion, and making functional relations. And they can do all of these types of encounters within a single activity, in spite of the fact that we have listed an activity under one, or perhaps two, types of learning encounters. As you read the actual observations on the children at play, you will see the fullness and richness of the child's inventiveness. The child makes guesses about what sorts of correspondences and transformations will occur and puts these guesses to the test in truly constructive play, play that builds on itself.

But how should we describe progress? If we are to understand the constructive nature of play, we will need some way to talk about development from one level to the next. We will devote the following section to what constitutes development.

PROGRESS

Six General Levels of Cognitive Development

As mentioned in the previous section, the problems that children encounter involve both correspondences and transformations. One way, then, to look at development is to consider how children improve in their ability to relate correspondences and transformations. We can observe what errors or successes the child has in his attempts to understand how two things are similar and how they could be changed to be different (or how two things are different and how they could be changed to be similar). If we submit the child's task to this sort of analysis, we can begin to see different levels of ability and, in like measure, different degrees of progress.

For example, say that Maureen, age 5, sees, in a book, a photograph of a seascape painting and a photograph of the sea itself. Because she assumes that both photographs are of the real sea, she cannot possibly understand questions about the style of painting the artist used to create the painted seascape. Her error is in making a correspondence between the real sea and the photograph without understanding how that correspondence was produced—that is, how the real sea was transformed by printing a painting in one case versus printing a photograph in the other case. Progress can be described, in this and many other examples, as learning how correspondences are produced and how correspondences are changed. Once Maureen thinks about the two ways that the real seascape can be changed, she can begin to understand the full range of differences between the two prints that she previously thought to be similar.

Now, what are the varying degrees of this ability in the preschool years? Piaget[3] has identified six levels of ability, more like six steps that children make from about age 1 to 7. These levels pertain to how children think about change itself.

TABLE 1-2. Piaget's Six Levels of General Cognitive Development

1. Level of Absolute Differences
2. Level of Opposition
3. Level of Discrete Degrees
4. Level of Variation
5. Level of Functions
6. Level of Exact Compensation

Absolute Differences. Sometimes an infant does not understand that an object has been changed. She is more likely to act in a way that indicates she believes that what she now sees is a completely new object. She may show great interest in a rolling ball but cannot care less the moment it stops rolling. It appears from her behavior that the stationary ball is not for her the same ball as before. The stationary ball has an *absolute difference* compared with that same ball when rolling.

To give another example, sometimes a 1-year-old will get upset if he sees his

[3] See Piaget's *The Development of Thought* (New York: Viking Press, 1977). The concepts are Piaget's, but the first author has coined the names of the six levels for purposes of easy discussion.

ball of clay gently rolled by an adult into a sausage shape. Does he think that the sausage shape is somehow an absolutely different object? It could be, of course, that he just doesn't like his balls rolled into sausages. But it is even more likely that he considers the process irreversible and that therefore he now has a different object. As far as his thinking is concerned, the adult has *exchanged* his ball for a sausage, rather than just *changing* the shape of his ball.

Opposition.   As children witness and create more changes themselves, they become more sophisticated about how things change. At this second level they understand that certain qualities of an object can change without necessarily exchanging that object altogether for a new one. Using the example above, a child at the level of opposition may say to the adult "Not long—make it round again!" These words indicate that the child understands that the object was not exchanged, but rather that a quality (shape) of one object was changed. What the child understands is that this quality was changed from what he wanted (round) to the *opposite* of what he wanted (long). He then says: "Long is not round. Make it back." Here it is clear that the child thinks of long as the opposite of round.

At this level of thinking any change is bounded by two extremes. There is round versus long, tall versus short. But there is not yet a middle term, an in between. The child has conserved the identity of the object; it is the same object. But the child does not yet consider intermediate states between the two extremes. His understanding of change seems to be all or none. Here are a few examples of this form of thinking, the level of opposition.

Aaron tries to bowl over a plastic bowling pin. The ball is rather light, and the bowling pin is filled with sand. When he discovers that he can empty sand from the pin, he decides to lighten the pin so that the ball can knock it over. Aaron feels compelled to empty all of the sand from the pin, even though this process is taking many minutes and is delaying his gratification of bowling again. It seems that Aaron thinks "If the pin is too heavy, I must empty the sand." The idea of emptying *some* of the sand does not appear satisfactory, or perhaps Aaron is not able to think about *some sand. Some sand* is in between *all* and *none.* To very young children change is a process of canceling out altogether—changing the presence of something into its absence, or turning one state (full) into its complete opposite (empty).

Here is one more example about the level of opposition, this time from a case of social interaction between two children. Hattie, age 3½, announces to the group at the sand table "Marika is my best friend." Jimmy, also 3½ and a close companion of Hattie's, says "What about me?" "You're my best friend too," Hattie replies to Jimmy. Then she adds "But not Herbie." It seems clear from Hattie's remarks that she has two categories of playmates, her best friends and her not-friends. She makes no distinctions within either group, and these groups are categorical opposites. This type of dichotomous thinking is typical for children this age.

Discrete Degrees.   In the third level children solve problems that require thinking about intermediate points between opposite extremes. There comes a time in the child's development when it seems funny to call everything either tall or not-tall, short or not-short. What is the child going to call intermediate states? Say the child sees three little wooden people, Daddy, Mommie, and Baby. Daddy is tall, Baby is not-tall, but what does he call Mommie? It seems funny to call her both "tall" and "not-tall" at the same time. So the child invents the term *"a-little-tall."* The Mommie doll is neither extreme.

At this level the child can actually think about degrees of some quality of an object, which is more than just thinking about the presence or absence of that quality. In fact, the child has begun to think about the quality itself, and not the object alone. When the child says "a-little-tall," he is concerned about tallness, not just the Mommie doll. You could say that the child has qualified a qualification. In truth, the child is beginning to think about how he thinks about objects, whether saying "tall" is sufficient to distinguish the middle-size doll from the largest doll.

We have not yet mentioned why this level is called discrete degrees. There are certain limitations to this level of thinking. The child thinks about these qualities—such as tall, a-little-tall, and not-tall—as if they are discrete, disconnected categories. He may understand that "a-little-tall" comes after "not-tall" but does not consider that "a-little-tall" is more of something (height) than "not-tall." This form of thinking can even occur when the same object is transformed, such as when clay changes from tall to a-little-tall to not-tall. The successive states are not yet understood as variations on a single continuum of change. It is as if the qualities made an absolute shift from one category to another. The term *a-little-tall* is more like the name of the object to which it applies, a label like a dogtag. Even though the child has invented a category that fits in between the two extremes, he still does not understand that there exists an infinite number of such categories. That is, he does not yet understand that "tallness" can vary along a perfectly continuous, unbroken dimension of change. Here is a good example of a child still at the level of discrete degrees.

Say the teacher creates three globs of finger paint on the table, each glob a different color. The blue glob is about the size of a quarter (call it Q); the red glob, somewhat larger, is about the size of a golf ball's diameter (call it G); and the yellow glob is about the diameter of a tennis ball (call it T). Jenny approaches the table and, as children often do, labels these globs of paint. "This one [T] is big, this one [Q] is small, and this one [G] is sort of big." The teacher picks up on Jenny's spontaneous remarks by asking "Which one has more?" (Unfortunately this is an ambiguous question, because both G and T are more than something.) Jenny points to T, perhaps because she equates *more* with *most*. Now the teacher, recovering from her ambiguous first question, asks "Is the red [G] more than the blue [Q]?" Jenny replies "It's sort of more," which indicates that she probably just substituted the word *more* for the quality of size itself.

To Jenny, the concept of more is not completely developed. Ideally, *more* implies a continuous variation that can be used when talking about all three globs. Glob T is more than G or Q, and G can also be called more if compared with Q. To say "sort of more" is to think that G does not quite deserve the label "more." The words *more* and *sort of more* are applied to T and G, respectively, as if that is their name. And names, while they can be arranged in a particular order, are discontinuous, discrete things; not variations along a single quality of size. This brings us to the next level of how children think about change.

Variation. At the level of variation the child understands that the state, or quality, of an object is but a point along a continuum and that between any two points there is always another point. There are points between tall and a-little-tall and even points between the betweens. The child begins to use words like *more, less, farther,* and *heavier* correctly, applying them to describe the continuous nature of change rather than to label the discrete and static state of objects and events. Jenny, on reaching this higher level, could understand that both the red glob and the yellow glob can be called more because more refers to the continuum itself rather than to some absolute amount.

Here are some other examples of children in either the level of discrete degrees or the level of variation. Several children are waiting their turn to bowl over plastic pins. Hattie says "I'm second." The first child takes his turn, and then the ball accidentally rolls through a ventilator grate and cannot be retrieved without the aid of a long stick. The game is temporarily interrupted while another person goes for a stick. Hattie gets very upset: "But I'm second. You said I could be second. I gotta be second." Of course, part of Hattie's distress is the fear that the ball cannot be retrieved and that she will miss her turn altogether. But it is interesting how she seems to be thinking about "second." She probably thinks about "second" in very concrete terms, such as getting the ball after Howie bowls. "Second" is her label for a discrete act at a particular point in time rather than any point on the continuum of time that happens to be next after the first.

A more advanced child, at the level of variation, could understand that, while second is always after first, it is not referenced by some particular action. On the continuum of time, if there are no ball throws after Howie's throw, the next throw is necessarily the second. Time passes continuously and does not start and stop in discrete degrees.

As in the above example it is difficult to say with certainty how much of a child's distress is due to such problems in thinking. Yet it is certain that these limitations in thinking do cause distress. "Your hands are very small," Trina says to Marc, who seems to shy at this remark. "Yes," a sympathetic parent comments from the side, "but Marc's hands will soon be bigger." At this Marc becomes even more distressed. "I don't want big hands!" he says emphatically. It is apparent that Marc is imagining adult-size hands on his wrists, as if these big hands just appeared all at once. An older child, in the level of variation rather than discrete degrees, would have understood that the hand—and for that matter the whole body—will gradually pass through an indefinite number of imperceptible differences until it is big. In other words, even though his hand will be *bigger* tomorrow than it is today, that does not mean his hand will be—by some discontinuous spurt of growth or in some absolute sense of the term—a *big* hand.

Functions.   Not too long after a child learns to think of variations, she begins to think about how two variations affect each other. This is called the level of *functions*.

Let's go back to the example of the ball of clay being rolled into a sausage. At the level of variation the child understands that there are an indefinite number of states between round and oblong. But she may not know that, at the same time the clay is getting longer, it is also reducing in height. She may know that, yes, it is less tall and, yes, it is longer; but she cannot coordinate both changes in order to reason that length is an *inverse function* of height. She does not yet understand that the two changes determine each other; that is, the greater the length, the lesser the height. This is what the child at the level of functions can understand.

There are many examples in the average preschool classroom and home of children's successfully dealing with functional relations.[4] Brian yells to his friend "Throw it harder. You have to throw it harder to get it all the way here!" Brian knows that strength of throw and distance traveled have a *direct* functional relation. Katie tells the teacher "Better close the window. The wider the window is open, the more wind blows in." She understands the direct functional relation between the opening and the wind.

At first, the child may be aware of two different variations but will not figure out their functional relation. This characterizes the child in the level of variations. The child knows, for example, that an incline board can be tilted along an infinite number of pitches from horizontal to vertical. The child may also know that a ball rolling down that incline can travel at many different speeds along a variation from not moving to very fast. Yet the child still may not be able to coordinate the pitch of the incline to produce the particular speed that he desires. Knowing that both variations exist, however, probably gives him the idea to experiment with their coordination and to discover the cause-and-effect relation between the two variations.

---

[4]We are using the phrase *functional relation* here in the same way that we used it to define one of the four general types of learning encounters.

Exact Compensation.   There is a level beyond the level of functions. But it will not overly concern us, because it deals with children more advanced than most pre-schoolers, children about 6 or 7 years old. This level bears mention, though, because it will help you understand where the previous levels are aimed. This sixth level is called the level of *exact compensation*. The child now adds a particular type of understanding to functional relations. She understands not only that one variation is functionally related to another variation but also that the amount of change in one variation is matched *exactly* by an equal amount of change—the *compensatory* change—in the other variation.

Take the example of a rope looped over a pulley hanging from the ceiling. In the level of exact compensation the child knows that, if the basket on one span moves down 3 feet, then the other span necessarily moves up exactly 3 feet. The child not only knows that the two variations function in an inverse direction, she also understands that a change in one is exactly compensated for by an equal change in the other. To use the example of the ball of clay, the child understands that, when the ball is rolled out, an increase in the length of the ball is exactly compensated for by a decrease in height. Because these variations are exactly compensatory, the child can then reason that the total amount remains the same throughout these changes. The total length of the rope looped around the pulleys remains the same; the total amount of clay in the ball remains the same. This is what Piaget calls conservation of quantity (see CCK, pp. 69–78).

Summary.   These six levels of thinking about change span the ages from about age 1 year to age 6 or 7. Each level builds on the previous level. Absolute differences come to be treated as opposites of each other. Up is not-down and tall is not-short.

But these opposites are all or none until the level of discrete degrees. Then, in-between categories are formed, such as almost-up, a-little-tall, and the like. But these categories are not yet true variations along a continuum.

During the level of variation the child begins to think of these categories as arbitrary points along a continuum of continuous change with an indefinite number of categories along it. Yet variations themselves are still treated as independent events. The child does not yet coordinate two variations to understand their functional relation.

At the level of functions the child can understand that a particular direction of change (increase or decrease) in one variation will cause a particular direction of change in some other variation. Yet the child still does not understand that the amount of change in one variation exactly compensates for a change in the other variation.

This happens at the level of exact compensations and is the source of conservation of quantity. At this sixth level the child now reasons deductively; that is, he knows that the changes *must* (by logical necessity) compensate for each other exactly. The deductive thinking is a totally new form, because the child has made an inference that goes beyond the raw experience. He has deduced, for example, that, because it is the same rope that is only being moved around the pulleys, the length of each span *must always* be the same length. He does not know this from some specific encounter with the rope. He knows it from the logic of relating facts to conclusions. While this last level—what Piaget calls the period of concrete operations—is the ultimate aim of all the prior levels, it will not overly concern us, because this book is primarily focused on the child from 2 to 5 years of age.

These six levels apply to cognitive development at large and will aid our attempts to describe the child's progress. In the chapters that follow we will identify, by citing our observational records, cases in which children evidence these different levels of thinking. This should help you understand how children are more advanced than they were months before yet less advanced than they will be in the future.

These six levels of cognitive development pertain to any and every case in which a child is trying to deal with what things are and how they change (correspondences and transformations). These levels express the progress that is potential in the child's spontaneous play. However, these six levels are so general that we decided to pull out from them some more-specific developmental trends. We did this in order to capture the vividness and immediacy of children in the act of playing, discovering, and inventing.

These developmental trends are derived from Piaget's six levels, but the trends are somewhat easier to see in actual child behavior. We will not spend a great deal of time explaining their derivation, but we trust that you will see their relation to general Piagetian theory.

Developmental Trends

On rereading everything that we had written in Chapters Two through Five, we ended up with a list of examples in which children were showing different levels of ability at the same task. We decided to list these examples at the end of each of the four chapters. We further decided to divide these examples into four categories of developmental trends. These categories, as we mentioned above, were derived from Piaget's general levels of cognitive development, but the trends are couched in terms that specifically relate to what we all see children doing. The fact that the same developmental trends summarize each chapter will help you see how all the activities deal with the same, unitary intelligence.

We will not labor over the definitions of these trends, because their full meaning will become apparent only after you read the activities and observational records in the following chapters. We present them here just to explain the organization of the handbook and to better relate our theory to practice.

Two Within One. At first, children have difficulty understanding how one thing can have two values or two functions. They later progress to an understanding of the double aspect of single states or events. This developmental trend occurs within a variety of task domains. Children come to understand that one line in a drawing can represent two edges of, say, two adjacent bricks; or that a pun has two somewhat opposite meanings; or that the number 3 is both bigger and smaller, depending on the comparison number; or that putting the cap "on" the toothpaste tube means both pushing in and twisting. These are all problems that can exhibit development in the ability to see the two within one.

Decentering from an Egocentric Perspective. At first, children notice states and events that directly relate to themselves but seem unable to take any other perspective, even when they are asked to do so. Eventually they learn how to decenter, to back away from an exclusive focus on themselves. Decentering from the egocentric perspective can take the form of a closer analysis of events that occur at some distance from the self. Or it can involve a better understanding of how another child is feeling. Or it can entail a greater facility in using conventional words instead of words the child herself invents.

From Opposite Extremes to Middle Degrees. As we mentioned in the earlier section on levels of development, children have difficulty thinking about the states between two opposite extremes. This difficulty is obvious when a child has to change something that does not work. For example, if a paintbrush is not spreading paint, the child either discards it for a new one or dunks it up to his hand in the paint container—he does one extreme or the other. Eventually, he learns to consider middle states and even states between the ends and the middle. This can take the form of pushing a toy car partway to the end of a track, filling a water glass only partway to reduce spills when carrying it, and compromising with a friend by waiting a *little* longer before having a turn. In these more advanced cases the children show an increased ability to think about middle degrees rather than to think only in terms of extreme opposites.

Seeing the Dynamic within the Static. Many situations require that the child remember or infer how something moves. A photograph, often called a snapshot because it is a static representation of a dynamic event, is understood only to the degree that the child can figure out what action "is happening." For example, a photograph of a little girl directly under a ball in midair could be a picture of "catching" or "throwing," depending on the context. Here are other examples of seeing the dynamic within the static: The child figures out how an elliptical wheel will roll by looking at the wheel's shape. The child figures out what made something fall just by looking at the static clues. Or, in the social realm, the child determines that a quiet child is still upset from a recent confrontation. All of these cases require that the child think about the dynamics of ostensibly static states, and the progress from failure to success in this ability can be considered a developmental trend.

Summary. These four developmental trends, as you probably sensed, match fairly well the four types of learning encounters that we have described. We took Piaget's six levels of cognitive development and matched them more specifically to the chapter headings for our learning encounters. By cross-referencing developmental trends and learning encounters, we hope that we have integrated the content of our curriculum with a means to define the child's progress.

PROCESS

We have described, in brief, the *content* of the activities by mentioning general learning encounters and have listed certain ways to define the child's *progress* from a Piagetian perspective. This last section is concerned with the learning and teaching *process.* Even if we have a good understanding of developmental levels, that does not in itself tell us what the child does to progress from one level to the next. Nor does it tell us what the teacher or parent should do to facilitate that development. Piaget probably has the most relevance to education when we begin to think about the process of learning and teaching.

How Young Children Learn

Piaget's work indicates that the world, to the infant, is a series of episodes, or snapshots. The infant can remember particular episodes, faces, and events but has difficulty remembering the order of these events in time. Even as the infant matures into early childhood, there are things that happen in the world that he cannot understand because of this episodic recall of what he observes. It is the gaps between the episodes that cause the young child difficulty.

Gaps. The child, given a supportive environment, will have ample opportunity to learn how to fill in gaps of all varieties. Here is a very powerful example of Kevin, a child at the School for Constructive Play, in the midst of dealing with gaps in his immediate world.

> Kevin is making imprints in rolled-out play dough using a small plastic piece shaped like a bow tie (two triangles pointing to each other). Kevin is holding his piece by one end so that, when he presses it into the play dough, all he makes is the rectangular shape, an imprint of the piece's butt end. The teacher, who has an identical piece, holds hers in a different orientation and makes several bow-tie impressions. Kevin stops abruptly, looks at the

teacher's bow-tie impressions with envy, and—as you might predict for a 2½-year-old—grabs the teacher's plastic piece. With her piece he makes imprints, with the apparent expectation that the bow-tie design will appear automatically after each press to the play dough! He shifts back to his own piece, presses this, and by accident makes the bow-tie design. Now he seems more attentive to how he is holding the piece rather than which piece he is holding. Upon this discovery he learns to make either bow-tie designs or rectangular designs with either piece.

Where are the gaps? What are the snapshots? We can discuss Kevin's initial problem in Piagetian terms. Kevin sees his plastic piece make a rectangular imprint (shot one). He sees the teacher's piece make bow-tie imprints (shot two). When he grabs the teacher's piece, identical to his own, he evidently misunderstands what procedure is required to fill the gap between shot one (rectangular imprint) and shot two (the bow-tie imprint). He initially thinks that this change requires an exchange between his piece and the teacher's piece. Eventually, he learns to fill the gap between shot one and shot two by changing the orientation of his own piece. Through experimentation Kevin learns, in this instance, to fill the gap between what he did do and what he wants to do by thinking about how a single object changes, rather than which object to exchange.

Many times each day the child learns how to span the gaps in her immediate world. At first, Lucy thinks that her piece of cake will not taste as good as her friend's piece. Her conclusion changes when she reconstructs just how the two pieces were produced—by cutting each from the same whole. At first, Aaron is confused, because the basket goes up when he pulls down on the pulley rope. After some experimentation he discovers that what he thought to be two separate spans of rope (the apparent gap in the immediate world) are really two parts of the same whole. Jimmy cannot understand how this butterfly ever was a caterpillar, because he sees before him a butterfly here and a caterpillar there. This gap seems irreconcilable until Jimmy learns that even the caterpillar in front of him will change into a butterfly through a natural process of metamorphosis.

In the social realm, Katie gets upset when she sees her mother get angry at a front door that is stuck. Katie is not sure that this angry person still contains all the love and nurturance so common in her mother. She learns to fill the gap between these "two persons" by doing something, such as asking her door-shaking mother "Is Mommie mad?" If the mother at least answers to the name Mommie, the child will probably feel a little better about the continuity between the angry person now and the nurturing-mother ideal. Katie has learned a procedure for filling in the gaps.

Procedures.   The process of filling gaps involves the discovery or invention of some procedure to get from one side of the gap to the other. The continuity between ostensibly separate things is restored by the construction (invention) or "reconstruction" (discovery) of a procedure.

Is this man with the flattened cheeks and nose Clayton's father? If Clayton sees his father slowly pull a nylon stocking over his face, he knows that it is still lovable Dad. If Clayton does not see the procedure by which the flattened face is created, then Clayton is not too sure. He must invent his own procedure for establishing continuity between the distorted face and Dad's face. Of course, the procedure could be the inverse of the procedure used to distort Dad's face in the first place. But if Clayton has no idea how Dad's face could be changed from normal to distorted, he initially will not be able to invert the transformation.[5] If Clayton is more interested than frightened, he will probably, by successive approximations, find out what procedures reverse the transformation. His explorations may begin with a straight-

---

[5] The term *transformation* in this example refers to the nature of the change from normal to distorted. The term *procedure* refers to the actual physical acts used to produce that transformation—pulling the nylon stocking over the head.

forward search for articles of clothing or physical features that "belong" to both Dad and this monster. Finding these features at least establishes the possibility that the two different "people" are really one and the same. And so it goes until Clayton invents some procedure by which he can convince himself of continuity between the two faces.

Once children have learned certain types of gap-filling procedures, they enjoy playing them out with other people. These games are frequent themes for social interaction. The common peekaboo game is a classic example. The toddler is delighted when she discovers a procedure for filling the gap between now-you-see-me and now-you-don't by moving her head back and forth behind some sort of screen. It is probably not the disappearance per se that makes this game so interesting as it is the child's sense of control over these events, the actions she uses to produce the alternation between the two very different states.

Here is another example of a social interaction, this time between a 5-year-old and her mother. Mother has asked her to eat all of her spinach. While mother is not looking, our clever Susan spreads the pile around on the plate. She deliberately hopes that mother will mistake the procedure of spreading for the procedure of eating, both of which could create a lower pile of spinach. Little brother George helps mother bridge the gap between the first pile and the flattened pile by clearly describing the procedure big sister used: "She just pushed it around, Mommie!" Since mother did not see the procedure herself, what little brother does, in essence, is represent the procedure to his mother in words. This brings us to the next aspect in the learning process, representation.

Representation. To fill gaps, children need some means to remember or to invent the procedures that relate the seemingly discontinuous states. A procedure is a sequence of actions and is not visible in the same way that states are visible. States remain stationary in the immediate present for a time sufficient for the child to study them—for example, the shape of a puzzle piece or the colors in a quilted blanket. Before the child can remember a sequence of actions, he needs some way to represent those actions. The representation, literally a "re-presentation," is what the child remembers or imagines. The representation may be a mental image, for example, of the older sister's actions. The representation sometimes, if we look closely, is an abbreviated imitation of the actions (the procedure). Graphic representations and words also help the child reconstruct or invent the procedures that explain apparent gaps in the immediate world of states. Here are several examples of children's using different modes of representation to think about procedures that fill in gaps.

Lauren watches a popcorn kernel heating in the oil. It pops abruptly. "It went POP!" Lauren exclaims, jumping up and spreading her arms at the same time. Lauren is representing the procedure of expansion that, in a sense, explains the gap between the tiny kernel and the comparatively large popped kernel.

In another setting, one child argues with a peer: "You didn't pull it. You yanked it!" This child seems to understand that the procedure of yanking is different from the procedure of pulling and is using words to represent what he is thinking. Not only do the words help him recall the procedure to mind; they also help him communicate what he means to someone else. A slightly less advanced child might use less conventional words to represent a procedure—for example, "The plane went whooosh, bang!" Here, the spoken word has a sound almost as long and then abrupt as the event the child is representing.

In another example, a child talks out loud to herself as she tries to fit a jigsaw-puzzle piece: "Turn it around. Turn it around." The words represent a procedure she has learned to literally fill the gap in the puzzle form board.

Summary. The learning process involves the construction of procedures to fill in gaps. The child uses various modes of representation, such as imitation, drawing, and words, to assist him in this process of construction. To bring this discussion together in a single sentence, we can say that the *gaps* are filled by constructing *procedures* with the assistance of *representation.*

While this definition of the learning process holds sway in all the learning encounters that follow, you may have noticed a particular relevance of this definition to the type of encounter called representing motion. The distinction between representing motion and representing procedures is subtle but important. By *motion* we mean primarily the displacement of an object through space, such as a rolling ball or the invisible movements of the pea under the walnut shell. The term *procedure* is more general in that it refers to any sequence of physical acts, at all levels of complexity, many of which are more complicated than the displacement of an object through space. For example, we would call "spreading the spinach into a flatter pile" a procedure. But it would miss the essence of the action simply to call this a motion of displacing the spinach in space. Motion, of course, is an aspect of any procedure, but the shape of the motion per se does not sufficiently define all procedures.

We apologize for such fine distinctions, but they are necessary if we are to have both a general theory of learning and specific learning encounters that are derived from that theory. In equal measure, a general theory of learning is necessary before we can make prescriptive statements about how to teach. This brings us to the next topic.

Rules of Thumb about the Teaching Process

In *The Child's Construction of Knowledge* you can find an extended discussion of how a theory of learning and development relates to actual classroom practices (see particularly Chapters Five and Six). We have abbreviated that discussion here into three rules of thumb. A rule of thumb, as opposed to a heavy-handed rule, should be applied as your clinical judgment dictates. We are asking you to consider these three rules as much as possible, but apply them as much as appropriate to give your teaching techniques a balance between what we are suggesting here and opposite techniques. We encourage you to approach teaching as an experiment in order to discover this balance.

Change without Exchange. Our first rule of thumb is something of a motto at the School for Constructive Play. In fact, we make a sign on poster board—"Change without Exchange"—and tack it to the wall, so all our teachers can refer to it during the day. The basic premise behind this rule is that children learn more about procedures when they physically change something about a single object than they do when they exchange that object for another.

Kevin is our best example. Remember that Kevin at first exchanged his plastic piece for the teacher's plastic piece so that he, too, could make bow-tie imprints. But even if he had made bow-tie imprints with the new object, he probably would not have understood just what made the imprint. He easily could have concluded that the imprint flowed from the plastic piece automatically. But when he experimented with changing his own piece from making rectangles to making bow-ties, he more clearly got the sense of the relation between the shape of a side and the shape of the imprint.

Take this example: Say a child rocks in a rocking chair, gets up, sits down in a regular chair, and jiggles back and forth in expectation that it, too, will rock. It doesn't, so he goes back to the rocking chair. He has learned which chair rocks, but does he know why? He may think that it rocks because it is red or because it is "lazy" or because it is on "skates." All of these are possible differences between the two chairs. If we, as teachers, can give this child some means by which he can change the regular chair into a rocker, then he will probably have a clearer understanding of why a rocker rocks. Helping the child to discriminate differences between the two chairs may be a good beginning, but giving the child the means to change a regular chair into a rocker is even more consistent with our emphasis on procedures.

At the School for Constructive Play we have designed many activities that have this potential for making a "within-object transformation" (changing something about the single object), as opposed to making an exchange between objects. A game called Weight Your Turn is a good example. We started with a commercially available set of plastic bowling ball and plastic pins. We modified the ball and pins by adding sand to them through a dime-sized hole that could be taped shut.

If the bowling pin is too heavy to knock over, the child can discover a procedure for making it possible to knock it over—drain out some of the sand from the pin. This procedure is within his level of competence and gives him a chance to make change without exchange. If we had not set the within-object transformation at his level of competence, he would no doubt have made an exchange when the heavy pin did not fall over. Had he made the exchange, he might have been more successful (assuming he chose a lighter pin), but he probably would not have understood the reason for his success. He might have thought that the new pin worked better because it was "more bouncy" or because it was "weak" or even because "the blue ones fall over better." Our emphasis on change without exchange is an emphasis on understanding and not exclusively an emphasis on success (see Chapter Three in CCK).

Down with Dichotomies.   In the section of this chapter on how children progress, we mentioned that Piaget treats as a landmark the child's transition from the level of opposites to the level of discrete degrees. Yet classrooms may present the child with an environment that works against this transition. Too often we ask the child to contrast pairs of objects. How often do we ask him to contrast two extremes with a middle item? If Piaget is right, this middle item is necessary to create the type of conflict that causes children to place opposites on a continuum. Recall the example of the child who named a middle-sized wooden doll "a-little-tall." The teacher who makes sure that the class has three of anything that varies on a continuum might be helping the child make that transition from the level of opposites to the level of discrete degrees. In other words, the teacher should add a middle item to dichotomies.

This emphasis on the middle term is no less than a central pedagogical principle advanced by Friedrich Froebel over a hundred years ago. Froebel, the founder of the kindergarten movement, instructed teachers to present the child with a wooden cylinder that was midway between the familiar ball and cube. The cylinder had some of the attributes of both the ball (mobility) and the cube (stability). It was intended to synthesize somehow the antithesis between the ball and the cube. It is not clear upon reading Froebel just what processes children would use to construct this synthesis. Perhaps if you combine our emphasis on within-object transformations (physically changing a ball of clay into a cylinder, and then the cylinder into a cube) with Froebel's emphasis on the middle term, you will have a rule of teaching better founded on principles of the learning process.

Classify with Good Causation.   Our last rule of thumb deals with the appropriate context for helping children to think logically. Preschool classrooms are filled with "logic games" such as attribute blocks, logo, number cards, and analogy cards. (For example, "What picture goes here to complete the analogy of Horse: Rider as Automobile: _____ ?") Besides the fact that some of these games are well beyond the average ability of 4- and 5-year-olds, we maintain that the format of presentation can be greatly improved. If you want your children to learn classification skills, give them "good causation" for doing so. Here is what we mean.

Young children, particularly in the range from 2 to 5, usually do not have the ability to think about how they are thinking. But they can think about what they are doing. Now, if there is a logic to the doing, even though the children cannot put that logic into words, perhaps a means to teach a young child to think better is to teach her to do better. We base this conclusion on the premise that the logic of action is the foundation for the later logic of spoken statements (see CCK, Chapter One). Furthermore, what makes an action "logical" is really how well that action leads to the causes that the child desires. Young children have little interest in classifying objects just for the sake of classifying them. But they certainly are interested in finding out how different classes of objects work within a particular cause/effect context.

Take the example of Tristan, who is playing on a game we called the Teeter-Totter Tube, a plastic tube taped lengthwise on a seesaw. Tristan experiments with rolling balls and cylinders down the tube. He discovers that he has to tilt the seesaw steeper to make the cylinders slide down the tube than he does to make the balls roll down. After a while he has made two piles, one with cylinders, one with balls. He has classified these objects with good causation.

If we had really been alert that day, we would have made sure that Tristan had cubes available. Then he could have classified with good causation in more than the dichotomy between slow and fast. Or, to summarize this discussion of the three rules of thumb, if we had been super alert that day, we could have given Tristan a batch of clay balls, cylinders, and cubes. Then Tristan could have experimented with the two extremes and the middle. And he could have made within-object transformations by sculpting one into the other. In a final summary statement, Tristan would then have been able to change without exchange, go beyond dichotomies, and classify with good causation. That's enough for any one day.

LEARNING ENCOUNTERS IN THE HOME

Even though the home differs greatly from a school's classroom and schedule, many of these rules of thumb can apply directly to what parents ordinarily do. For example, you can buy toys with an eye for those items that can be changed rather than exchanged. If a toy gets broken, we can repair it with the child's help. This is why wooden toys are such a delight. They offer many means to change the broken toy into a working toy rather than to buy a new one. The new plastic toys with complicated electronic circuits are beyond home repair. Not that electronic toys are without value, but a child's set of toys should at least be balanced between the two. The parent can also look for toys such as tinker toys and Lego blocks that can be changed from within, rather than exchanged, in order to render desired effects. As you will see in the subsequent chapters, it is important for the young child to construct a desired effect through putting a toy together and then changing the effect through later rearrangement of its parts. Children learn less if they have two toys that already perform the desired effects.

The rule of thumb represented in the phrase "down with dichotomies" also has implications for decisions parents make about toys they buy for their children. Whenever possible, try to have at least three forms of the same toys, such as a little wooden figure of a person, a middle-sized figure, and a large figure; or a little toy car, a middle-sized car, and a larger car. We are not recommending something that adds great expense to what parents already buy for children, but only that when parents make their ordinary purchases, to look for at least three degrees of variation within a set of objects like miniature replica toys or blocks, colors, or shapes. Note that a square, circle, and triangle are not three variations on the same shape, but a square, a rectangle, and a longer rectangle are. The chapters that follow will emphasize how the in-between or middle item can be used to improve the young child's ability to think about a continuum of change rather than a world of discrete and separate categories.

Parents can also become more conscious of their own use of adjectives such as *large* and *small*. What word does the parent use for "not-so-tall," "bigger-than-thin-but-not-fat," and so forth? Do these discussions ever come up at home? There are often opportunities to have a good conversation with the child about something that is neither hot nor cold, but somewhere in between, say the bathwater. There will be many episodes, indeed memorable episodes, in the home where parents can encourage children to think about degrees and variations rather than just about categories and opposites.

The rule of thumb represented in the phrase "classify with good causation" is perhaps more easily implemented in the home than at school, simply because things done at home are by necessity less arbitrary, less dissociated from a good reason for the classification. For example, children learn to put their toys in one box and their clothes in another, or shirts here and socks there. This is done so that they can find them later. This is a fine example of classifying with good causation. The child also bears witness to this in the kitchen; each utensil in its place; and in the shop, each tool in its place.

Of course, finding an object tomorrow is only one reason to classify objects and may be a reason that a three-year-old considers only with great difficulty. So we need to look for reasons that are more immediate. Say the young child is solving a jigsaw puzzle. Can the child first separate the pieces into pieces with a straight edge (the border pieces) and the pieces without a straight edge (the interior pieces)? Here is an example of classifying with good causation where the cause is more immediate to the child's purposes. Or say the child is building a tower of blocks. Can the child first eliminate all the blocks with round bottoms, knowing that they will not be useful in building a stack?

The parents' role during these encounters with classifying objects according to their function can simply be to summarize quietly the encounter, such as by saying, "You put the round ones aside because they would make your tower fall." Note that the child is not asked to agree or disagree, because such a question would distract the child from the constructive play. In the bathtub the child might put the objects that do not float on the rim of the tub. The parent comments, "All of these will not float," and that's it. Not "All of these will not float, right sweetums?" The upward inflection will destroy the threeway relation between you, the child, and the natural objects in the immediate present. The upward inflection will convert the encounter to one of two people trying to affirm each other rather than two people mutually and interdependently reflecting on the world together. Children need to feel free to ignore, expand, or even disagree if they choose, but the reaction should be about the observable event and not to the prowess or correctness of the adult.

Chapter Two

Establishing
Identity
and
Equivalence

ENCOUNTERS WITH IDENTITY AND EQUIVALENCE

Sometimes things that appear the same are really different. Conversely, sometimes things that are really different appear to be the same. When the child encounters some form of this general situation, we call it an encounter with identity or equivalence. Identity refers to the sameness or difference between two sightings of the same object. Equivalence refers to the sameness or difference between two separate objects, either seen at the same time or on different sightings.

Making the distinction between the apparent and the real is the fundamental objective of this type of learning encounter. For example, a large tube that a child has crawled through many times may look like a different object when it is standing on its end. If the child searches around the playground for the "missing" tube, then he has not conserved the identity of the tube when it is on its end. If he does not think to push the tube over to recreate the tunnel to crawl through, this, too, may be an indication that the transformation of the tube was so great that its prior function has not been conserved. This child has failed to consider the transformation. To him the tube on its end is not the same object. The following activities describe children encountering identity and equivalence problems.

IDENTITY: SAME OBJECT, DIFFERENT STATE

Children from 2 to 5 years old love to play in continuous media such as moist sand, water, and play dough. They knead, pour, push, build, press, flatten, scoop, and pull these media for many long minutes with a singleness of purpose that rivals the dedication of successful scientists. What is so fascinating about moist sand or limp clay or colorless water?

Perhaps the fascination comes from the many different states the child can create from the same object. Without having to grab some other child's possession, Jamie can change her clay from short to long. Without having to change her position at the sand table, Lisa can make a high mound and flatten it. The children playing with these continuous media have a control over variations that is like no other type of control. With blocks, on the one hand, the child often has to scout for the pieces she needs. With clay, on the other, the whole glob can do a great variety of things as it is. Clay, sand, and water give the child control of transformations without the frustration common with other forms of media, particularly discontinuous media such as blocks, puzzles, and Tinker Toys.

As children gain more command over continuous media, we notice that they begin to get involved with discontinuous media. Blocks and Tinker Toys are particular favorites. Children take five or six blocks and build them up, then knock them down; build them out, then collapse them inward. The same basic set of five or six blocks is put through a variety of states, first this shape and then another. The child seems amazed that so much can be gotten out of so little. Perhaps this realization that different states can be created from the same object(s) is a precursor to the later concept that different shapes can have the same area (quantity). The child at play with sand and blocks is certainly doing more than developing hand-eye coordination! The child reflects on his actions, the consequences to these actions, and the actions that undo those consequences. Let's look at some of the activities themselves.

SAND PLAY

Preparing the Environment

Sand should be placed in a sand table, a bin-like structure that is no more than waist high to your smallest children. When the sand is elevated in this way, the children have easier access to their work space. They do not get their own bodies in the way. Nor do they accidentally step on another child's work, as they sometimes do in a big outdoor sand pit or sandbox. They can see their own work better at this height, which seems to generate more pretend play with dolls and toy vehicles. They can dig in the sand table and discover a definite bottom, making holes that look like lakes. This, too, often generates pretend play.

Standing side by side with other children seems to make the whole area more social, more face to face, than a large sandbox, in which children crawl through one another's arms and legs. Conversation seems to increase when a child can work constructively to the completion of his own self-set goals without having to move continually toward and away from the other children. The conversations at the sand table seem to be the child's version of the adult's quilting bee. Some children, of course, will be completely engrossed in their own work. This is fine, too; the sand table can accommodate either parallel play or interactive play with equal ease.

The teacher can place a set of implements in the sand table. What she places depends on the type of encounter she wants to maximize. At the School for Constructive Play we have used the sand table as a gathering place, a "homeroom" area from which a host of encounters can occur. One week, when our theme was "balance," we had a variety of small balance beams in the sand table. Once, when our theme was "part/whole relations," we buried a life-size drawing of a girl under the sand, and the children dug to find each hand, each foot, and other body parts. For encounters dealing with equivalence, the teacher can place miniature representations of real objects such as cars, people, trucks, and trees in the table.

Entry

The children will come naturally to the sand table. They will begin to dig, build, and burrow, using their hands to scoop and sculpt. The teacher can sit and parallel-play with the children. He does not make any comments to them initially, but watches them and tries to get a good sense of their objectives.

The younger children (henceforth, we mean the 2- and 3-year-olds) will probably push the toy cars through the sand or dig and build with their hands. They will probably not develop a pretend theme, such as "going shopping" or "getting gas." The younger children are still somewhat at the level of exploring the medium as a medium, rather than using it to express a theme or as a ground for a pretend game. They see sand as the *figure*, as opposed to the *ground*.[1] In fact, for the younger children the sand *is* the object.

For the older children (henceforth the 4- and 5-year-olds) the sand can serve as a backdrop for pretend play, particularly if miniature objects are placed in the sand table. We will, for each of the activities we discuss, try to present encounters that are typical for both the younger and the older children.[2] We do this so that you can get a developmental perspective on the child at work.

Younger Children

Katie is digging in the sand. As she scoops the sand up, she smooths and pats the growing mound. Tom, one of our teachers, is playing parallel to Katie and begins to imitate her. Katie glances at Tom. She continues her work and then comments to Tom "I'm building a hill, see?" Tom nods gently without changing the pace of his work. After a few seconds Tom calmly says "I'm digging a hole." Katie has already noticed that Tom is doing the same thing she is doing. So why does he say he is digging a hole? "You're making a hill, silly," says Katie. Without any

---

[1] We are using the terms *figure* and *ground* here as they are used in perceptual psychology. *Figure* refers to the object of concentration; *ground* refers to the surrounding context in which the figure rests. For example, the white of this page is the ground, the black letters the figure.

[2] When we say "younger" and "older" children, we are referring to developmental ages. This means that you will sometimes find children of the same chronological age at different developmental ages in terms of their approach to an activity. However, you will also find that the same child has different developmental ages across different activities. Although most activities are divided into two sections ("Younger Children" and "Older Children"), such distinction has not been observed when it would have interfered with the flow of exposition or when age differences were not observed.

insistence in his voice Tom again says "Yes, but I'm also digging a hole." Katie then looks at her work. "There's my hole," she says, pointing to the scooped-out spot next to her hill.

Tom's objective had been to encourage an encounter with the different states of the same object (the sand, in this case). His entry was well timed and well modulated, and it seemed to work. The sand can be either in a high state—the hill—or a depressed state—the hole. The sand is still sand in either case.

The teacher can look for other opportunities to encourage learning encounters with identity. A child makes a straight path by pushing her palm through the moist sand. The teacher makes a curved path the same way. The child packs sand into a tall, skinny hill. The teacher packs sand into a long, skinny levee. The teacher does not ask the child to make the curve or the levee. These variations are there for the child to see and assimilate into her own play if she wants. The sand play remains, for the child, a self-regulated activity.

Older Children

Jimmie is driving a miniature car through the moist sand. He makes a road for his car, takes some of the miniature trees, and sticks a few along the side of his road. The teacher, Dianne, is sitting some feet away, making and landscaping roads, too. Jimmie carries out a monologue as he plays: "These trees. I'll put trees. Now the people can see the trees." Dianne knows that Jimmie trusts her enough to let her enter his play space. She takes from a separate part of the sand table a miniature tree. She shows it to Jimmie, saying "Can I put this near your road?" Jimmie nods, and then Dianne pushes the tree into the soft sand down beyond the trunk: "I'll make mine into a bush." Jimmie is amazed. How has she taken the tree and made it look like a bush? He smiles and then pushes down one of his own placed trees until it, too, looks like a bush. Dianne has, in this brief moment, staged for Jimmie an encounter with identity. The same object can be in either a tree state or a bush state, depending on how far one pushes it into the sand.

On other occasions a teacher would bury all but a part of some object to see if the children could recognize it. "Heck, we need the Mommy doll," the teacher might say. A child would spot a speck of yellow hair and dig out the needed object. These encounters with identity also occurred spontaneously at times. But they should always happen in the natural flow of the child's self-regulated play.

We will mention the sand table in many of the other learning encounters. As we said earlier, it allows for a great deal of versatility with a minimum of management problems. The few encounters mentioned above dealt only with same-object, different-state encounters with identity.

PLAY DOUGH

Preparing the Environment

Play dough is a mixture of flour, salt, and oil. The teacher may either prepare this beforehand (because some recipes require a curing period) or make it with the children as a class project. Even with the younger children the simple acts of pouring and stirring can be managed, and the children can produce the transformation from dry to moist ingredients. We have done this with success, letting the children add food coloring so that they can produce swirls of colors in the play dough until the whole batch becomes one color.

Sometimes we leave play dough in shallow bowls so the children can play with small clumps in any way they choose. On other occasions we make a large batch and roll it out over the entire surface of a table about 2 feet wide and 5 feet long. The rolled-out play dough, about a quarter of an inch thick, makes an excellent surface for taking the imprint of hard objects. We will discuss both the free-form sculpting and the rolled-out imprinting as same-object, different-state encounters with identity.

The teacher can have a small number of implements ready for the children to use. Cookie cutters, plastic shapes, rolling pins, and recycled materials—such as rubber sheets filled with holes and plastic gears—are all fun for making imprints in the rolled-out layer of play dough. And the free-form dough can be sculpted with or without the aid of these implements.

Entry

The teacher can make parallel entries in the play dough similar to the entries made in the sand table. (See pp. 184–185 in CCK for a discussion of parallel entries.) The younger children will probably want to gather a small batch of the dough to squeeze and pull it into different shapes. As we said in reference to sand, the medium itself seems to be the figure, the object of concentration. Older children will either create meaningful objects using free-form sculpting or make imprints in the dough with hard objects. Younger children will also make imprints. But often young children make imprints so deep that they get the idea of taking the play dough from the table in gouges. The younger the child, the more likely it is that she will need to have direct, manipulative control of a medium. This is why finger paint works better than easel-and-brush painting in the younger years. With the rolled-out dough the younger children have a little difficulty treating it as a surface to make marks on, rather than as an object to directly manipulate with their hands. To accommodate both types of exploration, we usually roll out a layer of dough on one part of the table and put some small clumps on another part. We then ask the children working on the side of the table with the rolled-out dough not to gouge it up.

Younger Children

There is not much need for teacher intervention when a small child is engrossed in pressing, pushing, and flattening a piece of play dough. A teacher may say, infrequently but with good timing, "Eva is pressing her play dough flat." This is a declarative sentence. It does not make any demands on the child. The child may assimilate the words as descriptors of her actions, or she may not. It is her choice. The words focus on Eva's actions. The teacher does not say "Eva is making a ball." The work *making* is too general. If children are going to learn a vocabulary for their *procedures* (recall the discussion of procedures in Chapter One), the teacher needs to select specific verbs.

Words are useful. They help children remember some past action. They help them communicate with other people. There is no other way children can learn specific words; they have to hear them from others.

Occasionally, a teacher might say "Clayton is pressing his ball into a flat shape." Here the teacher has identified the initial state (ball), the procedure (pressed), and the final state (flat shape). She deliberately does not interpret the final state by naming it something, such as "a pancake." This interpretation may offend Clayton, if that is not what he has in mind as he is working. He may have nothing in mind, and the word *pancake* may sound like an intrusion. It is risky enough to say "flat shape." Clayton may be thinking about how long the ball is getting, not how flat. Nevertheless, the teacher will make these comments on occasion just as a means to socialize the child into thinking about how objects change states. The teacher's comments do represent a slight intrusion. But to educate means to influence, to influence means to direct, and direction always involves a leader suggesting that the follower eliminate certain choices. All that we ask is that, as a sensitive teacher, you lead in such a way that your pupils can assimilate your suggestions.

Sometimes, the teacher does no more than provide an ever-receptive audience for the child's comments. The child knows that the teacher will share his joy and hear his remarks. In Photo 2.1 Tristan has a rubber sheet full of holes. By drawing the sheet tightly around a batch of play dough, he has made pips of dough protrude. Then he takes a different sheet of rubber with smaller holes. Now when he draws the sheet tightly around the dough, much smaller holes occur. He is delighted and shows this funny-looking transformation to our photographer, Arthur Mann, as you see in Photo 2.2.

PHOTO 2.1   Tristan makes one ball of play dough look like many small bumps.

PHOTO 2.2   Tristan shows Arthur this many-in-one effect.

Arthur smiled back at Tristan. Brief social exchanges often punctuate a transformation of media and make that particular final state more memorable for the child. Tristan was intrigued with the many-in-the-one, the many tiny pips from the one ball of clay. And this shared smile between him and Arthur could make this experience more memorable and therefore more useful as a prototype for similar experiences in the future.

Older Children

With our older children we encourage encounters with identity using implements and the rolled-out play dough. Children like to take an object and see how many different imprints they can make with just that one object. Once the children are involved in this game, a teacher may parallel-play so that she can gain entry into their game. Georgia, a teacher, played the following game with 4-year-old Lauren.

Georgia is making marks in the play dough with one of several objects. While Georgia does this, Lauren closes her eyes. After Georgia makes a mark, Lauren opens her eyes and tries to guess which object Georgia used. This game is somewhat difficult, because the child has to imagine what part of a whole object the teacher used. Because the same object, say a plastic spool, can make a variety of marks, there is no absolute mark that identifies the object. On successive trials, when Georgia uses the same object but in different orientations, Lauren is faced with an identity encounter: same object, different states.

After the teacher and a child play this game together, the child can pass it on to her playmates. It is interesting to watch 4-year-olds try to reconstruct the rules of the game. They are not often successful, but by 5 they have learned the purpose behind such acts as closing the eyes and using more than one object.

Nauman comes over to the play dough table and picks up a cookie cutter. He makes one impression in the dough in front of him and then makes another impression in a slightly different orientation. There is some overlap between the two impressions. He continues embellishing the design that is growing in front of him. We might venture to say that Nauman is intrigued with the fact that many different states can be created from the same object. Some minutes later Nauman gets the idea of using all of the different cookie cutters to make a composite design. He uses each cutter just once, making each mark overlap the previous mark. This excites him. He looks up at Georgia and laughs broadly. Through his spontaneous play, it seems, Nauman was experimenting first with a case of two within one and later with one within two (see Chapter One).

Nauman was a key figure in another learning encounter with identity. On this day, Nauman and Tristan are playing together at the play dough table. The teacher, Beverly, has made a small ball of dough. She tells the two boys that she is going to hide it. She then places a piece of flat dough over the ball and presses it down. Then Beverly asks if the ball is still there. Both boys insist that it is. When Beverly lifts the flat piece, the ball is "gone." Tristan regards the process casually, whereas Nauman obviously enjoys it and seems delighted by the mystery.

Beverly does it again, asking where the ball has gone and having the boys lift up the flat piece. First, Nauman says it rolled off the table. But when they all look for it on the floor and cannot find it, he seems more entranced than ever. Beverly then does it again slowly, so that the boys can see if the ball goes anywhere. They agree that it doesn't. Soon Tristan pipes up with "it's in there" and points to the flat piece. The boys then lift up the flat piece, and Tristan traces the outline of the smashed ball shape on the bottom of the flat piece. The boys then take over and start "hiding" shapes in more or less the same manner. (Because they don't push really hard, the smaller shape is much easier to find). Nauman even starts trying different shapes—a snake and a flat piece.

The staff felt that Beverly had successfully staged a good encounter with identity. The ball was transformed into a different state, but it was still there. Nauman initially confused a change of state with a change in position (thinking the ball had fallen to the floor). It is not clear that Nauman understood completely. But Tristan, when he traced the outline of the ball shape on the flat piece, did indicate his understanding of identity. Although this game was initially rather teacher directed, the children did eventually take the game over themselves. The fact that they did begin to make their own attempts and explorations justifies the initial phase of teacher-directed play.

SHADOWS–REAR PROJECTION

Preparing the Environment

A shadow gives a child no information about the color or the interior features of the object that casts it. Therefore, it is difficult for the child to know when a new shadow is cast by the same object (identity: same object, different state) or by a new object (nonidentity: different object, different state). The child cannot know by simply looking at the new shadow alone. She must either look toward the object that is in front of the light source or coordinate the various motions that the shadow made between the before and the after.

We have used two rear-projection setups for shadow play. In both cases the shadows were cast onto butcher paper hung vertically. The children could see the shadow through the paper on the side opposite the light source. Of course, in this position they could not see the object that cast the shadow.

In the first setup we used our indoor climber/loft. In Photo 2.3 you can see Lauren looking at some shapes that Nauman, inside the climber, is holding up to the paper. There is a slit under the paper through which Lauren can stick her hands and hold up shapes to look at. A Super-8 movie projector without film is being used as a light source. You can see the light of the projector through the triangular window on the right.

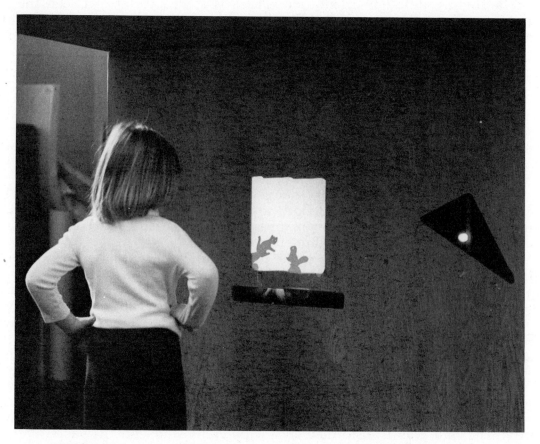

PHOTO 2.3   Lauren looks at shadows being made from inside the climber.

The climber setup attracted the children briefly, but it did not allow them easy access to both sides of the screen. Children who wanted to look alternately at a shadow and at the object casting it could not. Of course, they could see both the object and the shadow when they stood inside the climber, but this did not appeal to them.

The second setup was an improvement. This time we used a large (5 feet by 3 feet) Plexiglas easel—two hinged panels that rest in a scaffolding.[3] We placed one of the large panels vertically and the other horizontally. We papered the vertical panel and placed the projector about 4 feet from this "screen." The children could go behind the screen (under the "ceiling") and look at shadows made by any objects that passed between the screen and the light source. The lens on the Super-8 projector makes it possible to get a sharp edge on the shadows cast. With this setup the children could alternately look at the shadow through the paper or look at the object directly by moving their head around to the light-source side of the screen.

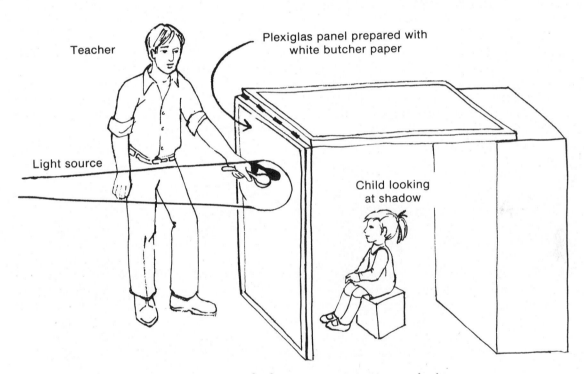

FIGURE 2.1   Shadows—rear-projection method.

Entry

Because the Plexiglas panels form a small, room-like structure that is airy and bright, the children find it an attractive place to go. Once inside, they notice the shadows that the teacher or a child is making. When this happens, they have a natural tendency to peek around the vertical panel to see what object is making the shadow. This is a good point to enter the child's play.

Younger children want to make the shadows themselves. If they see a teacher holding an object 4 or 5 inches from the screen, they ask for it. Often, they fail to keep a separation between the object and the screen. They place it flat on the screen as if it has to leave an imprint directly on the paper. Perhaps they have assimilated the making of shadows to some form of painting. Another common error is a failure to consider that their own body will cast a shadow. The younger children often

[3] We thank David Fernie of the University of Massachusetts for designing it.

stand directly in the line of the light source and hold the object up. In this position their own body blacks out the individual shadow of the object.

Older children consider their own body position and know to keep the object at least several inches from the screen to make a legitimate shadow. But they still have some difficulty recognizing the object when they see only the shadow.

Younger Children

Howie is standing on the light-source side of the screen. He sees his own shadow, runs up to the screen, and puts both hands on his shadow. He touches it in such a way that several observers conclude that he is trying to move it physically, as if it were a piece of dark cloth. What is this unusual "object" that moves across the paper but is not separate from it? Most things that move across paper of-a-whole, as this thing does, have an edge. Where is the edge? Howie continues to push on the shadow, but it relentlessly conforms exactly to the position of his hand, rather than moving some inches in front of his hand, as any other pushed object would. Evidently Howie does not understand that the shadow corresponds to himself—that the shadow, in a sense, is the same "object" as his body but is in a different state. Howie has not yet captured the identity between his hand seen directly and his hand seen in the state of a shadow.

George has been observing Howie pushing at his shadow. George stands to the left rear of Howie and casts the shadow of his hand at a spot Howie can easily see on the screen. George opens and closes his fingers to attract Howie's attention to the shadow. Howie runs to grab the moving shadow, not paying much attention to the fact that when he grabs it the shadow then lies across his own hand. But he does notice George standing there making funny movements with his hand. Howie then holds up his own hand, opens and closes it, but does not stand in the path of the light source. Howie seems to be imitating George's hand movements rather than trying to cast a shadow like George's shadow.

As luck would have it, Howie's flexing hand passes in front of the light source, and Howie notices the shadow that it makes. He seems to take notice of the moving shadow that his hand is making. George makes a "rooster" shadow by pressing forefinger to thumb and spreading the other fingers high. Howie looks at George's hand and does the same! His hand is, by accident or by design, still in the path of the light source. Howie moves his arm a little and the "rooster" shadow moves also. He continues this for many minutes. Perhaps Howie has discovered the identity between his hand and the shadow.

We might be tempted to call this an encounter with equivalence rather than identity. Technically, the shadow is not the same object as the hand. But neither is the shadow sufficiently different. A photograph is a different object from the real object photographed; it can be moved separately from the object. A shadow corresponds to its object in form *and* movement. Let us just say that Howie's experience represents an encounter midway between identity and equivalence. In fact, shadow play is a good activity to help children make the transition from identity correspondences to equivalence correspondences.

Older Children

With the 4- and 5-year-olds we have tried more sophisticated games. Sometimes we make shadows that are composites of several objects, such as one shadow made from two hands. The children see this shadow from the side opposite the light source. They then run around to the light-source side and try to produce that shadow themselves. Say the teacher makes a butterfly shadow by hooking her thumbs together. Will the child understand that this is a familiar pair of hands in a new state? Sometimes the teacher rotates a spoon to an unfamiliar perspective, thereby making an unfamiliar silhouette. Can the children predict that the object behind the screen is still a spoon? These are all encounters with identity: same object, different states. The teachers are quick to remove themselves from the game when the children begin to experiment on their own.

OVERHEAD PROJECTOR

Preparing the Environment

One advantage of being a laboratory school at a university is our access to good equipment. Down the hall from our classroom is an auditorium that contains an overhead projector on wheels. We occasionally borrow it for our children. Its horizontal surface allows for many encounters not possible with the Super-8 projector.

We place the overhead projector on the floor. The children can kneel beside it and place their hands or objects on the lighted surface. The housing above contains a mirror and lens that cast a sharp shadow on the wall 4 feet away. Sometimes we turn a free-standing set of shelves to face the wall and paper the back of its cabinet. This makes a good reflecting surface as well as one that allows the children to trace shadows if they like. The children are told not to look directly into the lens, because the light is quite bright, but they seem to avoid it reflexively anyway. When the children turn their back to the lens housing, they can see their own shadow on the wall. Thus, they have two ways of making shadows, one by placing things on the horizontal surface and the other by holding objects or themselves in front of the lens housing.

Entry

The older and younger children respond to this activity much as they do to shadow play. There are some special problems, however, for this apparatus. For one, the child who places her hand on the horizontal surface sees a shadow on the wall, not on the ceiling. The wall is not in direct line with the source of light. This dissociation of the object's position and the position of the shadow compounds the problems of identity for the younger children. For them it is somewhat better to project shadows by holding objects in front of the lens housing. Another problem is that the motion of the objects across the horizontal surface is reversed on the wall. There is no problem with stationary objects that are symmetrical, but asymmetrical objects, even at rest, are reversed 180 degrees.

These properties of the overhead projector can be frustrating to the younger children and can be a challenge to the older children. But it is interesting that in spite of these reversals in motion and orientation the children can still identify which objects make which shadows. They apparently use absolute cues, such as unique features of an object, or cues such as movement.

Younger Children

Matthew is sitting next to the projector. He is more concerned with watching the objects he is moving on its glass surface than he is with their shadows. This egocentric relation to the world characterizes the 2-year-old. Cathy, a teacher, gives Matthew a camel-shaped cookie cutter. She then places a small block on the left side of the glass surface. "Matthew, can you give the camel some food? He's hungry." Matthew still looks only at the glass surface below him. He moves the camel across this surface to the food. Because Matthew has responded to Cathy's idea, she continues. Cathy places the pretend food (the block) on the wall and asks Matthew if he can get the camel to move over to it for his food. Matthew picks up the camel and carries it over to the food on the wall. His camel starts eating. The teacher and Matthew then go back to the projector.

Matthew begins to play again, moving his camel cookie cutter on the glass surface, perhaps noticing how it is underlighted by the projector. Cathy points to its shadow on the wall and says "Matthew, can you make this *black* camel come to the food?'' Now for the first time Matthew watches the *shadow* as he moves the object. He cannot get the camel to the food (another shadow), but he does watch the camel shadow as he moves it up and down on the left side of the projection wall. (The food shadow is on the right side.) Matthew then takes objects and moves them in the air at random, looking to the wall in anticipation that they, too, will have a shadow.

A few minutes later Cathy gets the idea that the children do not seem to understand that the shadow is everywhere between the lens and the wall. The children have been trying to peel the shadows off the wall as if they were objects. So Cathy stands in front of the wall. She then reaches over to the projector and rolls a marble across the glass surface. The children notice that a shadow dot moves across the leg of Cathy's pants. Some of the children put other objects on the glass surface and look at the shadows they make on Cathy. Loren stands in front and looks down at his shirt to see the shadows. He can even hold his hand in front of his shirt and see the shadow of his hand. It now appears that the children are getting a better idea of the identity between the objects in the light source and the shadows that they cast.

Older Children

Tristan places a small chain, about 18 inches, on the glass surface. The chain makes very interesting shadows. Tristan enjoys changing the arrangement of the chain to watch the unpredictable patterns it makes. "This is a long chain," he says, and then he pushes it together in a coil to notice the shadow grow smaller. Not only does Tristan understand the relation between the chain and the shadow; he also understands the identity between the different states of this one chain's shadow. He then removes the chain from the glass surface altogether. "See, it's not shining," he says while looking at the wall. "Why?" the teacher asks. "Because it's not in the light," he answers. Tristan knows how to negate the shadow altogether.

It is interesting, however, that he uses the phrase *not shining* to describe the absence of the shadow. Does this mean that he thinks a shadow is like some sort of black light that shines on the wall? To Tristan, eliminating the shadow is like taking some object away (level of opposition), rather than allowing some "object" (the light) to enter. It is easy to overinterpret Tristan's words, but we have seen behavior that indicates that other children also make interesting errors regarding shadows. At least Tristan's concept of the shadow takes into account the fact that the shadow is everywhere between the light source and the wall. But he may not yet understand that the shadow is actually the absence of light, rather than the presence of some black light. Perhaps it is beyond the 4-year-old's ability to understand that this "object" we call a shadow is really negative light.

Jessica places a large circle on the glass surface. She notices the shadow that it makes on the wall. Then she places a smaller circle on top of the large circle. She is somewhat surprised to see that the addition of the smaller circle has not changed the shadow. Gary, the teacher, says "Only one shadow." Jessica takes the two circles off the projection surface and walks over to the wall. She holds them up separately. "Two shadows," she says. Perhaps she realizes that these two objects can be in two different states: a one-shadow state and a two-shadow state. In either state they are still two objects. As we have seen before, children are naturally intrigued with the case of two within one.

This learning encounter of Jessica's reminds one of how children become intrigued with a jigsaw puzzle. When a child seats a puzzle piece into its space, the piece virtually disappears and "melts" into the surface of the other pieces. The piece becomes one with the whole puzzle. Children often rub the flat of their hands over the surface of a completed puzzle, as though they are testing to see if any of the "two" protrude from the "one." Sometimes they, like Jessica, take out a single piece, put it back, and take it out again, just to confirm that in spite of the appearance of oneness there are actually "two." Piaget would argue that the child's interest in these contrasts has its source in the biological heritage of our species.

THE SILHOUETTE SORTER

Preparing the Environment

The Silhouette Sorter is a sorting box that we designed ourselves. This game is designed to improve what we feel is a fundamental weakness in the commercially made "shape sorters" on the market today. These commercial toys usually consist of a wooden or plastic box into which holes of various shapes have been cut. The child then places blocks of various shapes through their corresponding holes. Each block has but a single hole. The fundamental weakness here is that the toy does not encourage children to think about how shape can change. In our modification of this toy we have a single block but three holes; each hole is a different perspective of the one block. In this game the identity of the block remains the same, but the states of that block, the different perspectives, change. This means that the object has more than one absolute shape. The shape (the hole indicates the shape) is relative to how the child changes (rotates) the object.

PHOTO 2.4   Jenny puts an animal into the Silhouette Sorter.

In Photo 2.4 Jenny and Marc are playing with the Silhouette Sorter. Jenny is placing the object in the end of the box where the hole is the rear silhouette of the object. Notice that the top of the box has the top silhouette and the side of the box the side silhouette of this same object. Once Jenny places the object into the box, she can lift the lid, remove the object, and try another silhouette. We constructed this box so that different panels can be exchanged to present different types of challenges to the children. Some of the objects, such as the one seen in the photo, are composites made of parts that can be rearranged. The object in this photo is an animal form made from Connector Blocks.[4]

Our box is made of Masonite and wood. Less expensive and more quickly made versions can be made from a pasteboard box. Just trace the three views of an

[4] For your convenience we have listed the names and addresses of the makers of commercial material in the Appendix.

object on the sides of the box and cut them out with a sharp knife. Then, instead of exchanging panels to present new challenges, you exchange boxes. Several coats of enamel paint increase the durability of the pasteboard and prevent the edges of the hole from becoming worn. You should choose asymmetrical objects, so that each silhouette is different and at least some silhouette holes will be too small unless the object is rotated to the correct orientation.

Entry

Children are naturally attracted to holes. As nature abhors a vacuum, the child must fill in holes. Even the infant cannot resist placing hand into mouth or a block into a cup. For the younger children the Silhouette Sorter entices them to cram, push, and jam objects until they fall through the various holes. Their approach is more trial and error than pause and anticipate. The older children show a more deliberate and thoughtful approach. They can cope with a greater variety of challenges, as you will see in the discussion that follows.

Younger Children

For this age range objects with no removable parts work best. Objects such as a wooden boat or car are familiar and interesting to the child. The silhouette holes of these objects are also easily recognized, at least the side-view holes. The teacher can model the game once or twice, and then the children will play the game on their own. The teacher usually holds the box steady, if need be, or protects the child's work space, if other children are crowding in. Several children can work side by side if you have made several Silhouette Sorters. Because each box should have only one object, it is not possible to have several children working on the same sorter.

Older Children

After the older children have tried the solid objects, they will want more challenging objects. The composite object is the answer. For some of the sorters you can make the holes fit different *arrangements* of the same set of pieces.

For example, David, a 4½-year-old, is holding three pieces—a cube, a wooden dowel, and a rectangular block—from the Connector Block set. Tom, the teacher, has made a box that has holes cut to conform to the three different arrangements of these blocks seen in Figure 2.2. Holes (b) and (c) are actually different perspectives of each other; hole (a) requires a rearrangement of the parts of the object.

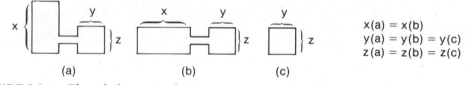

FIGURE 2.2   Three holes cut in the sorter correspond to silhouettes of a three-block object.

Tom rotates the Silhouette Sorter so that hole (a) is directly in front of David. David studies the hole momentarily and then arranges his three pieces to fit that configuration and pushes the composite object through the hole. Tom returns the object to David and then rotates the box to hole (b). David quickly disassembles the composite object and rearranges its parts to conform to the configuration of the new hole. With each trial Tom returns the object and rotates the box to present David with a new challenge. On some trials David has to rearrange the pieces; on other trials he needs only to reorient the composite object. David enjoys the quick pace of the game. This activity is a good example of a child's encounter with identity correspondence of the same-object, different-state variety.

Our one reservation about this game is that the whole setup is a little too "academic." That is, the game is played on a table top in isolation from anything more meaningful than these specialized actions themselves. You should try to find ways to *embed* this game in some social context, some more naturalistic setting. For example, you might place a wooden partition between the kitchen cabinets and the dining table in the role-play area. Cut holes into this partition that conform to the different perspectives of common kitchen implements, such as spoons and teapots. Then a child in the kitchen can pass the, say, teapot through the appropriate hole when a child on the other side of the partition asks for it. The transfer through the holes can go both ways.

Here the focus on same object, different state is embedded in a social context of communication between two children or between a teacher and the children. We never tried this; but we felt that, knowing our children, it would have worked. We always preferred games that had this quality of purpose to games that were too isolated from everything else that children do. Of course, fitting a key into a lock is a naturalistic encounter. Perhaps some variation of an unlock-the-lock game would be a more meaningful way to stage an encounter with same object, different state.

This plea for you to embed encounters in naturalistic settings is a general plea that we maintain, albeit at times implicitly, throughout this book. (Remember our rule of thumb about classifying with good causation.) But we are not obsessed with the plea, either, because what looks isolated and ad hoc to the adult is sometimes fraught with purpose for the child. For example, there is no need to embed painting in some more meaningful context, such as painting a piece of furniture or painting a picture. The medium itself offers its own purposes to the child. By closely observing children's behavior—their eagerness and intensity—you should be able to discern when an activity is too "academic" for them.

Variation

One of our students, Lindsey Peach, did invent a variation of the Silhouette Sorter that was not so "academic" as our table-top version. She came up with the clever idea of using a giant cardboard box, such as a refrigerator crate, and cutting out actual silhouettes of one child. She used four silhouettes: a front view with arms to the side, a front view with arms spread out at right angles to the body, a side view, and a fourth view made by tracing the head-on view of a child in the crawling position. These four silhouette holes in the box were then used as gates into the box. The box was placed in the front of a large tunnel that communicated with the inside of the climber/loft.

The children had great fun figuring out how to posture their own bodies in order to get into and out of the box. We found that two boxes worked even better—one with little silhouettes for the small children and another with larger silhouettes. These giant Silhouette Sorters gave the children an opportunity to think about different transformations of their own bodies. We might call this a *within-self* transformation. It was fun to see the children anticipate how to hold their arms out or to assume a crawling position in advance of entering or leaving the giant box.

PAINTING

Preparing the Environment

If you can consider a portion of finger paint an "object," then painting is an ideal activity for transforming an object into different states. The same portion of paint can be swirled into spirals, stroked into lines, and smeared into spots. Once we began to think about painting as an encounter with identity and equivalence, we designed some new variations on painting. We felt that the paint alone was too amorphous to define changes from one state to another. So we devised means to have the states change more dramatically—from one state to an extreme, usually opposite, state. Take, for example, a stencil of a familiar object such as a motorbike. Turn the stencil one way and brush it with paint, and the image is facing to the left. Rotate the stencil and brush it, and the image is facing to the right. The stencil is the same, but the states (two orientations) are different.

Variations

Inasmuch as we have already cited many examples of how a teacher can enter activities that encourage the child to encounter problems of identity, we will shift here to a discussion of variations on this theme of same object, different state, using various forms of painting.

The child can take a piece of red construction paper, cut a hole out (with teacher's help), and place the stencil over yellow paper. Then he can brush red paint over the stencil, leaving a red circle of paint on the yellow paper. Alternatively, he can take this same stencil and glue it to the yellow paper, leaving a yellow circle with a red background. When children work in groups to create these scenes—they can be called, say, the sky and the sun—they may begin to notice that different combinations of the same objects create opposite effects. If painting is too difficult to manage, the same four combinations can be made from red and yellow construction paper alone. Other scenes, such as a white bird on a blue sky or a blue bird on a white (clouds) sky, can be attempted.

We also found in a recycling center some rubber sheets filled with holes. The children could place two of the sheets, one on top of the other, on a table covered with paper. They could then brush paint through the holes. If the holes in the top sheet were aligned with the holes in the bottom sheet, the paint left a matrix of circles. If the two sheets were deliberately misaligned, the paint left a matrix of ellipses or even no paint marks. With two sheets the children could align or misalign them and create *variations*, rather than just the *opposites* of circle and no-circle.

We also use a thin layer of semimoist sand. The children can etch in the sand. The sand does not take imprints as clearly as rolled-out play dough, but neither can the children peel up the sand into clumps. Therefore, the activity is better defined as one of etching. The rubber sheets make hundreds of little mounds. Of course, if the sand is too deep, the children bury the stencils or just dig in the sand. This activity of etching in sand is not popular with the younger children, perhaps because of the limits it sets on their preference for digging.

IDENTITY: SAME OBJECT, DIFFERENT USE

We now shift to the second form of identity correspondences. The same-object, different-state encounters just discussed involved one object changing its shape, such as the play dough or shadows. The second form of encounter—same object, different use—involves a change in the use of a given object. Encounters of this kind, as you will see later, may also include a pronounced change in the state of an object, but the defining feature is that this change is related to a new use of the object. For example, you could use a shoe to put on your feet for walking down the sidewalk, or you could use that same shoe to hold in your hand for cracking walnuts on the porch steps. The use of the shoe has changed from stepping on cracks to cracking on steps.

The teachers at the School for Constructive Play keep this objective in the back of their minds. When they see an opportunity to stage an encounter with same object, different use, they do so. These occurrences are most often serendipitous. The "prepared environment," therefore, is, in effect, the prepared mind of the teacher. On other occasions we do prepare the environment in advance. We will mention both types of encounter.

TUNNEL TO WELL

Preparing the Environment

These first encounters with same object, different use occur out of doors. We bought a large, blue sphere made of durable plastic called the Blue Bubble. The sphere is hollow and has holes at both ends, so that a child can easily crawl inside.

In fact, two children can curl up inside. When the sphere is sitting on one of its holes, it becomes a container. It looks like a bulging, blue well. In Photo 2.5 you can see Tristan reaching down into the open hole of the well. Some minutes later he has turned the sphere onto its side. Now he can crawl into and through the sphere as if it were a tunnel (see Photo 2.6). The sphere works all right, but some of the children do not like that it rolls so easily. Once inside they feel too dependent on the whims of this unstable ball.

We also have a few sona tubes—large, cardboard tubes used as forms for making concrete bridge pilings. We use them for wells and tunnels. These tubes on their side are more inviting than the blue sphere, because they are more stable. But as a well—on one end—they present a different type of problem. Once a child is inside "the well," the teacher has to be ready either to lift him out through the top or raise the tube so he can slip out the bottom. The children enjoy this game with teachers nearby but are somewhat timid—as well they should be—when other children approach them in this vulnerable position of being up to their necks in a well.

Entry

George is playing with Bobby outside. Bobby sees the sona tube lying on its side. He crawls inside and out the other end. Then he returns to the same entrance and begins to crawl into the tube again. With this, George makes noises like a choo-choo train. Bobby seizes on this idea and pretends to be a train going through a tunnel. After Bobby has made a few passes through the tunnel, George sees an opportunity to stage an encounter with same object, different use. With Bobby's help, George stands the tube on its end. Bobby uses new words in reference to the well. He wants to "get inside" the tube. (He had talked about the tunnel using different words, such as "I'm going through.")

George lifts Bobby and gently lowers him into the well. Bobby smiles, ducks down in the tube, and then pops up so George can see him. As some other children approach, Bobby ducks down again. When they are just passing by he pops up again and laughs. One of these children wants to get in the tube with Bobby. George lifts Nauman and puts him in. It is like their little, private room. They slide their backs down the inside walls, bracing their knees against the other's knees. They talk to each other and giggle at the resonance of their voices down in the tube.

George then peers over the edge of the tube and says "Helloooo down there." Bobby and Nauman shout back. Then George asks them if they want to see out the bottom. They say yes, so George lifts the tube about 2 feet. They are now, in effect, sitting knees to knees in the middle of the whole playground. This rather small change in the position of the tube makes a tremendous change in effect, from privacy to publicity. George lowers the tube slowly, and then Nauman asks if he can get out. George says OK and lifts him out through the top.

Bobby, although missing Nauman's company, is not that eager to leave the well. George, knowing that Bobby is generally a daring boy, asks him if he wants to be let out of the well a different way. He agrees so George asks him to lean against the inside wall of the tube. As Bobby does this, George begins to gently tilt the tube over on its side, until the tube—and Bobby—are lying flat on the ground. Voilà! The well becomes the tunnel again! Bobby crawls out one end with ease. Other children see this game and ask George to "do it to me." He does.

In this manner the teacher has transformed the function of the object by a mere change in its orientation. The fact that Bobby was inside the tube throughout the transformation was a good idea. It probably helped Bobby to understand just what had to be done to the tube. If he had not been in the tube, or even if he had not seen the transformation, he might not have conserved the identity of the object.

The tunnel-to-well activity was something that happened accidentally. But since that activity occurred, we have begun to rethink the purpose of playground

PHOTO 2.5   Tristan looks down into the "well" of the Blue Bubble.

PHOTO 2.6   Now the Blue Bubble is like a tunnel.

equipment. We would like to have, but have not yet built, more equipment that the children themselves can change. A slide that can be changed into a plank walk would be better than a slide and a plank walk separately. This ideal fits our theme of *change without exchange:* give the children control over the transformation so that they do not view the world as a set of static objects. A swing that can be changed from short arcs to long arcs by changing the place from which it is attached, a seesaw that can telescope inward or outward to change its length, a jungle gym that can be rearranged—these are all within-object transformations. This form of transformation, as we have explained, is more educational than a between-object exchange. For these reasons the large cardboard tubes are good playground equipment. Here in Photo 2.7 you can see yet another use of the same tube. Katie is pushing Aaron, who is rolling inside the tube. Eva watches. The tube is sometimes a well, sometimes a tunnel, and sometimes a drum to roll.

PHOTO 2.7   The sona tube becomes an outdoor ride for Aaron.

INVERTED FURNITURE

Preparing the Environment

A kitchen pot turned upside down can be a drum to beat; a table turned on its side can be the wall of a fort. The object remains the same, but the use changes. These encounters with same object, different use involving indoor objects were sometimes staged and sometimes occurred naturally.

In one case where the teachers did prepare the environment in advance, several chairs were removed from around the play-dough table. There were fewer chairs than children who usually play at this table. On another day the sand table was removed from the classroom. The following anecdotes pertain to these two cases.

Entry

Clayton approaches the play-dough table. Other children are sitting in chairs, kneading and rolling dough. Two buckets are against the wall. Clayton says "I want a chair. I wanna sit down." Barbara, the teacher, says "I think all the chairs are being used. Can you use something else?" Clayton stands playing with his dough. He makes no answer but repeats "I wanna sit down."

Barbara: "How about using that bucket."

"Bucket?!" Clayton exclaims.

Barbara: "Sure, use the bucket as a chair."

Clayton: "You can't use a bucket. You'd fall in." He laughs.

"Turn it over," Barbara says.

Clayton gets the bucket and does just that. He pushes it near the table's edge

PHOTO 2.8   Clayton uses a bucket for a chair.

and sits on it almost matter of factly. Of course, had Clayton not been on the brink of complete frustration, Barbara would have encouraged him to invent the new use himself.

On other days the other children caught on to the idea of using buckets as chairs. But the younger children did not like to use them. They had a little more difficulty forgetting that the bucket is a bucket. For example Nuffy, a 2½-year-old, vehemently insisted "No, it's a bucket!" when Peter suggested it could be used as a chair. And later, when Nuffy did move it to the snack table to sit on, he did not think to invert it and fell in. Eventually, he understood that it worked better if you turned it upside down.

On the day the sand table was removed, the children entered the large room to find one of our worktables inverted and filled with sand. They saw the sand and immediately knelt beside the table and began to dig (see Photo 2.9). None of the children commented on the fact that this was an unusual position for a worktable. None of the children even commented on the legs sticking straight up in the air. Why not?

PHOTO 2.9   Two inverted worktables make an unusual sand table.

For one, there was no reason to talk about the table in its ordinary position, even if the children had noticed it. If a child had come over and asked "Where's the play-dough table?" then David or Jenny might have said "We're using it here." But this would not be a likely thing for a child to ask. At most the child would have asked "Where is the play dough?" The children take the furniture for granted. The *figure* is the small objects on a table; the table is the *ground*. Because tables are usually not changed, they are usually not seen as the *figure*.

For another reason, the children did not witness the transformation. This was our mistake. Had we teachers inverted the table with the children's help and then filled it with sand, the identity of the table might have been conserved. Then, instead of the children's thinking that they had a new sand table, they might have thought that they had a new use for the worktable. The use changed but the object remained the same. From that day on we tried, as much as the logistics of moving furniture around would allow, to engage our children in the changes we made. Through this process we hoped that we were developing in them a sense that even pieces of furniture are not static, divinely placed surfaces, but rather objects that can be changed.

Rethinking the role of furniture in the classroom generated some of our most novel activities. The easel, for example, is usually a surface on which the child paints. It is the ground. But this use of the easel as a stationary surface is an arbitrary role assigned to it by convention. Why not have the surface move and the paintbrush remain stationary? So we invented an easel that spins. It will be described more fully in a later section. The point is that the surfaces that children use are taken for granted by both child and adult. We feel that a whole range of encounters is missed if the teacher and children resist changing the furniture and the walls and the ceilings of the space in which the children play.

We did not find that these changes confused the children. Children are incredibly accepting of change when they take part in it with adults whom they know and care for. Of course, the rearrangement of furniture and equipment was always done within a certain amount of constancy. The climber/loft, the windows, and the doors all served as anchor points. The children always knew where they were, even though furniture was sometimes rearranged to serve new functions.

OPPOSITE USES[5]

Sometimes an object shifts from one use to another use that is a natural opposite of the first. For example, one cup can first be used to pour water and then to receive water. The act of emptying the cup is the opposite of the act of filling it. The cup in the right-side-up state functions as a receiver; the cup in the inverted state functions as a deliverer. We, like all teachers of young children, have noticed how long a child will stand at the water table and pour water back and forth between two plastic glasses. Perhaps the child is intrigued with the double use of each glass. She begins to anticipate that, as soon as the left glass gets full, she can return that water to the glass on the right. The glass that is momentarily not-full can soon become the glass that is full. We may be witnessing in these simple actions the child's explorations with *opposition* (see the discussion in Chapter One).

The teacher does not need to do very much during these times when the child is exploring the change of uses. She may protect the child's play space. She may facilitate his play by making sure that he has two plastic glasses, that the water is deep enough to allow him to fill his glass, and that the water is not too cool from the tap. And she may imitate him just to reassure him that he has permission to do as he pleases.

On several occasions we staged an encounter with same object, different uses that involves a bucket brigade of sorts. We separated two water tables by about 10 feet. One was full of water and the other was empty. The children would dip their buckets into the water table to fill them, walk across the room to the empty water table, and empty them. Not only did this activity encourage the use of a bucket in two different ways; it also established a need for children to work cooperatively.

Another week we staged an activity in which the children had to exchange colored water between colored glasses. The child was given red juice in a blue glass and blue juice in a red glass. She was then asked to switch them around so that the red juice would be in the red glass and the blue in the blue. The child, of course,

---

[5] Occasionally the discussion of an activity, because of its special nature, does not follow the usual format.

needed a third glass, empty, in order to perform the exchange. This third glass had two uses. First, it received the red juice from the blue glass in order to make the blue glass empty. Then it emptied the red juice into the red glass, made empty by pouring the blue juice into the blue glass.

We had hoped to stage this during snack time as an activity with some greater purpose than just pouring liquid from glass to glass. But the other children were distractions to the child trying to solve the problem, so we played the game with individual children in a quiet corner of the classroom. The younger children would sometimes pour the red liquid directly into the blue liquid, spilling the mixed liquid everywhere. They did not think the process through to the point of realizing the necessity for the third glass. Some of the 3-year-olds made the exchange without any difficulty, but they seemed to just pour liquid from any full glass to any empty glass. Sometimes they would even, after two moves, end up with the red liquid back in the blue glass.

So we used half-filled glasses. This way the 3-year-old would not avoid pouring the red liquid directly in the red juice glass for fear of spilling it over. With half-filled glasses he could mix liquid without spilling it over. Some of them did choose this strategy. The 4-year-olds, even with half-filled glasses, understood that the empty glass was a necessary intermediary. Even when the teacher had hidden the third glass out of sight, these children would leave the table in search for an empty glass!

Many events happen spontaneously during the school day that have this quality of one object's functioning in opposite ways. A child accidentally drops a sheet of paper onto some finger paint. When he moves it out of the way of his work space, he notices that the paper smears the paint in an interesting way. He continues to explore the patterns he can make by rubbing the sheet of paper over the white expanse of the papered table top. The teacher notices his interest and begins to imitate the child, and the learning encounter is expanded into a ten-minute activity.[6] This child has invented a new use for a sheet of paper directly opposite to its ordinary use. The paper has shifted from "applicatee" to "applicator," if you will. We suspect that part of the child's interest is due to the "funniness" of using paper as an applicator, and by funniness we mean that the child senses the oppositeness of these events.

Many of our children are also intrigued with the fact that their own finger can serve a double function. Wipe a finger across the finger paint, and it makes an etching (vacant space). Wipe that same finger across the clean surface of the paper, and it makes a paint stripe (filled space). They even notice and explore the fact that paint off of the paper equals paint onto the finger; paint onto the paper equals paint off of the finger. How can one motion do two things (two within one)? When they watch the etching their finger made, they are surprised to see the paint on their finger. When they concentrated on the paint building up on their finger, they are surprised to see the etching. As we will discuss more fully in the next section, young children have difficulty understanding simultaneous uses. This surprise, however, is the source of their explorations, and the explorations will eventually help them understand how one motion can do two things.

EQUIVALENCE: DIFFERENT OBJECT, SAME STATE

With equivalence correspondences we shift to similarities between separate objects, as opposed to two different sightings of the same object. Photographs, miniature objects, and videotapes are all objects that correspond to some other set of objects. In other words, these things are representations of other things. The corre-

---

[6] See CCK, Chapter Seven, for ways to expand and generalize a learning encounter in progress.

spondence between the one and the other is a correspondence of form (state) rather than a correspondence of use—something we will discuss in the last section of this chapter. A miniature table corresponds to a real table in form, but not in size. Children recognize correspondences of state, and—more in keeping with our approach to education—they like to create them.

The technical problems are great for younger children trying to create a correspondence of state. Even when it is clear that they are trying to draw a person with their crayon, we notice their failure. And it is too glib to say "Well, that is how the young child sees a person." This is not true. They are the first to say that their drawing does not look like the thing they are trying to draw. Their ability to recognize equivalences far outstrips their ability to produce equivalences. For this reason, we decided when dealing with children 2 to 5 years old to concentrate on the recognition of equivalences, at least when the forms involved are complex.

We will not discuss all types of representation in this section. Imitation, for example, is a form of representation. A child who imitates a teacher during movement games is creating an equivalence between himself and the teacher: different objects, same state. Nevertheless, because imitation also involves one person's taking the perspective of the other, we have decided to discuss it in the next chapter, on changing perspective. Similar reasons are behind other decisions regarding where to discuss types of equivalence correspondences.

SCALED-DOWN PLAYGROUND

Preparing the Environment

During the summer before our school started, Tom Healy, one of our lead teachers, built a 4-foot by 3-foot model of the playground. He glued rocks to a piece of plywood to simulate the graveled areas. He used balsa wood and tiny wooden dowels to make the jungle gym. The cargo-net climber he made of pipe cleaners. The whole scene was done to scale and looked quite realistic.

At Skinner Hall, where our program takes place, we are blessed with a large bay window that gives the children a 270-degree view of the playground outside. We have placed Tom's model in the bay window, so that the children can easily compare the scaled-down space with the outdoor space. In Photo 2.10 Seth is showing Barbara a correspondence he has recognized. His right hand is touching the miniature jungle gym, while his left hand points to the real jungle gym outside.

The model works best when we place it on a low table. This way the children can see both the model and the outdoors. The table also prevents the younger children from climbing into the model. The miniature pieces can be moved about, so the children will have a number of things to do. Also, children are given tiny wooden people. With this diversity of objects, the game can easily accommodate three or four children.

Entry

The model sitting in the bay window created mild interest from the children. This was a little disappointing to us, because we found the model so delightful. Our delight came from our study of the exactness of its scale. Perhaps the children did not study it in this way. We saw the cleverness of using pipe cleaners to represent ropes. They saw something that in a more global sense looked like the cargo-net climber. Our minds could see the analogy between the cotton texture of a pipe cleaner and the hemp of a large rope while at the same time consider the identity of the pipe cleaner as a pipe cleaner. We adults sensed the paradox; the children did not (see CCK, p. 112).

In any event, the children knew that the model was the playground and did enjoy walking the toy people through it, jumping them from seesaw to jungle gym and pretending that the people were sliding down the slide. The younger children

PHOTO 2.10   Seth points outside to the real object that corresponds to the miniature object in the Scaled-Down Playground.

were less interested in the correspondence of the model with the outside playground. They played with the toy people, naming them "teacher" and children's names. It seemed that the glued rocks were frustrating to them. They wanted to pick them up and found it unusual that, in spite of their loose appearance, they were all stuck together. This focus on the physical properties of objects, as opposed to the creation of thematic play, typified the difference between our younger and older children in many activities.

Younger Children

Lilly is driving a miniature tricycle down the sidewalk in the model. Sometimes she drives it off the sidewalk and onto the grass. The teacher asks "What will happen if you drive your tricycle on the grass?" He expects Lilly to say something like "It will get stuck" or "I'll have to pedal harder." Lilly ignores the question. Perhaps she is not really involved in the full pretense of how a real tricycle would move across real grass as opposed to real concrete.

We concluded that the question was far too difficult for a 2½-year-old. Besides, the question called for a comparison between two surfaces. This might be hard even in the world of real objects.

Nuffy is playing with a toy person. He has placed it on the platform of the miniature slide. The teacher asks "Where is your little person now?" "On the slide," Nuffy replies. The teacher parallel-plays with Nuffy and some other children. She occasionally makes a comment about her own little person, such as "I'm going through the tunnel."

As it turned out, these games were a good opportunity to teach children the vocabulary of spatial relations. We saw two advantages of the scaled-down space for this purpose. First, the children, from their bird's-eye perspective, could see the movements of objects easily. This is not always possible when the child himself is walking between two structures. Second, the children could generalize what they had learned in the model to what they would do outside. We noticed that certain concepts, such as *opposite* and *balance*, were first learned with miniature objects and then transferred to body-size activities outside. Sometimes it worked the other way, with children learning concepts outside and then applying them to the scaled-down space. We felt that the two types of spaces complemented each other. The scaled-down space helped the children study the global relations; the life-size space gave these spatial relations personal meaning.

Older Children

The older children sometimes used the model to reenact scenes on the playground. One episode was particularly vivid to the children. On Monday a sidewalk steamroller from the university maintenance department came to make some asphalt repairs right outside our window. The children watched the big cylinders of the steamroller press the hot asphalt. They inspected the sidewalk after the steamroller had gone and the asphalt had cooled.

On Wednesday the teaching staff made sure to have a miniature steamroller in the scaled-down space. Several children recognized this new toy as the steamroller they had seen two days before. So they set about pretending to roll the asphalt, going back and forth many times as they had seen the big roller go. Most of the talk centered on the man on the machine and the way the sidewalk was being flattened. As they rolled the toy machine, they pressed down very hard. The weight of the real steamroller had obviously made an impression. The scaled-down version of the real-life situation gave the children an opportunity to express their knowledge and perhaps learn even *more* about what they had seen by virtue of this enactment. As Piaget repeatedly tells us, when a child imitates something that she sees, she learns new things about what she is trying to imitate. Imitation is a creative act of reconstruction, not a copy of something completely understood or perfectly remembered.

One of the favorite games that the older children enjoy is treating the little wooden people as if they were teachers or other children. Here is a case in point. On a sunny day Brian, a graduate student in our early-childhood program, is walking just outside the bay window and says hello to David, who is sitting inside at the playground model. David says hello in return. Brian is the only person on the playground. He walks over to the jungle gym and perches very conspicuously on top of it. Tom, a teacher, asks David "Can you put your little person where Brian is sitting now?" At first David just points to the miniature jungle gym. After a bit of pretend play with the "Brian doll" Tom asks David again to place the wooden person where Brian is sitting now. Brian has moved to the cargo-net climber. David has no trouble playing this game. Wherever Brian walks and perches, David makes the correspondence with the "Brian doll."

The purpose of this activity is to confirm the notion that the people figures can represent current events and current states of real objects. We feel, but have no systematic data to prove, that these types of games increase the amount of representation that the children use spontaneously on other occasions.

In addition to this purpose we discovered an interesting use of the scaled-down space that dealt with the coordination of three points in space. When the children were asked to place a doll at some site that corresponded to the current position of a real person, they had no trouble. When they were asked to position one of the pieces of playground equipment within the general playground area, they had great difficulty. They might be able to place, say, the jungle gym on the correct side of the scaled-down yard. But they would fail to place it the correct distance—or even an approximate distance—from the rear boundary of the model. In other words, they could make a point-to-point correspondence, but they could not make a point-within-a-plane correspondence. The latter is more difficult because the location has to be constructed by the intercept of two distances, the distance from the right boundary and the distance from the rear boundary. We did not push the children to attempt point-to-plane correspondences. We felt that games on the point-to-point correspondences were sufficient and would eventually help children to solve the more difficult problem in their own good time.

FACE TO FACE

Preparing the Environment

Arthur Mann took pictures of the teaching staff and printed each picture as a life-size face. We then mounted these prints on cardboard to make masks. We were curious to see how the children would react to, say, Lisa's face on Tom's body. We predicted every reaction from offhandedness to delight. We were also concerned that it might frighten the younger children, so we were very careful to put the masks on slowly while the children were watching. We did not get any fearful reactions. We did get a lot of delight and some offhanded amusement. Most of these activities took place outside, because we had predicted that the masks would generate too much excitement for an indoor game. After the novelty had subsided, we did play with the face-to-face masks indoors. We should have taken photographs of the children to make masks, but the expense and shooting schedule prevented this.

For some of the masks we cut holes in the eyes, so the wearer could see through the cardboard. For others masks we simply cut out the outline of the hair, so that the photograph looked like a head. We also placed the head on various incongruous objects, such as dolls and stuffed animals. Again, we had some reservations about raising fears in the children, but we also did not want to presume problems where none might exist. Evidently, all of our children were sufficiently familiar with photographs not to be disturbed by this rather unusual use.

Younger Children

There is not much to say about the younger children. They showed no special reaction to the picture of George's face on a baby doll. In Photo 2.11 little David lifts the picture but does not ask questions about it. The teaching staff, on the other hand, found this whole thing very comical. It was as if George were sitting there with his own clone on his knee! The adults could sense the paradox in this arrangement. The younger children could not. Perhaps they were not yet advanced to the point of being able to construct the contradiction of one person's being in two places at once. The adults sensed the comedy, even though they knew one of the persons was a fake.

Older Children

The older children were amused. In Photo 2.12 Hattie recognizes that Tom looks like Lisa. "No!" Hattie exclaims with a mock insistence, "You can't do that. Put it back." She wants Lisa to wear only her own picture. Clayton comes over to Tom and Lisa, looks thoughtfully at Lisa, and then looks at Tom with Lisa's face. After a pause he turns to Lisa and declares, while pointing to Lisa's picture, "That's your name." How perfect! Lisa's face is her name. Words have this type of concreteness for children. Piaget calls it verbal realism, which means that the words are not understood as something separate from what they represent. Perhaps Hattie is experiencing a similar discomfort around violations of pictures. Piaget calls this picture realism, where the picture is not clearly separated from the thing it represents. The correspondence between the picture and its object is too strong to play around with. The correspondence, for Clayton, between a name and a face is so strong that he is perplexed by the mismatch. Perhaps these encounters with the face-to-face masks will give the children a reason to reconsider the nature of the correspondence between pictures and their referents and between words and their referents.

PHOTO 2.11   David wants to lift the photo mask of George on the doll.

NOW-PHOTOGRAPHY

Preparing the Environment

We have taken photographs of the children at other times, and we keep no other type of picture in the classroom. We feel that the medium of pictures should be introduced in a personal way. How often children learn the names of animal pictures and then fail to name these real animals correctly on a trip to the farm. If pictures are used to present unfamiliar content, then children develop some unusual expectations. Derrick, on seeing his first real pig, said "It's too big." He had seen many paper pigs printed on the small pages of children's books. In order to accentuate the fact that a picture corresponds to real things, we try to present the real things first. Thus the name of this activity, Now-Photography.

PHOTO 2.12   Hattie tells Tom that he cannot wear Lisa's face.

We have another reason for wanting to use photographs of the children themselves at play. We want to give them at least the opportunity to think about the photograph as a moment in time. Not all children are able to think of photographs in this way, but at least we have prepared things so that this is a possibility. A picture of Eva pushing the big sona tube the day before makes it possible for her to think about the whole event. If she sees a drawing in a children's book, she has no personal event to recall. Therefore, the drawing in the book is probably no more than a static picture rather than a frozen moment in an activity. At the School for Constructive Play we are very conscious of the need to assure that children understand that static states can change in time (see CCK, pp. 52–53).

Younger Children

The younger children look at a picture and name the objects in it: "Ball. Girl. There's Kevin." Less frequently they comment on the action implied in the photograph: "She's throwing it." This tendency to name objects, as static forms, is directly opposite to their approach to real objects. When they see a resting ball out of reach they say "Throw it" or "Roll it." It is rather curious that they do not at least comment on the action potential of the ball in a photograph.

We suspect that their tendency to name static features in photographs is a product of how photographs are presented to children: unfamiliar content is introduced by an adult asking "What's that?" Content that has no correspondence to children's own past actions makes it more difficult for them to think of the dynamic aspects of photographs. This fact—combined with most adults' habit of asking "What's that?"—contributes to the child's tendency to treat photographs as static representations.

Older Children

The older children not only name objects but also, with equal frequency, describe the action. The quality of these descriptions is richer and more embellished if the photograph shows a recent activity in which the children took part. For example, one day we all went outside and held the edge of a huge parachute. We collectively raised and lowered our arms to make the silk bellow up and gracefully fall from dome to bowl.

Several days later the children looked at a photograph of this activity. Some of them reenacted the raising and lowering of their arms. This reenactment was quite individual; that is, none of the children attempted to form a circle or even a partnership with other children in the classroom. This led us to believe that the group activity with the real parachute might not have impressed the children as a cooperative venture. Nevertheless, the correspondence between the photograph and the real activity did elicit attempts to reconstruct some aspects of the parachute game.

As we said in the previous sections, these attempts to reconstruct past events can themselves lead to *new* knowledge. Perhaps if the children had continued to reenact the motions of the parachute game, they might have joined hands in the process. Several children's lifting and lowering of an *imaginary* parachute would greatly accentuate the cooperative and coordinated nature of this activity. Without the real parachute the children would not have the silk itself to guide the timing of their actions.

We did try to enact catching imaginary balls and tugging imaginary ropes during movement period. Our head teacher, Peter, applied whiteface, as all mimes do, and played these imaginary games. The intent was to have the children mentally construct the movements rather than respond reflexively to the constraints of real objects. We will talk about our few successes and many failures with this game in the section on self-to-object perspective in Chapter Three.

EQUIVALENCE: DIFFERENT OBJECT, SAME USE

Primarily, equivalences of use differ from equivalences of state in that they involve cause and effect. Two objects can cause the same effect—an equivalence of use—without looking the same—having the same state. Both a hammer and the heel of a shoe can drive a tack into a board. Problems can often be solved by figuring out new uses for old objects, by seeing an equivalence of use between an unfamiliar object and a more familiar one.

CREATIVE PROBLEM SOLVING

Preparing the Environment

Here, as in many of the activities that we have described, the best preparation is a prepared mind. The teachers are sensitized to opportunities to support the children's attempts to find a creative solution to some problem. It is true that some problems are beyond the resources of 2- to 5-year-olds, such as a broken tricycle or a stuck zipper; in these situations the child must rely on an adult. Classrooms are different. They exist because of the forethought that adults use to arrange them for the sole purpose of educating the child. This means that the teaching staff considers the abilities of individual children and then stages problems that are within their resources.

A teacher might deliberately make a table wobble by screwing one leg into its socket a little too far. She anticipates that the children will find the wobbly table annoying and try to find some way to prevent it from wobbling, such as putting folded cardboard under the short leg. These resources do not exceed the manual and mental competence of the preschooler. Adding "length" to the leg with cardboard has an effect that is equivalent to adding length by unscrewing the leg a little.

Entry

For younger children equivalent functions are best practiced in reference to a whole object. A cup can be used as a shovel; a wooden cylinder from the block set can be used as a rolling pin in the role-play area. Young children are quick to assimilate new objects into familiar schemes of action. But they would be hard pressed to solve problems, such as the wobbly table, that involve an addition of parts or the modification of parts of a whole object.

The older children are better able to make creative modifications in the parts of an object to make it work. For example, if the axle of the Tinker Toy truck is missing, the older child may grab a pencil from a table top and jam the wooden wheels onto either end of it, thereby solving the problem. She is able to see the equivalence between the missing dowel and the pencil—both whole objects—even though the dowel is only a part of the whole truck. The younger the child, the more difficult it is for her to *diagnose* the subparts of a problem. This characteristic goes back to our earlier comments that the younger children are more likely to *exchange* whole objects when the one they have does not work. They have difficulty diagnosing the *change* required to improve the broken object.

Younger Children

Elaine, the head teacher, has prepared the environment by removing all the sand from the sand table. She has placed the sand, about 50 pounds, in a big pasteboard box. When the children arrive they find the sand table empty and see the sand in the box. "Who did that?" Jenny asks the sand table itself. She and Katie set about transferring the sand by scooping up double handfuls from the box and walking the 4 feet to the table.

Loren, an older child, tries to pull the big box over to the sand table with no success. Jenny then realizes that the handful approach will take a long time, so she scouts for containers. Elaine has made sure that some such things are accessible. At first the children, now as a group project, use ordinary objects such as spoons and shovels. This is not much better than the handfuls in terms of the amount transferred per trip.

Katie runs to the kitchen area and gets a cookie sheet. By pushing the rigid sheet under the sand she can lift a large quantity and carry it, as on a tray, to the sand table. The other children follow up on Katie's idea. They understand that one does not need a container to transfer the sand. A rigid sheet, even though it has no rim, can serve the same function. The children use other cookie sheets, shallow baking trays, and planks from the block area. Loren even tears off a cardboard flap from the box that is holding the sand. He jams its edge into the sand and carries it to the table like a load of mortar, cradled in the V of the cardboard.

All of these children solved the problem by sensing the potential use of objects—that is, different objects have the same use. Loren's solution was more advanced, because he sensed the use of part of an object—the flap of the pasteboard box. Loren's was a real act of creativeness, given that the flap was part of the very object that was the problem. Loren, in effect, had transformed the obstacle into a solution!

Older Children

Chris is building a two-story tower in the block corner. He first places a double unit flat on the floor. He then takes two doubles and stands them on the floor at each end of the first block. Because he does not stand them on the flat block itself, it is impossible for him to span the two uprights with another double. See Photo 2.13 for his solution. After trying to place a double between the two uprights, he searches for a larger block. He uses a triple unit with success, but he keeps one end of the lintel

PHOTO 2.13   Chris uses a large lintel to span the bottom two uprights.

flush with the upright on his left. Finally, he stands two triples upright on the opposite ends of the block serving as the lintel. This time he is forced to place the uprights on the foundation block itself (there is no floor under this lintel). Next (after this photograph was taken), Chris places another triple across the uprights. This time it does not fall through! He is very pleased. He studies his two-story tower. What has he learned? He knocks it down and starts over.

This time, Chris builds the structure you see in Photo 2.14. We will describe the sequence and what we feel is the significance of Chris's construction.

Chris begins with a triple flat on the floor. Then he takes two uprights and, instead of standing them on the floor adjacent to the opposite ends of the triple, stands them on the triple itself. Now he has avoided the classic mistake. He will be able to use a lintel that is neither too short nor too long for the distance between the two uprights. He takes a triple and places it on top of the two uprights with great satisfaction that *both* ends of the lintel are flush with the outside edge of the respective uprights. It is perhaps an arbitrary fact that the uprights are themselves doubles. He has only certain blocks nearby. Alternatively, he may be anticipating that, if he uses two triples as uprights, his remaining doubles will be too short to span the uprights.

After building the first story of this tower he adds two more doubles upright, again forced to place them on the lintel, rather than on the floor. He caps his tower with a triple placed across the two uprights. He leaves this tower standing for a good while before he takes it apart.

We observe here the beauty of self-regulated learning. Chris, due to the constraints of the physical environment, was forced while building the first tower to place the two second-story uprights *on* the ends of the lintel. If the environment had given him the option, he would have placed the uprights *next to* the ends of the block

PHOTO 2.14   On his second try, Chris places the bottom two uprights on top of the block on the floor.

below. But once he had been forced to place the uprights this new way, he evidently understood the improvement in symmetry and stability of the whole construction. With uprights *on* the ends one can make an exact fit with a lintel. So, on the second tower he placed the uprights on the foundation block, *even when he could have done it otherwise.*

Now, here is the essence of learning. Chris added a constraint that was not there in the environment. He constructed the constraint (no uprights on the floor) because he felt it was needed to reach his goal. Learning, in all its complexity and sophistication, is generally no more than learning what *not* to do when there are no physical constraints for not doing it.

Although this episode is a good example of self-regulated learning, it also portrays Chris dealing with equivalent uses. He understood that the block on the floor could function in the same way that the lintel functioned. Both of these blocks could be a support for uprights. If he had persisted in seeing the floor itself as the primary support, he would never have placed the first-story uprights on the ends of that block flat on the floor.

If you feel that this discussion of Chris has been too analytical, as we have been told by students and teachers, then please consider what this complaint means. Does it mean that this level of detail is too difficult? Yes, it is difficult. Does it mean that the analysis might be inaccurate? Yes, it could be inaccurate. Does it mean that the analysis is not worthwhile? No, we hope this is not true. We feel strongly that a close analysis of children's behavior is necessary to understand them. We grant the difficulty and the many mistakes that we, as teachers, will make, but the alternative seems to be less desirable. Teaching children with a complete faith in our gut reactions seems like a huge waste of our body from the neck up.

SIMULTANEOUS USES

The difficulty level of a problem doubles when the child must understand that two different objects serve the same use simultaneously. The problem of building a three-block bridge is not too difficult. The upright blocks' use is to support something; the lintel's use is to be supported. Try to have the child construct a two-block arch, leaning one block against the other and releasing, so that the arch remains. In this arrangement each block serves the same use—support—simultaneously. The left block supports the right, and the right block at the same time supports the left block.

In Photo 2.15 you can see Marya trying to construct the arch she saw George make a few minutes earlier. She is using the same blocks that George used, so any difficulty cannot be reasonably attributed to them. Notice how she has placed the block in her right hand under the side of the other block. Her blocks here make the statement "Right supports left and left is supported by right." Each block has one use, apparently. When she releases her grip, the blocks fall to the table. She may even try it by switching the uses, the left becoming the supporter and the right the supported. The arch still falls. To solve this problem, the children must understand that each block has the same use simultaneously, not successively.

You see Marya solving the problem in Photo 2.16. She gently places the blocks edge to edge and makes the adjustments necessary to have them remain in an arch. She evidently realizes that two objects can have the same use at the same time. The blocks support each other.

When the younger children see a teacher make such an arch, they attempt to reconstruct it in the most interesting ways. One child just stands the two blocks upright on the table with a space in between. Another child places one block upright and holds the second at a right angle to it in an inverted-L formation.

Each child got half of the solution. The first made the block free standing but had no "ceiling" to pass under. The second made the "ceiling" to pass under but had not made the structure free standing. To think about both uses at once exceeds the capability of the younger children (level of opposition). The older children, with some trial and error, solve the problem (level of variation).

The discussion of Marya is included just to define what we mean by simultaneous uses and to outline why these problems are so difficult. We are not recommending that the arch-building task become a standardized curriculum item. We are asking that you be sensitive to the structure of the child's play so that you can better understand why a child might be having problems. The following is an example of this type of sensitivity facilitating a learning encounter for a child. Embedded in the child's free play is an encounter with different-object, same-use equivalence.

We have rigged a set of swings in the classroom. The swings consist of two seats on opposite ends of a nylon rope. The rope passes through two pulleys about 3

PHOTO 2.15   Marya tries to balance these blocks by placing one on top of the other.

PHOTO 2.16   Marya solves the problem by placing the two blocks against each other.

feet apart, anchored to a ceiling beam in the classroom. The pulleys and rope are visible to the children. Any extra weight placed in one swing makes the opposite swing go up.

Aaron pushes down the right seat to the floor. He turns and notices that the left seat is up. He pushes the left seat down. As he starts to walk away, he stops short when he notices the right seat once again up. So he pushes it down a little more vigorously. The left seat goes up. He is greatly perplexed. From his level of understanding (level of opposition) he is looking at two independent seats, each hanging by its own rope. So why can't he get them both down?

The teacher catches a glimpse of Aaron's perplexity, so she watches him. He alternately pushes one seat down, shifts, and pushes the other seat down. She realizes that Aaron is making a false assumption about the separateness of these two seats. She stands ready to protect Aaron's space so that he has an opportunity to work this problem out. The teacher is aware that the problem is typical for children Aaron's age, about 3 years old.

Aaron then does a most interesting thing. He stands midway between the two seats, turns sideways, places a palm on each seat, and simultaneously pushes down on each seat! Now, as foolish as this is, it is quite clever. It is quite consistent with his belief that the two seats are on separate ropes but are for some reason being contrary. To see his logic, think of a mother having trouble with two contrary children in the grocery store. She would, no doubt, take both children, one in each hand, to bring them down, metaphorically speaking. That's the best way to bring two independently moving objects to rest in the same place.

In spite of Aaron's objective, the absolute resistance of these two seats when he attempted to move them simultaneously might have given him the information he needed regarding their connectedness. The simultaneous resistance of the seats could result only if the two seats were connected. Both seats have the same purpose of making the other move.

Aaron explores with this new scheme of behavior. He pushes slightly on the left seat, feeling the right rise slightly; he pushes slightly on the right seat, feeling the left seat rise slightly.

It never became apparent that Aaron really figured out that these seats were on a common rope. But his explorations were probably leading him into a better understanding of their connectedness. As we said when we discussed Marya's trying to lean the two blocks together, the difficulty level doubles when the child encounters simultaneous uses. Aaron could not imagine that the seats cause each other to go up and therefore cancel each other out. The teacher should say very little, even though she recognizes the structure of the problem. She might have ventured, when Aaron was pushing down on both seats, "They are both going up." Chances are, Aaron would learn more from his own actions, but sometimes words help the child to bring his actions into a coherent set of relations.

EQUIVALENCE THROUGH PRETENSE

Children begin pretend play around age 2 and seem to use pretense with increasing frequency up to 3 or 4. Then it levels off in frequency, even though the form may change. At the earlier stages pretense consists mainly in using whole objects as pretend objects. A wooden disk can be a pretend cookie, and a Popsicle stick can be an airplane. One object serves the use of the missing object in a manner of pretense.

The older child seems to require more exact correspondence for objects to substitute for each other. He will fly a pair of crossed Popsicle sticks around the room but will not be satisfied with a single stick representing an airplane. We would be reluctant to say that the older child is less creative and more rigid. We prefer to think that the older child is being creative in the way he represents those aspects central to the use of the missing object. For example, the older child is more likely to think of representing the wings of an airplane. The essence of the airplane is a little more precise for the older child, and the means of establishing the correspondence between that essence and the pretend object is more complex, not less creative.

Preparing the Environment

Pretend games can be encouraged in a variety of ways. We have found two ways to be exceptionally successful. In our role-play area, set up as a child-sized kitchen and dining room, we mix meaningful objects and amorphous objects together. We have miniature toasters, plates, teapots, and saucepans mixed with play dough, pieces of wood, and wads of paper. The children do not hesitate to use the amorphous objects as imaginary knives, forks, bread, pie, and "whipped cream" (the wad of paper placed on top of the pretend pie). In the atmosphere of pretense children easily establish correspondence of the same use for different objects (the amorphous object that is present and the real, nonpresent object for which it stands).

A second procedure works even better to generate pretend play. We bring all of our children into the large classroom just after snacks. They sit down as a group and watch the staff act out a two-minute skit using props such as hats, real objects, and amorphous objects. Then the children are free to play with these props in any manner they like. They can reconstruct what they have seen the teachers perform or invent new scenes or do whatever else they want. After the skit the teachers blend into the wall, protect the safety and happiness of the children, but do not direct their play. The following is an example of one day's success.

Entry

Tracy and Fredi are to act out a skit. Norine is to narrate the action. They have prearranged the room before the children come in from the smaller room where they are having snacks. The theme is "rescue." Tracy and Fredi, women, have on fire hats. They are standing inside a cardboard box that is painted like a fire truck. The other teachers bring the children in and have them sit on the platform in the middle of the room. The children are used to this routine; they know they are to watch the skit for a few minutes and will be allowed to play immediately afterwards.

Norine, from the sidelines, begins her narration. "Tracy and Fredi have been working at the fire station. They decide to take a break and go to the ice cream store." Norine continues her narration while Fredi and Tracy walk through the motions with much expression and animation. The children are delighted. Then there is a scream from the climber/loft. A mother and child are in distress. Tracy and Fredi jump in their fire truck and clang-clang to the loft, where the mother yells down for help. The firefighters tell her to lower her baby into the stretcher. The mother does, and then the firefighters help the mother down. They make a few dashes back and forth from the water table to the climber/loft, throwing pretend water on the imaginary fire. End of the two-minute skit.

The children now converge on the props. Bobby and Nauman put on the fire hats, put the doll in the stretcher and, with Lauren looking on, also in a fire hat, they play "rescue" by walking the doll to a pretend hospital under the climber/loft. The hospital is completely their own invention.

Matthew, a younger child, runs from the water table to the climber and yells "Fire! Fire!" He returns to the water table and runs back to the climber, still yelling "Fire! Fire!" and laughing as he does so. He repeats this by himself six or seven times, with no less joy on the seventh run than the first.

Loren goes to the ice cream table and starts to take everyone's order of ice cream. Cardboard cones (usually used as funnels in the sand table) are used as the ice cream cones. A spoon functions as a pretend ice cream scoop. Loren holds a stick and uses it as a pretend pencil to write down the orders. Loren is embellishing what he saw. There was no "waiter" in the skit. However, there had been a waiter in a skit some days earlier.

For 30 minutes the children reconstructed, ad-libbed, invented, and embellished the skit. Many new objects were assimilated into the pretense. We felt that the two-minute skit was an excellent means to set a certain amount of structure without destroying the self-regulated nature of pretend play. The skit was a priming device that the children could use to get themselves started in some type of pretense that they could do as a group, if they wanted. Because they had all seen the same skit, the theme was set for the several who wanted to play in small groups. Individual children, such as Matthew, were also free to do things in their own way. And many objects, in this atmosphere of pretense, were employed to correspond to the use of a missing object.

LEARNING ENCOUNTERS IN THE HOME

The concepts of identity and equivalence are encountered quite often in the family setting. For the very young child it is obviously important to know that Mom in a new hairdo is still loveable, protecting Mom. For a younger sibling it is important to know that this is his or her glass of juice, not Sissy's juice, even though the glass was moved. The smooth flow of play between siblings often depends on their respective ability to establish the identity of something or create an equivalence when needed.

Parents can suggest games for their children or prepare the environment slightly to increase constructive play with these concepts. The following paragraphs present several useful ideas along these lines.

A wooden chair can become a make-believe jail or cage if the child crawls under it instead of sitting on it. The identity of the object remains the same, but its function changes with a change in the spatial orientation the child takes to the chair. Creativity is fostered by parents who find value in this sort of childhood fantasy.

A bed is something to sleep on; but underneath, the bed becomes a secret room. The surface that was previously under the child now becomes the surface over the child. The dual role of that surface (the mattress) is a good example of two-within-one, and fosters the child's sense of getting more from less and two for one. Bunk beds are also particular delights for children because of the change in perspective they afford.

A doll house can be made that looks like the floorplan of your own house. Then the miniature floorplan becomes an equivalence to the child's own home. With this type of play space the child will be able to act out scenes that actually happened in particular parts of the house and can get a better sense of how his or her own house is laid out. It is interesting that children, when asked to draw the room in their own home, show very little understanding of how one room is related to another room. A personalized doll house could remedy this. An afternoon's work by a parent with some sturdy cardboard or wooden partitions could yield a doll house that allows for the same type of activities we described earlier in the Scaled-Down Playground.

A variation on Now Photography is eminently possible within the family. Photographs of family outings are perfect examples of how children can be helped to understand the equivalence, but not identity, of a photograph and the event it represents. Parents can, and naturally do, talk with children about the real events that the child participated in that are portrayed in the photograph. And parents might deliberately take a sequence of snapshots with the idea that it might be fun for the child to arrange the snapshots in chronological order for a family album. For example, a shot of a child approaching the diving board, then one of a child springing up in mid-air, and then one of a child entering the water could be assembled. This family activity is not only a natural way to re-experience the joy of being together outside, but also is a learning encounter with equivalences and, as you will see in Chapter Four, an encounter with the representation of motion.

Outings are also well-suited for other extensions of classroom activities. A trip to the beach can lead to games with containers used in the sandbox at school or even the Buried Body game we describe in Chapter Three, in which the child tries to figure the location of a hidden bodypart. An upside down bucket is equivalent to a rightside up sand castle tower. A toy can make a variety of impressions in the smooth sand in a manner similar to the holes in the Silhouette Sorter. These encounters with the medium of a sandy beach can ebb and flow in a naturalness identical to the oceanside itself. A parent who plays next to the child without directing, but merely by having fun in parallel with the child, will find that the child's explorations of the medium will be constructive and inventive. The parent does not say, "Hey, look at what I can do," or even, "Look how the sand comes out of the upsidedown bucket." The parent simply plays in a manner that is interesting to him or herself and occasionally says, "The sand looks like the inside of my bucket." The parent says this to the sand rather than to the child. This gives children the freedom to listen without fear that if they listen they will be tested for paying atention. Of course, the parent will try to find some form of sand play that is a slight variation on something that the child is doing, but is also in some intellectually honest manner interesting to the parent. This double sensitivity to the child and to yourself will make the play more constructive and more authentic.

SUMMARY: IDENTITY AND EQUIVALENCE CORRESPONDENCE

In the activities in this chapter children deal with various forms of correspondence. We have identified four forms, the combination of *identity* versus *equivalence* and *state* versus *use*.

A correspondence can occur between the same object on two different occasions (identity) or between two different objects (equivalence). For example, a turtle in one room may look exactly like the turtle in the next room. The child is confused. Is it his pet, Herbie, or is it another turtle? Does the child say "There's Herbie" or "Who's that?" If he runs back to his room to see if Herbie is still there, we can say that he is using a procedure to distinguish a case of equivalence from a case of identity correspondence.

These two categories can be further subdivided into correspondences of states versus correspondences of use. The following are two examples of equivalence. Say that a child recognizes that a toy shovel looks vaguely like a paddle mirror. So she says "This looks like a mirror." She has made a correspondence between the shape of the shovel and the imagined shape of the mirror (correspondence of state). Then she may use the shovel as a pretend mirror, commenting on her imagined reflection. Now she has made a correspondence between the pretend use of the shovel and the ordinary use of a real mirror (correspondence of use). Both of these examples deal with cases of equivalence (two different objects).

The child who can make such correspondences can be more creative in her play and more effective in her work. She can recognize and create similar states across a variety of objects and media; and can use a variety of objects to solve problems when resources are limited.

We always try to stage the activity so that the children can use their own procedures for creating and checking correspondences. The shadow box, overhead projector, rolled-out play dough, scaled-down playground, Silhouette Sorter, and blocks are good examples. In each of these activities the children have control over the procedures that produce the correspondences between one state (or use) and the other. We deemphasize the passive matching of states (and uses) often found in other preschool curricula. But in some activities, such as those dealing with photography, the children cannot produce the correspondence. The camera does it automatically. In these cases we at least try to use photographs of recent activities in which the children have taken part. We hope that this type of photography increases the probability that the children are using the photo as an equivalence to the more complete and more kinetic real event (see Now-Photography).

If we made some general statements now about how children at different developmental levels behave, then you should be able to recognize these same trends in most any activity you design yourself. This way, the handbook should be more useful for you and the particular constraints of your own school. All of these trends refer to encounters with correspondences, but you will see similar trends in the chapters to follow.

DEVELOPMENTAL TRENDS

TWO WITHIN ONE

Children pass from a level of not understanding that one thing can be two things at once to a level at which the two-within-one condition is obvious. These relations occur in a variety of contexts.

Cases where object is both itself and something else:

The younger children did not show any particular surprise when a table was both itself, but upside down, and also a sandbox. Older children would probably have commented on the "funny" way we were using the table.

The younger children did not sense the ingenuity of using household objects, such as pipe cleaners, to represent outdoor equipment in the scaled-down playground, such as the cargo net. Our older children also did not show much reaction, but our teachers were amazed. Perhaps children only slightly older than our 4-year-olds would sense the twoness within one, the pipe cleaner as both itself and a rope.

Our 2- and 3-year-olds showed no particular reaction when one teacher's photograph masked another teacher's face. The older children, around 4, laughed at the incongruity of, say, Tom's being both himself and Lisa at the same time.

The younger children were more likely to treat a case of two within one as if the two were completely different. A party hat was a hat, and the same object inverted was a funnel, but the 2-year-olds did not call the party hat on the head a funnel. They might call both the hat and the funnel a triangle. But the common label for both positions in no way indicated their appreciation of twoness within oneness.

Cases where one object is both a whole and several parts:

The younger children's pretense consisted of creating correspondences between global qualities, such as using a ruler for an airplane. The older children would create correspondences more definitively, such as by adding a cross stick to a ruler to make a pretend airplane. The airplane, for the older children, was both itself and the two parts, fuselage and wings.

The younger children could solve problems creatively by substituting an entire, unfamiliar object for a more common, unavailable object. The older children could solve problems creatively by diagnosing the subpart of an entire object that was not working and making a creative substitution for that part alone. In other words, the older children could "conserve" the whole while changing the part. This means that the new part was not, in itself, a complete and sufficient whole. It was, indeed, both itself and its relation to the whole. For example, if a sand shovel was not working, a young child might throw it aside for a new object (exchange). The slightly older child might try to push the loose blade more securely onto the handle (change rather than exchange).

The younger children's use of objeccts in the scaled-down playground duplicated the action of life-size objects (whole object here corresponds to whole object there), but they did not make more subtle part-to-part correspondences. For example, Lilly could move a miniature tricycle the way a real tricycle moves as a whole. But she showed no evidence that she could represent the relation between the pretend hard wheels and the pretend soft earth (a part-to-part relation within the whole theme of tricycle riding). The older children included these more subtle part-to-part relations within a general theme of pretense.

The younger children could match the orientation of a whole object to different perspectives in the Silhouette Sorter. They had difficulty when the hole in the Silhouette Sorter called for a rearrangement of the parts within the whole. The older children could handle both changes in orientation of the whole and changes in the rearrangement of the parts.

Cases where one point has two references in space simultaneously:

In the scaled-down playground the younger and the older children alike had difficulty placing miniature objects in locations that were determined by reference to two other points—for example, the jungle gym in reference to both a side and back wall. The older children could make point-to-point correspondences—for example, place the "Brian doll" on the jungle gym itself.

Cases where one object has two actions simultaneously:

The younger children had great difficulty thinking that each block in a two-block arch has two uses, supporter and supported. The older children were able to construct the two-block arch after some groping.

DECENTERING FROM AN EGOCENTRIC PERSPECTIVE

Children pass from focusing on those attributes and perspectives of objects and people that are most closely aligned with themselves (egocentrism) to a greater use and understanding of attributes and perspectives that they do not currently hold.

Cases where the child centers on effects that are close at hand (proximal) versus cases where the effects are beyond physical contact with the self (distal):

The younger children preferred to control media such as sand, play dough and paint directly with their hands, whereas the older children became equally interested in how different implements affect these media.

The younger children liked to touch shadows on the wall, as if they thought the shadows were objects. The older children would stand back and cast shadows with their hands some inches from the wall.

Cases where the child centers on a single aspect of an event that has personal relevance versus cases where the child includes the perspective of other objects and persons:

The pretense of the younger children was often the repetition of one impressive aspect of a scene they had observed. For example, Matthew ran back and forth yelling "Fire! Fire!" The younger children center just on the thing they do themselves. Their pretense is idiosyncratic. The older children try to act out roles and events that include other children and role-play in small groups that collectively carry out a theme.

The younger children tend to explore the physical properties of the sand and the play dough. The older children are more likely to treat these media as the "ground" for thematic play. That is, the older children decenter from the immediate properties of the media and treat them more as a backdrop for interobject and interpersonal events.

SEEING THE DYNAMIC WITHIN THE STATIC

Children pass from seeing a stimulus as not much more than a particular static configuration to seeing the action that is potential in that particular configuration.

We saw one case of this dimension in Now-Photography:

The younger children would name objects in a photograph, whereas the older children, in addition to naming, would relate actions implied in the photograph. The older children more clearly understood that a photograph is a static representation of a dynamic moment in time.

We will see many more examples of this dimension in Chapter Five, such as when children do or do not anticipate how objects of different shapes will roll in different ways.

FROM OPPOSITE EXTREMES TO MIDDLE DEGREES

Children have a tendency to transform events to their terminal state—that is, all or none. Only later in development do they understand that there are middle states along a continuum of change.

We saw a clear case of this dimension in the Two-Block Arch:

The younger children would change the support block into the block that was supported. That is, they changed the supporter to its opposite value. Had they been able to consider some middle state, halfway between supporter and supported, they might have solved the two-block-arch problem. The older children began with these same alternations between opposites, but they eventually considered the middle state of partly supported and partly supporter.

We will see many more examples of this dimension in Chapters Four and Five such as when children can or cannot consider how to make water flow "a little-fast" or a ball roll almost all the way.

We think you should use these developmental trends to guide your observations of your own children. We hope that you do *not* use them to make games that try to accelerate development from one stage to the next. If you place your emphasis on a graduated curriculum, you will quite probably interfere with the self-regulated nature of child development. But if you understand these general developmental trends and emphasize the natural child in all his or her completeness of spontaneous exploration, we think that you will be a better teacher. Knowing what children of a given level are likely to be struggling with will help you make a more judicious entry into their world.

Chapter Three

Changing
Perspective

ENCOUNTERS WITH PERSPECTIVE

Between the ages of 2 and 5, children make a great deal of progress in their ability to consider perspectives different from their own. At the younger end of this age range children assume that what they see is what people nearby see.

Peter asks 2-year-old Lilly to hold the mirror so that he can see his face. Lilly holds the mirror up all right, but she has the reflecting side facing herself. Matthew is playing with a paddle mask, a clown's face. He approaches Cathy, holds the mask up to his face, and looks through the eye holes at her in apparent expectation that she will say something about his mask. But he has the back of the mask facing Cathy and the painted side facing himself.

These are forms of centration on what the self can see. As children grow older, they learn to decenter from the self-perspective and consider the other person's point of view. Four-year-old Genielle sees Barbara's necklace, a small gold chain. "You can't see your necklace," Genielle says. Barbara asks why not. "Because your chin is in the way," Genielle replies with confidence. Even though she can see Barbara's necklace, she realizes that Barbara herself cannot.

We have divided our activities dealing with perspective into two broad categories. The first category, self-to-object perspective, involves encounters that require the child to think about her position in space relative to some object. For example, the child is about to release a tether ball suspended from the ceiling. She wants to knock over two bowling pins in one swipe of the ball. To do this, she must stand in a particular position. She must stand so that both pins are in line with the arc of the ball when released. There are only two places within a full circle that she can stand to make the ball hit both pins.

The second category, self-to-other perspective, involves encounters that require the child to think about the timing of an action relative to some other child's action. For example, two children are playing a game of ice fishing. Both have their fishing lines lowered through the same hole in a wooden platform. On the end of their lines is bait, which is just a bit smaller than the hole in the platform. If both children want to check their bait at the same time, a bottleneck will result at the ice hole. At least one of the children has to decenter enough to coordinate the timing of his action with that of the other child.

Not all of the activities listed under the self-to-other category are strictly cases of good timing. Sometimes, perspective refers to the needs of another person. For example, a teacher with her arms held in slings cannot scratch her own face. A child who volunteers to help the teacher has, in effect, taken the teacher's perspective. This, too, is an example of self-to-other perspective.

These activities involving taking another's perspective emphasize what has traditionally been called social development. It is unfortunate that social development has often been listed as a curriculum objective separate from cognitive development. One commonly finds curriculum models for early childhood divided into social, cognitive, and sensorimotor development. This division gives the impression that cognitive development pertains only to the academic subjects, such as prereading and premath skills. The false separation of these domains of development can also be heard in the everyday talk of parents. "I want my child to learn to share and get along with other children. I don't care too much right now about cognitive skills."

We certainly agree that getting along with other children is a high priority for early-childhood education. However, we treat these social skills as just another problem to be solved by the child. The child uses the same intelligence to solve problems of a social nature that he uses to solve other problems. In fact, there is some evidence that learning to consider his relation to the physical world helps a child make more accurate judgments about the social world.

For example, if Kevin realizes that his plastic block can make the same designs in the play dough that Marika's block does, he will not feel the need to grab her block. In perspective taking, knowledge of the physical world may be still more closely related to making good judgments in the social world. Kevin has realized that Catherine cannot see his new tennis shoes from where she is sitting. This knowledge enables him to understand that she may not feel the same excitement and pleasure that he is feeling. At this point in Kevin's social development he may expect that, when Catherine does see his shoes, she will have feelings similar to his. Later, he comes to know that, even when Catherine's physical perspective enables her to see his new shoes, she may feel different than he does. He may even anticipate that she will feel disappointed or jealous that he has new shoes and she does not.

SELF-TO-OBJECT

BURIED BODY

Preparing the Environment

The "body" in this case is really a life-size outline drawing of a child that is "buried" in the sand table. The drawing has clothing and features, so that, when parts of it begin to be uncovered, children will infer that it is indeed a picture of a person under the sand. The drawing is taped to the bottom of the emptied table, and then the sand is put back over it.

This activity evolved from earlier efforts to create perspective taking at the sand table. That site was appropriate because several children stand around a common space, each of them having a slightly different point of view. In these early efforts we used small, wooden dolls (such as the Fisher Price people) and pieces of cardboard decorated as walls and fences to discuss what each doll could see. For example, a doll with its eyes facing a wall could not see the doll on the other side, and a doll lying face down in the sand could see only sand. Typically, younger children believed that their figures would always see what they themselves could see, no matter which direction the doll's eyes were facing. Older children became involved in the idea of varying points of view and created dramatic situations.

After a few days of playing "what can you see?" and "peekaboo" with these small figures and barriers, we noticed, many children became comfortable discussing what the figures could see looking directly across from them—which is what they were doing most of the time. But the children were less adept at considering perspective in other planes. That is, they used the notion of seeing as if it were a horizontal beam of light from the eyes. Thus, views from a downward glance or a sideways look were not considered. Further, the figures usually "saw" what the children could literally see themselves.

This brings us to how the Buried Body came to be. In replacing many small figures, each having its own viewpoint, with one large figure that was initially seen only in part and whose identity was not immediately obvious, we changed the encounter in two ways. First, there was more cooperation involved. By eliminating the figures and props that had led to a series of mostly individual actions and setting out only a few implements for digging, we shifted the focus to a group project to uncover and identify the unknown thing at the bottom of the sand. Second, there was a shift from "seeing" to "identifying." To identify what was buried in the sand table, it was necessary to reason from a part to the whole. Could a child in seeing part of the uncovered figure—say, a hand—know that the hand might be part of a larger thing, a drawing of a child's figure that was lying under the sand?

Entry

Of course, the children are initially unaware that anything is hiding under the sand. They begin to dig and mold as usual. The teacher realizes that a clue is needed, so she announces she is going to "dig deep." As often happens, several children imitate her and also begin to dig deep. The teacher, Fleet, is digging near where the figure's hand is, and Genielle is digging near its shirt. Genielle gets down to the bottom first, but she makes no comment on what she has uncovered. Fleet looks over and says "Good grief! There's something down there." The children then begin to offer guesses about what it might be. Because the figure's shirt is striped, parallel lines are visible. Genielle proudly concludes that it is a fence, making a thematic link to the previous play with figures and barriers.

Without commenting on the correctness of this guess, Fleet finishes uncovering her area and reveals the hand. To her surprise, no one immediately realizes that it is a hand. Nor do the children indicate that they think the two uncovered areas are connected. However, several children become interested in the bottom of the sand table. This exploration even leads one child to peek under the table itself when asked what he thinks is under the sand. Some children say that nothing is under the sand. Clayton looks at Fleet and says "The table, silly."

Eventually, the buried body is revealed and the children reach a consensus that it is a girl. At this point the conversation begins to focus on what the buried body can see lying on the bottom of the sand. Clayton says she can't see anything because she has sand in her eyes. Although most of the sand has been cleared away and piled up around the leg and foot areas, there are a few grains in the figure's eyes. A younger child, Katie, announces that the buried body is looking at her. Immediately, all the other children standing around jump on the egocentric bandwagon and call out "Me, me." In reality, although they are all looking at the figure, the eyes of the figure are looking straight up at the ceiling. So Fleet looks up to the ceiling without saying anything. Katie and Clayton also look up. The teacher does not correct a wrong response or even quiet the "me" chorus. She nonverbally adds the possibility of another perspective.

Most of the children in this age group exhibit what we call physical centration. That is, they concentrate on one aspect of an object, usually the part they are looking at directly. In this case the focus was on the sand, and few children simultaneously held in mind that there was something else below, be it table bottom or drawing. This was especially true for the younger children.

Younger Children

Younger children might have benefited more from this activity if they had witnessed the process of burying the life-size drawing. As it was, it seemed hard for them to imagine anything of such size below all that sand. Kevin became absorbed in clearing away as much sand as possible in front of himself, but he lost sight of the goal of identifying the buried body, even after other children had revealed the shirt and both hands. Katie thought she had found a tree, but she quickly accepted Genielle's conclusion that it was a hand and raced around to the other side of the table to find the other hand. This indicated that she had a sense of the proportions of the drawing and of where she herself should be in order to find the matching hand.

Several times Katie and Kevin imitated the actions of older children and teachers, in digging deep, in searching under the table, and in looking up at the ceiling. It was Katie who announced that the drawing was looking only at her, but she was also the first one to look up to the ceiling. In general, most of the younger children who came to this activity did not grasp the nature of the part-to-whole identity problem. They used the sand in familiar ways—digging, shoving, spreading, and so on.

The activity that preceded the Buried Body, using small figures and barriers, seemed more appropriate for the 2½- to 3½-year-olds. Their imitative, reconstructive, and spontaneous play eventually became full of many examples of visual perspective taking. Months later, there were still reports of what the small figures could see in many other contexts than the sand.

Older Children

It was the older children who seemed most interested in the buried body and went to work on the problem of what it was. David remembered the occasion when the sand table was empty (see Chapter Two) and went off in search of containers to put the sand in. Jenny and Genielle moved a lot of sand down toward the legs and feet, so that the torso and face could be cleared. They were able to construct the whole figure in proper proportion. Clayton became very involved with the drawing's point of view, noticing the sand in its eyes and reasoning that it was therefore unable to see anything. He was also mindful that the bottom of the sand table was below the sand and was mildly exasperated with the question of what was there under the sand. He knew with a feeling of certainty that the bottom of the sand table had to be there. A *bottom* is really a relative term that identifies something in space below something else. Most of the younger children did not think about the possibility that anything was below what they could see.

BOTTOMLESS BOTTLES

Preparing the Environment

In the Buried Body activity many children neglected to see the drawing as a whole with many parts. They centered on the aspect they could see before them, the sand itself. This tendency to center on the closest physical aspect of an object precludes noticing other perspectives about objects. The next two activities, the Bottomless Bottles and the Funny Funnels, are designed so that children will think about and look at the part of the object that is not immediately before them.

Bottomless Bottles is an example of how ordinary classroom materials can be easily modified. It requires no construction and, once completed, can remain a permanent part of the collection of items used with sand and water. We took several pairs of plastic bottles and jars that had screw tops and cut the bottoms off half of them. This was done carefully, so that, if the bottle was sitting on a table, it was not easy to tell that the bottom was gone. Some bottles with bottoms had holes punched or poked in the sides. These modified containers were placed in the water and sand areas along with a few other items for pouring and scooping. We tried to avoid cluttering the area with too many other objects, so that attention would be drawn to the bottomless bottles.

Entry

Unless the water and sand tables are in an inaccessible, poorly lit area or have been set up so often with the same objects that they have become boring, children will come frequently to these areas. We observed that the black liner of our water table made it hard to spot translucent objects under water. A sheet of Mylar (translucent silver plastic) was attached to the liner bottom adding sparkle that renewed interest in the area.

If a teacher was zoned to be near the water table, he would play simply with the bottles, pouring water back and forth or screwing on and removing tops. As a child entered the area, the teacher could hand a bottle to her. Mark recorded such an experience with Marika, age 2½.

Mark gives Marika a normal bottle and asks her to fill it. She does, transferring water from a cup. Then Mark switches bottles and gives her an open-ended one. She does as before, "filling" the bottle. She pours cupfuls in several times. Each time, the water drains into the table. Soon after, Chris, 3, comes over and chooses a bottomless container to fill. He holds it near his body instead of over the table. He manages to get himself fairly wet without realizing it because of his concentration on filling up the bottle from the top. The bottomless bottles prevented Marika and Chris from doing what they expected to do—fill up bottles with water. This is another example of how a violated expectation induces mild conflict.

To expand this encounter and take advantage of the conflicting expectations, Mark models screwing on a top and turning the bottomless bottle upside down so the top is now at the bottom. Now the bottles that Marika and Chris were unable to fill can be filled.

On other occasions older children spontaneously discovered that this was the way to fill such a bottle. Younger children think of the *top* in absolute terms as an object, the *piece* that is screwed on. But in this case the top of an inverted and filled bottomless bottle is what is *at* the top. *Top* is a relative term whose identity is determined by its function.

Younger Children

Younger children consistently center on the top of the bottles and, even when the water is pouring out onto themselves, do not realize that there is no bottom. Alythea was given a bottomless bottle to fill and tried to remove the screwed on lid. When she could not, she gave it back to the teacher to take the lid off. It never occurred to her to invert it and fill up the open end. Many times the younger children would repeat this mistake for days, oblivious to others who realized how to fill such bottles. Rather than tell or show such children how to invert the bottles, we let the materials be self-correcting. This meant that some children would exchange their bottle for another, while others quietly began using the open end as a scoop to fill a normal bottle.

Older Children

The silliness of pouring into an open-ended bottle struck the older children quickly. When Jessica was given a bottomless bottle, she examined it, turned it lid-side down, and began to fill it. She had come to expect that some of the bottles would not have bottoms and that it was necessary to inspect before pouring away. In other words, it was harder to fool an older child.

On another occasion Fleet plays a game with Hattie. She holds a bottomless jar halfway under the water while she fills it. It looks filled because the open bottom is jammed against the table bottom, temporarily sealing it enough so that it holds water. Then she hands the jar to Hattie, offering her a bottle of water. Hattie looks puzzled at the now empty jar, so Fleet repeats the process. Next time, Hattie smiles, takes another bottomless jar, and says to Fleet "Don't look, I'm playing a game. I'm going to fill up a jar." Later, Hattie plays this trick on Kevin, a younger child. But he is not amazed that the filled jar becomes empty as she hands it to him.

Even though many of the older children demonstrated that they could fill an open-ended bottle by inverting it, most of them, when asked to point to "the top," stuck to the idea that the top was the screw-on lid. It is not uncommon for verbal expression to be more limited than or to lag behind physical actions. Teachers often assume that, if a child is unable to answer a question correctly about a certain matter, she doesn't know. Careful observation of children's actions broadens a teacher's understanding of the extent of children's knowledge.

Another way to encourage a child to think about different aspects of a jar is to use one that has a bottom but also has a hole punched in the side. Thus, water flows out the opening, and it is impossible to keep it filled above that level. Especially if the hole is facing away from the child, the child may pour and pour, not knowing why the bottle cannot be filled. Few children realize that force is exerted sideways against the walls of the bottle and not just downward. Of course, someone on the opposite side of the table may see that the water is streaming out the hole. Hattie saw this happening at the sand table. David, across from her, was frustrated in his attempts to fill his bottle. Hattie knew that sand was "leaking" out the side, but she didn't know that David could not see it. She kept saying "Silly, silly" to him, and finally in exasperation told him to turn the bottle around. She had realized that he did not know what she knew. Hattie's comments indicate that she experienced this encounter as both a self-to-object and a self-to-other perspective problem.

FUNNY FUNNELS

Preparing the Environment

Funny Funnels is really a form of Bottomless Bottles. It involves changing a funnel by clogging up the drain hole. We plug the drain end of a funnel by inserting a tightly wadded piece of Nerf sponge into the hole and putting duct taping over the bottom. Water and sand are held in such a funnel as if it were a cup. These modifications are done to encourage children to think about the part of the funnel they cannot see, the drain hole. Younger children, especially, have absolute expectations about common objects. When these expectations are not met, taking an unfamiliar perspective clears up the mystery.

Entry

These funnels can be used in the same manner as the bottomless bottles. In fact, they can be used at the same time. The reactions of the children are very similar. The youngest ones do not exhibit surprise at the nondraining funnels. They may not even notice that the funnels they are holding are still full. Older children notice immediately that something is wrong.

For example, Hattie waits for a few minutes for her funnel to empty its water. When this doesn't happen, she turns it over and discovers the taped-up hole. Tom then asks her how to make her funnel empty out the way that his is emptying. Hattie thinks of several possibilities. First, she suggests turning the funnel upside down. Then, she suggests taking off the tape and pulling out the sponge. Her final idea is quite unexpected. She takes a clear plastic tube, inserts it into the full funnel and begins to blow hard in the other end. The water surges over the side of the funnel. A still older child, say, 6 or 7, could be questioned about whether such a funnel is really a funnel at all. Is the essence of being a funnel eliminated by plugging it up? Is it now a cup, even though it is shaped like a funnel? These questions pursue the equivalences contained in this learning encounter. The funnel plugged up has the same use as a cup, but it really does not look the same. (See the section in Chapter Two on Equivalence: Different Object, Same Use.)

There is one final comment to make about Funny Funnels and Bottomless Bottles. You may have noticed that these activities involve many objects, each somewhat different from the other. Objects are exchanged, not changed within themselves. As we have mentioned, we would prefer it the other way. But physical limitations prevented us from creating transformable objects. Perhaps you can invent a way to make a funnel whose drain hole gradually opens and shuts or a bottle whose bottom is detachable. We did have duct tape around for taping up the punched-out holes in the sides of the bottles and funnels. This allowed the children possibilities for changing the way an object works and then undoing that change. The child who initiates an action that changes the use of an object is more likely to be aware of the relation of the physical characteristics that determine an object's use.

GATE GAME

Preparing the Environment

The Gate Game requires the child to consider the position of his own body in space. That is, the child must decenter away from himself enough to take the position of "me" into account. This game is set up so that changing the position of the self affects how well the child plays the game.

A sturdy piece of cardboard is cut with inverted U shapes along the bottom edge. The cardboard is sandwiched between two identical tables and held in place with duct tape below (see Photo 3.1). We use three-sided tables that form a hexagon when put together. One or two objects are set up behind a gate, and the child tries to roll a tennis ball through the gate to knock over the object. The ball is wrapped with tape a few times to highlight its movement. The teacher stands so that he can reposition the objects after the child's ball knocks them down.

PHOTO 3.1   Chris takes aim at the Gate Game target.

Entry

This game quickly attracts children. The teacher simply challenges the player to knock over a certain object. Once a child has mastered a simple, direct-line path from himself to the gate to the object, the teacher can make the game more difficult by putting the object slightly at an angle to the gate. This way, a straight throw misses, and the child must move his body slightly to one side to realign. An impossible setup can also be tried—that is, putting an object close behind the wall. Older children will realize that they cannot possibly hit such an object. Younger children will think that, if they can see it, they will be able to knock it over.

Younger Children

A variety of strategies is exhibited by younger children trying to play the Gate Game. Lillian throws the ball several times, rather than rolling it, but is not successful. She climbs up on the table to reach the gate. Even at this range her ball is not hitting the object. So she climbs down, walks around to the other side, and knocks down the object with her hand! The student teacher, Maria, wisely realizes that the goal of knocking over the object by rolling the ball through the gate is too difficult for Lillian, so she removes the object and suggests that she and Lillian *roll* the ball to each other through the gate. Later, Lillian is able to roll the ball through a gate and knock down objects that are directly centered.

Climbing up on the table is a common response to a series of misses. If this becomes a safety problem, you can put the object on the child's side of the cardboard wall. We also tried elevating the table on a platform for better sighting but found that it made the table a little too high for the shortest children. Another way of making the game easier for herself was done by Sydney. She moved the target object up close to the outermost gate. Because of the hexagonal shape of the table she was able to stand very near this gate and knock down the plastic cow.

Older Children

Even if their control over the ball is not accurate, older children know that they need to line up their bodies with the target object. You will see them squatting down to put their eyes close to the edge of the table, the way a golfer does when putting. Seth played with Tom by instructing Tom to move the target from gate to gate so he could sharpen his aim. Jessica enjoyed setting up her own target, but she always put it right in the gate itself. Hattie stuck her arm through the gate on the outside to roll the ball toward an object in the center of the table. She apparently thought this was easier than rolling the ball through the center gate. After several tries her aim improved, and she moved back a bit. Every child observed modified his or her approach quickly, even within a few minutes' time.

CRAZY BRUSHES

The School for Constructive Play designed four unusual paintbrushes to use with the Plexiglas easel. Crazy Brushes requires the user to accommodate her actions to the actions of the brush. The first of these variations is made by connecting two brushes to one handle. A coat hanger is bent in double thickness and attached to the brushes with duct tape so that the brushes look like a U with a handle at the bottom (see Figure 3.1). The second variation is made by adding an extended, L-shaped handle to a single brush, again using coat-hanger wire and duct tape. The third version is made by attaching a long-handled brush to an adjustable belt, so that the belt, when buckled in the back, has a brush jutting out the front. The final brush is attached to a plastic army helmet from the dress-up collection. It protrudes from a hole drilled into the forehead area of the helmet.

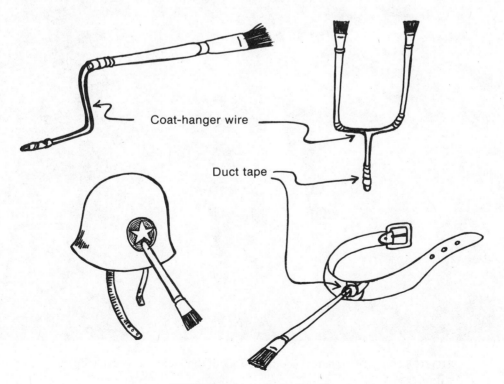

FIGURE 3.1   Crazy Brushes.

The purpose of modifying ordinary paintbrushes is to amplify and exaggerate the child's hand movements. Most children paint or draw with brushes as if they were extensions of the fingers. In Crazy Brushes the action and resulting paint marks of the moving brush are different from the action of the moving hand. Therefore, the child has to decenter from hand movements alone in order to think about the movement of the brush. It seems incongruous or unexpected that making a small circle with the wrist produces a much larger circle of paint. These exaggerated and amplified paint marks help the child notice the shape of the motion, both of the hand and the paint. In order to produce a particular pattern of paint, the child must coordinate the action of the brush with the action of her body.

As you can see in Photo 3.2, Kevin is able to reach the Plexiglas panel above him by using the brush with an extended, L-shaped handle. This gives him the

PHOTO 3.2   Kevin paints on the ceiling of the Plexiglas easel, using one of the Crazy Brushes.

unusual perspective of painting above his head. Later, he looked down on the same panel from the climber/loft and spotted his paint marks. With this brush a simple twisting motion of the wrist produces a large arc of paint. Some children prefer to use the original handle or grasp the brush with both hands.

A child using the double brush often does not realize that there are two brushes and holds one of them by its own handle rather than using the newly constructed handle. Especially when trying to reload the paint, the child finds that the presence of the second brush makes it impossible to do the usual dipping in and lifting up to paint. This frustration leads some to discard the brush. But others eventually figure a way to manage and begin to enjoy the results. The pleasure involved is much like that derived from holding two pens together and making two lines with one stroke.

As you can imagine, the brushes that are worn by the children either around the waist or on the head lead to comic movements and contortions. Rich laughter and giggles accompany intense efforts at moving in just the right way to paint on the Plexiglas panels. In using hats and belts as paintbrush holders, children experience painting from a different perspective. The difficulties of achieving the results that are so easily obtained holding brushes in ordinary fashion make children aware of how different parts of their body can be controlled. Helmet painting comes out zigzaggy, whereas belt painting looks mostly like splotches. The shape of the paint mark is determined by the motion of the brush. In ordinary painting children commonly center only on the motion of the hand. Using Crazy Brushes encourages the child to think about the relation between self and object.

VIDEO VIEWING

Preparing the Environment

Because our program takes place in a lab-school setting, we are fortunate to have the use of videotape equipment. We began using video by making tapes of episodes of children's play to sharpen our observational skills. The equipment was highly interesting to the children, of course, and it was somewhat of a disruption from the planned activities. So we decided not to fight this natural curiosity and brought the monitor in. Once we decided that it was all right for the children to use videotape, too, lots began to happen.

Initially, we placed the equipment in the smaller, quieter of our two rooms. The only other activity going on nearby was at the sand table. We did not want to drain participants from other activities.

Entry

Children get very excited when they recognize themselves on television. Many of the younger children, especially, yell out their names at their own image. It is as if they were talking to a twin of themselves, rather than an image. Kevin does not say "There's me!" but rather "That's Kevin." Cailin, 2½, sees herself on the monitor and says to Tom "She has my shirt. She's outside."

"Are you outside?" Tom asks.

"No, I'm inside."

"But she's outside?"

"Yes."

Cailin was seeing the object on the screen as a separate being in another place. That is, she correctly recognized the correspondence, or similarity, between herself and the television image. But she was still grappling with the problem of whether the correspondence was identical or equivalent. Cailin treated her TV image as an equivalence—that is, another person very much like, but not identical to, her.

This encounter helped us realize that what was missing for Cailin was an understanding of the role of the camera and of the nature of television itself. Thus, to draw attention to the camera and encourage recognition that it was from the point of view of the camera that the image was projected, we invited children to look through the lens. We assumed that an understanding of camera's point of view would help a child realize where she had to stand to be within range and what the relationship between the three points in space (camera to child to monitor) was. We even doctored up the camera to look like a person, complete with one giant eye (the lens), some yarn hair, and a smiling paper mouth.

Another way of helping make the camera more noticeable was to turn it sideways, so that the image on the screen was projected on its side. Most of the children leaned over when they saw themselves this way. Even though the children were unable to do physically exactly what their image was doing (such as stand completely upside down), we are not sure that they realized that it was the tilt of the camera that made them appear that way.

Younger Children

A row of chairs is lined up in front of the monitor. Four children are seated in them and watch as the camera moves slowly from one child to the next, beginning with the faces and moving down their bodies to linger on their feet. A game develops in which the camera moves from shoe to shoe, with the children trying to outguess one another over whose feet are on the screen. One child begins to kick his feet, and the others soon follow in a mellow, sit-down "dance." Then the camera, held by George, also begins to dance with a slight sway. This back and forth goes on for a few minutes until the camera turns away to scan the room. The kickers continue their dance, but now the image they see is no longer their own.

Later, Aaron returns to the chairs when no one else is there. The camera is focused on the sand table. Aaron starts kicking his feet and watching the monitor expectantly.

Older Children

Genielle has been watching herself on the monitor for quite a while when David enters the room. The camera follows him as he walks toward her and stands next to her. David watches for a while and then begins to leave. Again the camera follows him until he has gone, and it remains focused on the empty doorway. Genielle has continued to watch the monitor. When she sees the empty doorway on the screen, she turns and runs into the next room after David.

It seemed as if the image was more powerful than the reality. She did not act as if she knew that David was gone until she saw it on the screen.

Another example illustrates that some children are aware of the perspective of the camera. This time the camera is set up to look down on the sand table. The monitor is nearby, so that Nikos can stand on one side of the table and watch himself on the screen. He has a block in his hand and discovers that he can see it in the monitor. He waves it around a bit but then holds it toward the camera. He gradually lifts the block higher toward the camera until he can stretch no more. All the while he is looking directly at the monitor.

Nikos acted as if he knew that the camera was the source of the image that he saw on the monitor.

Photos 3.3 and 3.4 show videotape being used in a more social setting. This encounter is a two-way experience for Aaron and Genielle, the children kneeling in front of the monitor. First, there is the relationship between themselves and the image on the monitor, a self-to-object issue. The image on the monitor is of another child, Nikos. In this case, the TV image is clearly not a mirror to whatever is in front of it, something that both Aaron and Genielle have previously expected. Aaron, who is pointing to the image on the monitor, has recognized his friend Nikos. Aaron then turns and points to the real Nikos, standing behind. Now the experience is a self-to-other one and a problem of correspondence. How can Nikos be standing here while he is also there on the screen? Are there really two Nikoses?

PHOTO 3.3   Aaron and Genielle see Nikos on the video monitor.

PHOTO 3.4   Aaron and Genielle turn to see the real Nikos in the room.

For Aaron and Genielle to figure this problem out, they must understand the procedures involved; that is, they must understand that the camera is the source of the image. Admittedly, this is beyond the complete comprehension of young children. But the perspective of the camera can be recognized. The children must also know that there really cannot be two Nikoses—a question of identity. Like the confusion between a shadow projected on the wall and the object making the shadow, this dual sighting raised questions of equivalence and identity. Some children (Cailin, for example) treated the television image as if it were identical to the real person. Others, like Aaron, recognized the image for what it is, an equivalent representation of the real person.

PIPE PUT TOGETHER

The material for this activity is a commercial set (see Appendix) of about 45 life-size plastic pipes and joints that can be put together in endless ways for use with water or sand. The pieces screw together, which is too difficult for some of the youngest to do for themselves. But this feature also makes it possible for others to build elaborate constructions.

Preparing the Environment

On several occasions the water table was set up before the children arrived with a complicated, maze-like structure of pipes and joints. Children poured water into several openings, and they could predict where it was going to come out and race to catch it. Sometimes, one child instructed another to stand ready at the other end. This situation called for imagining the pathway of the moving water and anticipating the speed of the flow. It also provided a game that several children could participate in together. They could alter the water's flow by plugging up an opening or twisting a downspout to point up. For the youngest children, though, this was really too many variables to hold in mind at once.

Simpler setups involve two or three connected pieces in many configurations. Some of these are shown in Figure 3.2. These constructions are easier to use. They

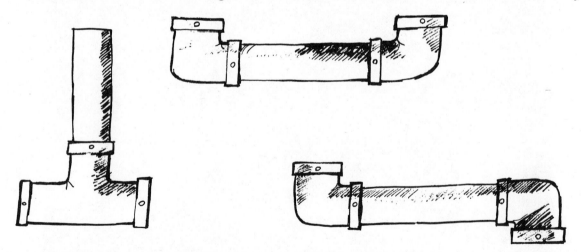

FIGURE 3.2   Pipe Put Together—variations.

can be held with one hand while the other hand is pouring water into them. By moving or twisting one joint piece, the child can change the flow of the water. Holding the pipe in a different orientation also changes the water's movement. All the children enjoy feeling the water wash out over their hands as it comes out an exit hole. Many of them reach inside the various-shaped joints and pipes, acquiring a physical sense of the interior space.

Entry

One variation of Pipe Put Together uses two water tables side by side. When the activity begins, one table is empty; the other has water in it, in which pipes, joints, and containers have been placed. Lauren and Chris both question the student teacher, Maria, about why the first table is empty. Maria shrugs, and Chris asks for permission to fill the empty table. Maria asks Chris how he will do it, and he suggests using a bucket. After a small amount of water has been added to the empty table, Jessica comes over. She wants to pour her pitcher of water through a pipe pivoting on the flush edges of the two tables. She holds the pitcher with her right hand, which she normally uses for pouring, and the pipe with her left hand. Alas, the water goes back into the full table! (See Photo 3.5.)

Jessica did not anticipate the limits or perspective of her own body. Pouring water from her right hand always results in the water going to the left side. Few children are aware that using one side of their body determines the direction of a motion.

Jessica's second try (not pictured) is also an example of centering on her goal without accounting for her body in space. She continues to hold the pitcher in her right hand and the pipe in her left hand. But she crosses her right hand over her left, trying to reach the other end of the pipe. This awkward position results in little water going into the pipe and none into the empty table. Finally, Jessica switches hands, putting the pipe into her right hand and the pitcher into her left (see Photo 3.6). She has finally figured out how to orient her hands vis-à-vis the pitcher and pipe to achieve her goal.

In Photo 3.7 Aaron notices that the water he is pouring into a funnel is draining out onto the floor. He has been centering on one aspect of the plumbing setup, the funnel. Because he is using both hands to hold his bottle, it is physically impossible for him to catch the outflow water. Chris steps up and places a bucket under the pipe to catch the outflow (Photo 3.8). His participation has made this encounter become both a self-to-object and self-to-other situation. With Chris catching the water, Aaron's behavior is more socially directed. He pours the water through the funnel in order to fill Chris's bucket.

Variation—Backward Buckets

All experienced teachers and parents know how easily younger children accidentally spill liquids. As we saw in Bottomless Bottles, many children do not even notice their own spills when the water is rushing down themselves, and they notice even less when water trickles to the floor. They are intent on something else. After observing many hours of videotape and discussing this phenomenon we began to see a difference between the physical actions of our youngest and oldest children. Younger children do not seem able to anticipate the path of the water flow. Because of this they are always pouring toward themselves to watch the water coming out. Since they are unaware of how far the water will arc toward their own body, they are often standing in the direct path of the water.

In Photo 3.9 we see a good example of this. The child is pouring the bucket toward herself and looking down as it splashes against the table. This tendency we labeled *proximal*, meaning toward the self. Now look at Photo 3.10. This is an example of a more experienced child's actions. Chris, 3 years old, pours in a more conventional fashion, away from his body. This we called a *distal* action, meaning away from the self.

Even though Backward Buckets is not really a complete activity, it is a learning encounter, and we feel it is important to understand its significance. It is a spontaneous occurrence that illustrates how younger children's inability to anticipate the spatial relations between their body and a moving object (flowing water) leads to what adults sometimes consider a nuisance. As the child grows in her ability to understand the properties of moving objects, she constructs the spatial

PHOTO 3.5   Jessica pours water into the full, rather than the empty, water table.

PHOTO 3.6   Now Jessica pours water into the empty water table by reversing her previous actions.

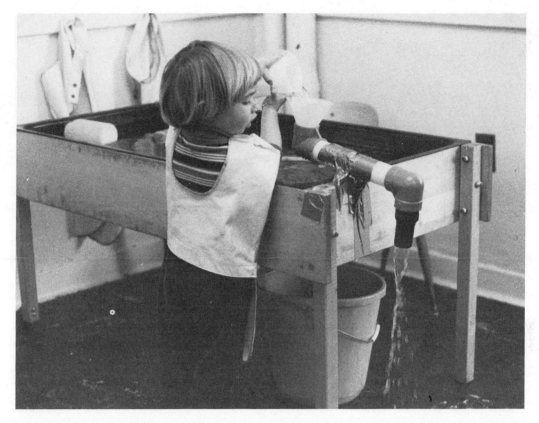

PHOTO 3.7   Aaron is so involved in pouring water into the funnel that he is unable to contain the water spilling out from the end of the pipe.

PHOTO 3.8   With Chris holding the bucket, Aaron now watches both ends of the pipe.   **83**

PHOTO 3.9   Lillian empties the bucket toward herself in order to see the water come out.

PHOTO 3.10   Chris empties the bucket away from himself in order not to get himself wet.

relation between her body and that object. Eventually, she arrives at the distal solution; she no longer needs to watch helplessly and in fascination as water pours toward herself. She has enlarged her perspective to include that of the water moving away from herself.

THE "I'M IT" GAME

The School for Constructive Play uses creative movement sessions in ways that reflect the overall and specific goals mentioned in Chapter One. The movement leader wears whiteface and mimes during the entire session to focus the group on action instead of dialogue. The "I'm It" Game is an example of a movement activity that uses careful observation and perspective taking. This activity encourages children to pay attention to the movement of an object so they can reproduce that action with their own bodies.

During one movement session the entire group has been watching the popcorn maker and has seen Peter, in whiteface crouched behind, do his own imitation of popcorn popping. Now Lauren does her impression. She clearly has observed the action carefully and does a good representation of the upward pop and the opening out of a single kernel. Younger children tend to choose one dominant aspect of such an action and approximate that, while ignoring other, more subtle properties of an action. Thus, in the case of popcorn the younger children jump up and down as fast as possible.

This type of activity helps children observe an object's movements in relation to the movement of their own bodies and to think about the correspondences and perspectives involved. There is a correspondence between the action of the kernel and the similar action of Lauren's and Peter's movements. Their physical representation is an equivalence similar to the kernel but is not the kernel itself. Further, imitating another object's action forces children to consider the perspective of making their own body look like that action while taking into account the nature of their body in contrast to the object.

PENDULUM BOWLING [1]

Preparing the Environment

Pendulum Bowling is a great favorite with all ages of children and staff. It offers so many possibilities that the point of saturation that is usually reached after two weeks with an activity does not apply. As with many other of our favorite activities, this one takes place in the sunny bay window. In the center of the ceiling beam a long rope is tied to a screw eye. The other end of the rope is knotted and inserted into an opening cut into a tennis ball. The ball hangs down to within about 3 or 4 inches of the top of a large platform. The platform, about 5 feet by 15 feet, forms a boundary for the pendulum users and protects spectators from the action. One child stands on the platform and releases the tennis ball. It swings back and forth, perhaps knocking over objects that are placed on the platform. The targets include three or four block constructions, weighted bowling pins, and foam cubes with Sesame Street figures on them.

Entry

The teacher involved in Pendulum Bowling has two roles. One is the physical management of the activity. This means setting up the target objects, regulating the flow of children taking turns at releasing the ball, and keeping the spectators out of the way of wild pitches. The other role consists of commenting on the action of the ball and the position of the child releasing it. If Seth throws the ball and it careens wildly, the teacher comments "Seth threw the ball and made it go way out. Maybe

---

[1] We thank Constance Kamii, of the University of Illinois at Chicago Circle, for the idea of Pendulum Bowling.

next time he'll *let go* of the ball to see what it does when it goes slowly." As David lines up his body on the opposite end of the platform from the block structure he hopes to knock down, Barbara says "David is standing in a straight line with the blocks." These comments help children reflect on their own actions and perhaps on the relation between the position of their body, the target object, and the moving tennis ball.

Younger Children

Younger children threw the ball instead of releasing it. Then it bobbed up and down, eventually evening out its motion if everyone could stand back long enough to let this happen. We noticed that younger children persisted in this a long time. They apparently were not figuring in the limits of the string on the movements of the ball. Younger children often got in the way of the backswing of the ball, too. They chased after the ball, not knowing that it would return to them if they stayed put.

Kevin, age 2½, takes several turns with the pendulum and hurls it forward. Barbara finally models for him how to release the ball and let it swing toward the bowling pins. She asks Kevin to try to knock down the pins. Kevin holds onto the ball, walks through the arc of the swing, and, as he comes up to the pins, he knocks them over with his other hand. Kevin can concentrate on one thing at a time. Remembering how to release the ball and aiming for the pins is too much. His solution is quite reasonable. He stops the wild throwing and knocks down the pins.

Later, Katie, also 2½, is challenged by Barbara to knock over three pins that are placed beyond the path of the ball, so that it is impossible to hit them. Katie tries several times and then leaves. Four-year-old David comes over and tries, too. He then walks to the other end of the platform and knocks over the pins with his hand. He sets them up again, this time within range. He swings the ball and knocks the center pin over.

This episode illustrates how older and younger children handled the same problem. The younger child did not try to change anything about the placement of the pins; she probably did not know that it was impossible to hit them. The older child somehow knew that the pins in the first position could not be knocked down with the pendulum, so he did it by hand. In moving the pins within the range of the swinging ball, David illustrated his ability to imagine and reconstruct the pathway of the ball. Just as the older children crouched down to take aim in the Gate Game, David paused to correctly position his body in a line with the bowling pins. Younger children rushed to release the pendulum ball, so eager for their turn that they neglected to look toward the object at the other end.

Older Children

Hattie, age 4½, catches on quickly to the impossibility of hitting pins that are too far away. She takes one or two trial swings and then moves the objects closer in. When Barbara questions her about why she is moving the pins before she knocks them over, Hattie replies emphatically "Because I have to hit them." She speaks with the certainty that there is no other way to accomplish the goal. Barbara then moves the pins over to the side of the platform, but within range of the pendulum. Hattie stands as before in the center of the platform and lets go of the ball. It goes straight out and returns to Hattie without touching the pins. Hattie holds onto the ball and walks down to the pins, moving them back to the center of the platform. She has just made an inverse reversal by directly undoing Barbara's action. She stretches the pendulum rope tight and sets the pins at a point of contact with the tennis ball. Then she steps back to the other end of the platform and confidently releases the ball. Hattie could have made a reciprocal reversal if she had moved her body over to the side straight across from the pins.

A variation using two double-unit blocks as targets presents a complex problem for the older children. They are asked to position the pins one behind the other, so that the first one, when struck by the pendulum ball, will fall in such a way that it knocks down the second one. We tape a wrist band with bells to the top edge of the second block to distinguish it from the first. This also defines the goal as making the bells ring.

This variation is more complex because it requires the child to think about where to stand so that the first block when falling will knock over the second block and make it sound. It is a problem that is similar to that of the Gate Game, requiring the player to line up his body exactly behind the target block so that the pendulum ball will hit it dead center and make it fall straight backward. There is only one place that this can be done from. The easier version of this game—knocking one pin over—allows a choice of release points.

SELF-TO-OTHER

The preceding activities were all designed so that children will consider the perspective of their own body in space relative to an object. Adults are often surprised at how oblivious a 2- or 3-year-old is to what they consider to be obvious. The child does not realize that, in order to knock down a pin with a thrown object, you must line up your body. He does not know that what you can see of an object facing you is not necessarily what that object looks like from the other side. These are self-to-object problems. The following section deals with self-to-*other* problems, which join two or more children in activities that work only when some cooperation exists between the participants. What we call "tied thighs," or you know as a three-legged race, is especially illustrative of the nature of this self-to-other category. With their legs tied together, neither child can walk very well without coordination with the other child. The two must talk and tug together to evolve a walking relationship.

Another childhood classic that requires social cooperation is using string telephones. Two paper cups are connected by a long string tied to the bottom of each cup. For this "telephone" to work, both children must simultaneously pull in opposite directions to make the line taut, while alternating as speaker and listener. The children must time their actions with each other for the conversation to really happen. We observed our 2-year-olds talking to each other at the same time. Because neither was listening, neither realized that the line was slack and the voices were not being transmitted.

The self-to-other activities are really of two types. An example of the first is the three-legged race. Such an activity cannot be done alone, and the children must time their actions with each other. Included in this type are many examples of the use of large-scale vehicles by several children at once. It is true that a single child may be able to propel the Moon Buggy, a metal-frame vehicle, for example, but it is not a very good ride alone. Working as a group, children can have an exciting ride with more momentum.

The second type of self-to-other experiences deal with children's understanding of other people's feelings and states. These encounters are the beginnings of the development of empathy. Many of them occur spontaneously as children sort out their misunderstandings about their peers and adults in the classroom. This second type of self-to-other perspective is illustrated by the example, mentioned earlier in this chapter, of the child with new shoes who recognizes that his friend will not feel the same pleasure he feels.

THE CO-OP BOARD

Preparing the Environment
The board itself is made from ¼-inch plywood, cut about 2 feet by 6 inches. Rounding the corners is advised for safety reasons. Our board is covered with contact paper. A further improvement would be to paint half of it with one color and

half with another. This would highlight the midpoint and make it easier for children to put an object in a spot that would balance. About 2 inches in from the ends of the board small notches are cut. Strong nylon cord is tied around these notches and, as you see in Photo 3.11, runs up to the climber/loft overhead. Two screw eyes are placed in the top railing of the loft, so that the raised board reaches the platform where other children are waiting. This way, an object on the co-op board can be delivered to the children upstairs. Choose an object that will not hurt anyone if it falls, because it will surely be spilled off the board many times. A Nerf animal or stuffed toy is a good choice.

PHOTO 3.11   Jenny and Marc successfully lift the Co-Op Board to Katie and Marya in the loft.

Entry

The object of this encounter is for two children to raise and lower the board between them without spilling the object that is resting in the center of the board. Initially, a teacher must model the use of this board. He might ask a child to help him lift up the board by pulling the rope. This suggestion immediately sets an encounter in motion. Only if two people skillfully time their actions can the board get all the way to the top. If someone is waiting up there, this provides some motivation, but it takes more than eager receivers to make the Co-op Board work. Younger children, in particular, have a lot of trouble working the board successfully. It is the 4- and 5-year-olds who figure out ways to raise the board while keeping it level.

Younger Children

Many younger children try to use the Co-op Board alone. For instance, Matthew grasps both strings, one in each hand. He pulls both strings down to the floor and watches the board go up. He repeats this, doing it fast and slow. Jake tries to pull the two strings but gets them tangled. She pulls a little bit, but the board will not move. She grabs the bucket resting on the center of the board and runs up the ladder to the top of the climber. This action is characteristic of many younger children on many activities. Finding it difficult to use an object to achieve a goal, they do it themselves instead.

Matthew pulls the strings in opposite directions, down on one string and up on the other. The ends of the board tip back and forth. Loren tries to pull it with one rope. And Taneka, positioned on the top of the climber, pulls the strings from above. She is trying to raise the board by lifting it toward herself. These examples illustrate how many different ways are tried by the younger children to raise the board by themselves.

Even when two children were working side by side at the Co-op Board, it was not always a coordinated effort. Both Chris and Lauren yelled at their respective partners when the board tipped or fell. At least they realized that the other child's pulling had disrupted the board. But they showed no inclination to instruct the other children how to correctly time their pulling. Even when Chris and Lauren were working with a teacher they were not able to *produce* the correct coordinated actions that would lift up the board without a spill. They seemingly knew that both partners have to work together, but they did not know exactly how to do that. This was an indication that Chris and Lauren were almost at the level of functions (see Chapter One) in their understanding of the relation between the two ropes. They knew that pulling on one side affected the other side and the stability of the board, but they did not quite grasp the inverse nature of the functional relation.

Furthermore, the Co-op Board presents something of a social problem. The participants have to agree to work together to achieve a common goal. This type of activity is not one that most preschoolers have often experienced. Therefore, difficulties of physically understanding how the board works are compounded by difficulties in socially accomplishing the task.

Older Children

Norine had several interesting encounters with older children at the Co-op Board. Loren is at the top of the climber and tells Norine to make the board come up to him. She asks him how to do it. He points to the wall behind her and says "Walk that way." Norine and Loren repeat this a few times. Loren says "I want the board up, so you just walk that way," pointing to the wall behind.

Later, Tristan comes over, takes the two strings, walks backward and makes the board go up. Norine asks "What happens when you walk backward?" "It goes up," Tristan replies. A few minutes later Tristan goes up to the loft so Norine can send him a bucketful of sponges. The following dialogue takes place:

Norine: "When I pull my arms down, what happens?"
Tristan: "It goes up."
"And if I pull my arms up, what happens?"
"It goes down."
"And if I pull just one arm up what happens?"
"It goes tippety."

Both Loren and Tristan have sensed the inverse functional relations involved in the Co-op Board. Walking away makes the board come toward the person above, pulling down lifts it up, and raising up lowers the board.

Norine's questions are a good example of the "predict strategy" of teaching (as discussed in CCK, p. 198). Her questions to Tristan gradually lead him to anticipate how varying his actions will affect the performance of the Co-op Board. Such dialogue encourages Tristan to use mental imagery and language to reflect on and organize his actions.

As you see in Photo 3.11, Jenny and Marc (5 and 4, respectively) have gotten the board to the height of Katie and Marya. They coordinated their movements by compensating when one of them pulled too fast. Clearly, both Jenny and Marc were accounting for each other's actions.

TWIN-LINE TENNIS[2]

Preparing the Environment

Twin-Line Tennis is a game very similar to the Co-op Board. A weighted tennis ball is attached to the midpoint of about 20 feet of nylon cord. The rope's two ends are threaded through two screw eyes in the ceiling beam about 10 feet apart. The end pieces of the cord are knotted around small metal rings so they cannot slip through the screw eyes. The rope hangs from the ceiling in the shape of the letter M. A bucket is placed on the floor below the midpoint of the distance between the screw eyes. The object of this game is for the two children playing to work together to lower the ball into the bucket below (see Photo 3.12).

Entry

Even though this game is of the same form as the Co-op Board, it is more interesting to our younger children. Perhaps because they can stand or sit facing each other, their actions are more coordinated. Also, there is no object that falls off when the children do not time their actions together. The larger scale of this activity also magnifies the effects of even small movements. We know that large-scale activities are particularly exciting to young children. This is why it does not make sense to divide up an entire classroom into lots of small spaces.

One observation illustrates the approach younger children take to Twin-Line Tennis. Jake and Taneka are sitting across from each other, holding the ends of the rope. Jake pulls hard on her end, and the ball lifts up to her side of the ceiling, jamming against the screw eye. Taneka wants the ball on her side so badly that she makes Jake trade seats with her. Taneka has not realized the relationship between the two ends of the rope. She thinks of the two ends as being absolutely different, so that in exchanging one end for the other she will get what she wants. A child more experienced in playing Twin-Line Tennis or other similar games would exhibit more sophisticated thinking about this relationship and would understand the transformation brought about in tugging and releasing the line.

Taneka does get Jake to trade seats with her. But, of course, this does not have the result Taneka expects. Jake pulls the ball up to her side again. Taneka begins yelling at the ball, telling it to come over to her side. She does not understand that, if

---

[2] Jack Tulloss, of the University of Massachusetts, gave us the idea for Twin-Line Tennis.

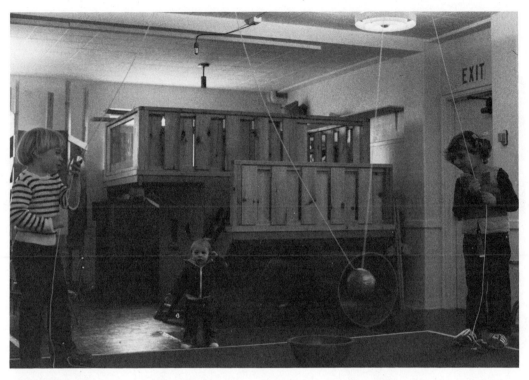

PHOTO 3.12   Jenny and Marc cooperate in order to lower the ball into the bowl.

she pulls harder, she might get it over to her side. Jake is too intent on her own objectives and will not let go of the rope and allow the ball to slide down into the bucket.

Taneka's actions—trading seats with Jake and yelling at the ball to come over to her side—are characteristic of a younger child's more egocentric schemes. Her thinking was at the level of opposition (discussed in Chapter One). Jake's actions also indicated an unawareness of the functional relations of this game. You will find Taneka's approach to the Solomon Swing (Chapter Five) very similar to Jake's.

The other thing we noticed that differentiated younger and older children is how they talked about what happened when the ball did go into the bucket. Two younger children yelled out at the same time "I did it. I did it." Two older children said together "We did it." This is an example of how a younger child sees a cooperative activity from only one perspective, her own.

CO-OP CITY

Preparing the Environment

Co-op City is a form of one of most children's favorite activities, road and train play. Its material design illustrates a principle that we found very successful: take a known "winner" and modify it slightly to encourage or highlight one aspect. Children love to drive toy vehicles. However, they do not follow pathways, but drive wherever they please. Co-op City constrains the child to drive along a defined route and to have head-on conflicts with other vehicles. These head-on conflicts can only be solved by a negotiated solution.

The base of Co-op City is a recycled water-table top. If this is not available, a plywood board of similar size (2 feet by 4 feet) can be used. A slightly smaller board is cut to fit on top of the lip of the table, so that there is a 2-inch hollow space between them. Using a saber saw, cut intersecting pathways in the smaller plywood piece, as you see in Photo 3.13. Make the pathways end in 1-inch-diameter holes.

This will be the beginning spot where children insert their cars. The whole piece is now painted and screwed securely to the inverted water-table top. The islands that form the inside of these pathways are securely screwed to pedestals underneath.

PHOTO 3.13   Nikos, Marika, and Loren play at Co-op City.

Small wooden cars are used as vehicles. Drill holes in the bottom of the cars in which to glue dowels 2 inches long. Glue round Tinker Toy hubs to the other end of the dowels. The two cars are inserted into the entry holes on either end of the pathway, and the hubs keep them in the pathway while they are being moved along by a driver. A few accessories—such as a tunnel, roadblocks, some houses, and other small buildings—provide additional possibilities for use.

Entry
The teacher can parallel-play with a single child or be a reflective observer when two or more children are present. Another strategy that encourages children to notice the road layout is to block the forward progress of a car when it is trying to

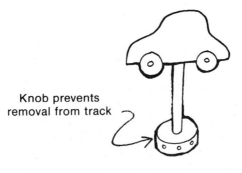

Knob prevents
removal from track

FIGURE 3.3   Co-op City car.

reach a certain destination. To reach this destination, the child must choose an alternative route. If this happens, the teacher can say "You are going the opposite way." Such language modeling is often imitated by children later on. Loren said once to another child he had just collided with "You go your opposite way, and I'll go my opposite way." He was overgeneralizing the use of the word *opposite*, characteristic of many younger children.

A third strategy is to arbitrate during conflicts. If two children are smashing their cars into each other, the teacher can start by verbalizing the fact that there is a conflict. She might say "Loren's and Bobby's cars can't get to the tunnel. They're bumping into each other. Maybe there's another way to get to the tunnel." It is the younger children who tend to get stuck in their conflicts without being able to sense the possibilities of other solutions.

Younger Children

Younger children used the cars as if they were racing vehicles. This made them jam up somewhat. They also inserted other things into the grooves to "drive," such as telephone poles and road signs. Especially when locked in a conflict situation, they tried to lift their car out of the groove. Aaron even wondered aloud "Why is it [the knob on the bottom of the car] there?" Also characteristic of younger children is extreme possessiveness. All of the loose pieces, houses, trees, roadblocks, and so on were identified as belonging to someone. And the first thing that almost everyone tried was to have a deliberate crash with the other car. Few of the younger children realized that there were other options in playing Co-op City.

Older Children

Several examples of Tristan's behavior will illustrate the approach of an older child. Peter asks Tristan to come to his "office." There are two routes, one long and one short. Tristan chooses the shorter one. Then Peter drives the other car and comes to the tunnel. In order not to knock down the tunnel while using it, it is necessary to switch hands midway. Tristan, knowing how often the tunnel gets knocked down, holds it for Peter, while he peers through the end. He chuckles as the car comes toward him.

While playing with another child, Tristan imitates another teacher's actions. He sets up a roadblock for the other child and says, as the other car comes up to it, "Oh, you want to go the opposite way."

When Tristan's car came in contact with another child's car, he would quickly turn and go the other direction. Tristan understood the layout of the track enough to be able to extricate his car from useless conflict situations. Furthermore, he did not "need" to engage in collision driving or territory staking as the younger children did. His grasp of the spatial relations of Co-op City permitted him to understand that detours, even when longer in distance, facilitated the social use of this material. This example illustrates how physical knowledge of a detour helps the child make more equitable, less absolute judgments about the social world.

CONES IN THE HOLE

Preparing the Environment

The cones were cardboard recycle items; the hole was cut in our "good maple table." The cones were painted two different colors so they could be identified as the blue one and the orange one. Nylon cord about 4 feet long was attached with duct tape to the tip of each. The size of the cones determined the size of the hole in the table. The hole had to be big enough to accommodate one cone at a time but too small to let two through at the same time (see Photo 3.14).

We had first tried to use a large glass jar for a genuine bottleneck situation, but our cones were too small and didn't really bottleneck. Besides, the jar tipped over with any fast tugs, making us anxious about the glass. As it turned out, the table hole led us to make other activities (the Shell Game, Chapter Four) and also

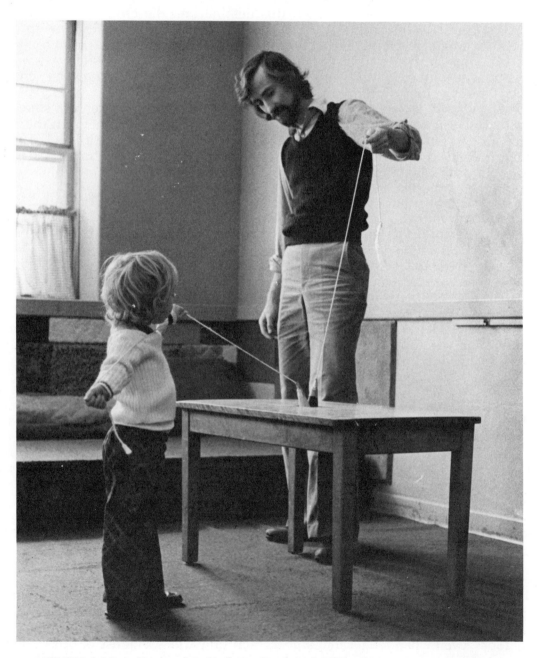

PHOTO 3.14   Tom and Cailin face a bottleneck while playing Cones in the Hole.

led to impromptu encounters. One of these involved a child's hand stuck up through the hole. The hand did a finger dance and then disappeared after shaking hands with the audience. Perhaps this was fascinating because the part (the hand) became a new whole. A hand dissociated from its body prompts a question of identity. Is the hand still the person who "owns" it? The paradox of this encounter is similar to that of the Face to Face encounter described in Chapter Two. Is a person really the same person when part of her is being someone else?

Entry

The cones are placed underneath the table with their strings extended upward through the hole in the table. A child holding a string tries to retrieve his cone without creating a bottleneck. In order to do so, he must coordinate his actions with the other child, so that one cone is pulled out first and then the other. Both children must decenter to the point at which they realize that, in order to get their cone through the hole, they might have to let the other child get his cone out first.

Younger Children

Cailin played Cones in the Hole alone in a self-to-object encounter. She pulled both strings back as far as possible, walking backwards as she pulled. This was done by many of the younger children, whereas most of the older children pulled out their string by standing still and pulling hand over hand. Cailin seemed intent on exploring the length of the strings stretched all the way out. Perhaps she was noticing how the edge of the square hole in the table was affecting the motion of the cones. As she pulled *back* the cone lifted *up*. The motion of the object, the cone, became slightly dissociated from the motion of the subject, Cailin.

Older Children

Tom had several interesting conversations with older children. He asked Eva if she could make both cones come out at the same time. She answered "No, 'cause the hole's too small." Later he asked Hattie if she could put them in at the same time. She also replied no. Tom observed Hattie telling another child to wait while she pulled her own cone out. Then she reversed it and let the other child "win" while she waited.

We recommend that those of you who try Cones in the Hole figure out a way to embed it in a dramatic play episode. We found that children would come for a short trial and then move on to something else. It would probably have interested them more if the cones had been decorated as fish or figures with funny expressions. Another untried idea was cutting a small hole in the floor of our climber/loft through which items suspended on string could be pulled from one level to the next.

BODY-SIZE BALANCE BOARD

A board of medium length (3 to 4 feet) is mounted on two arches from a unit block set. Duct tape proved strong enough to hold the arches in place, even with two 40-pound children rocking away on the board.

One child can use the board to try to balance himself as he stands and wobbles. Experiencing his own body off balance may be the first way for a young child to structure the concept of balance.

When two children are sitting on the Body-Size Balance Board, it becomes like a teeter totter. Keeping it balanced now requires each child to think about the other. This social setting may encourage children to discuss weight as the variable that makes them go up or down.

In Photo 3.15 Jenny and Marc have brought out the weights to use. These weights are computer tape disks that have been filled with sand and taped closed. Each weighs about 5 pounds. When a child uses a piece of equipment first with her own body and then with objects, she may be generalizing her knowledge from the self to objects.

PHOTO 3.15   Jenny and Marc explore the balance of weights on the Body-Size Balance Board.

TILT-A-HOLE TRAY

The Tilt-a-Hole Tray is an exciting cooperative game. A lightweight board about 18 inches by 24 inches forms a base for the tray. Small strips are nailed around the edges to make a lip. A square hole, slightly larger than a tennis ball, is cut into the center of the tray.

The tray is held on either end by two children who may either be trying to keep the ball from going into the hole or trying to get the ball to drop through the hole. Switching the object of the game keeps it from becoming repetitive, and even the youngest children were able to vary their strategies quickly.

In Photo 3.16 Marya (3½) squats down to get the ball to roll in her direction. She has experimented with various tilts and discovered that bringing the tray way down gets the ball to come toward her very fast. Katie, 4, is holding both her hands on the side edges, trying out sideways tilts.

On a few occasions, when the children were not so closely matched as these, the older child got frustrated that his partner did not understand how to work with him to control the ball. In this case a teacher tried to encourage the older child to instruct the younger child in the proper tilting technique.

TOTE TOGETHER

Tote Together is another case of a spontaneous happening that, once noticed by the teacher, can be staged as a regular activity. The School for Constructive Play has a set of large, hollow blocks that have rope handles at either end. These blocks are often taken outside for large-scale building projects. At cleanup time many

PHOTO 3.16   Marya and Katie try to get the ball to drop through the hole in the Tilt-a-Hole Tray.

children are eager to help carry the blocks inside. Some grab a rope handle and drag their block along behind them. Others, generally the older children, seek out another child to help carry the other end. This way they can tote the block together. Sometimes two children grab the same rope handle and pull the block together. Or two children may hold onto the ropes at both ends and walk in opposite directions, getting nowhere.

Gradually, though, even the younger children construct the scheme that with large objects two can carry together what one alone cannot. This way, all sorts of big objects can be moved around. To stage an encounter like this, an obstacle that can be moved only if several children cooperate is placed in a heavily trafficked location. Toting together solves the problem.

STRETCHER TOGETHER

The stretcher is simply made from two poles with a cloth taped around it. It has become a real favorite for rescue games. In order to carry an object, such as a doll in need of hospital care, two children must hold the ends of the stretcher's poles and walk together. Some children, especially the younger ones, try vainly to carry the stretcher alone and then leave in discouragement. Older children are likely to recognize the futility of a solo attempt and call for an assistant.

In one case, the fire fighters are carrying a doll to the "hospital" during a fire at the climber/loft. On the return trip to the burning loft, Nauman finds himself walking backward. As he gets closer to the loft, he turns his head around to look behind him. After three rescues Nauman no longer needs to turn his head to see how much farther he has to walk backward before bumping into the burning loft. He understands the spatial relations between the hospital and the loft from both a forward and backward perspective.

CO-OP FIRE ENGINE

This activity and the four following ones all use large vehicles that move successfully when children collaborate. The Co-op Fire Engine, the Sharing Chariot, and the Ladder Train are games involving homemade vehicles; the Moon Buggy and the Blue Bubble Ride use commercial items (see Appendix).

The Co-op Fire Engine is made from a large cardboard carton with no top and no bottom (see Figure 3.4). It is cut down so that, when standing on the floor, it comes about to the children's waist. Rope handles are tied on around it. These are held onto by the children, who stand inside the carton and reach over the edge. Red paint and black trim around the edges give the carton a fire-engine reality. Even the very young children can participate because of the relatively light weight of the box. A couple of children lift it up around their bodies and walk or run around. Because the paint clearly defines a front and back, the children do not pull in opposite directions.

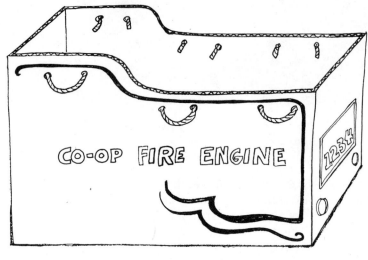

FIGURE 3.4   Co-op Fire Engine.

LADDER TRAIN

Unlike the Co-op Fire Engine, the Ladder Train has no distinguishable front and back. It consists of a long, wooden ladder that is lashed to two identical plastic wagons at either end (see Figure 3.5). The children stand between the rungs and propel the train by shuffling their feet along.

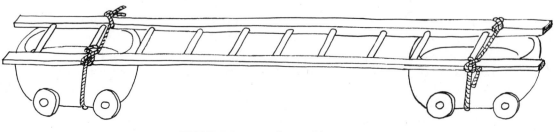

FIGURE 3.5   The Ladder Train.

The activity begins with the Ladder Train parked at a station. Five children get tickets from the stationmaster and board the train. The stationmaster signals them off and instructs them to travel to the other terminal across the room. Reaching the other terminal requires that the passengers face the same direction and move their feet along together. When they reach the other station, the stationmaster sends them back the other way.

Because either end of the train serves as a reference for both front and rear, depending on the perspective of the child seated at that end, interesting questions arise. Is the train going forward or backward? Who is in the front and back?

SHARING CHARIOT

Double ropes are attached to the two handles of a wooden wagon. The center of each rope loop is padded with foam and then wrapped in duct tape. The padding becomes the harness for the "horses'" waist. Student teachers were surprised that few children wanted to get into the harnesses by having them slipped over their heads. They hypothesized that, if the children had been asked to step into the harness rather than stand passively while it was put on them, they would feel more secure and in control. This is just what happened when Mark got Lauren and Bobby to give Lillian a ride. They did not object to wearing the harnesses and skillfully avoided several obstacles around the yard.

In Photo 3.17 you see Marika and Aaron pulling the ropes rather than wearing them. With two children pulling two children, the progress was slow. So Lillian got out of the wagon and went around to the front to help Aaron and Marika. With three pulling one, the wagon moved right along, giving a faster ride.

The Sharing Chariot also encourages taking turns and peer regulation. Everybody wants to ride in the chariot, but fairness dictates that everyone has to give rides, too.

PHOTO 3.17   Marika and Aaron pull Lillian and Lauren in the Sharing Chariot, but progress is slow.

MOON BUGGY

The Moon Buggy can hold as many as four children and requires cooperative efforts from each rider. Photo 3.18 shows the additions some of our student teachers made to the Moon Buggy to make it more appealing. The construction at the top is the "rocket engine." Nauman is holding a space-light emitter and wearing a space helmet. The buggy's casters rotate 360 degrees, allowing for movement in any direction. Of all the cooperative vehicles this one allows the greatest variety of perspective to its riders.

BLUE BUBBLE RIDE

The Blue Bubble can be seen in Photo 2.5, where it is being used in the game called Tunnel to Well. For use indoors during the time focused on balance, one of the student teachers, Tracy, put a shiny silver strip around its middle. This created a

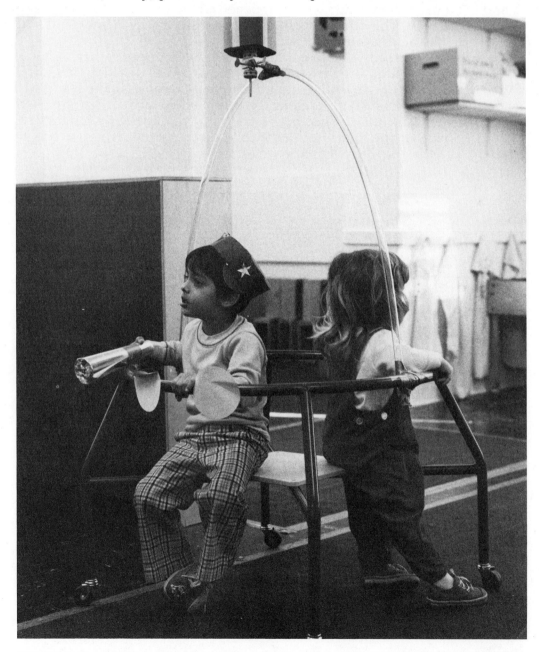

PHOTO 3.18   Lillian and Nauman must work cooperatively to make the Moon Buggy go.

guideline to help the children roll it. The bubble is rolled as a combined effort of two children. Small objects that are put inside create a rattling sound as it turns. If the Blue Bubble is rolled counter to the direction of the silver strip, the objects fall out.

Tristan and Marc are standing side by side pushing the bubble. It goes off the silver guideline. Tristan tells Marc to get it back on the silver line. They are joined by two other children, and together they roll the bubble over to the large sona tube that opens into the climber/loft. The bubble fits right into the tunnel hole, and the children line up its smaller holes with the full-size opening of the sona tube. Then they climb through the bubble into the tunnel and into the loft.

Later, Tristan and Alythea are at opposite ends of the bubble, rocking it back and forth between them. They are both yelling into the bubble's holes and listening to the echo of their voices. Alythea leaves, and Marc returns to join Tristan again. Together they roll the bubble over to a platform edge and push it up onto the platform. Tristan then pushes the sphere off the platform and it bounces. "The big Blue Bubble bounces!" Tristan exclaims with delight.

SPINNING SPACE

Preparing the Environment

This game of changing perspective uses a large, flat, circular tray that is divided down the middle by an upright partition. The tray is mounted on a lazy Susan and sits on a table top. Small manipulative objects, such as Lego pieces, Cuisenaire rods, or colored cubes, are placed in duplicate numbers on each side. Ten or fifteen pieces of one set is plenty. A tilting mirror tile is hung on the wall next to the table, so that a teacher playing the game can see the other side of the divided tray, where a child is working.

Entry

The teacher plays the troublemaker in this situation (see CCK, pp. 113–114). While the child opposite her is playing with the materials, the teacher observes and copies the child's actions. When the child has made a small structure and the teacher has copied it, she rotates the lazy Susan. To the child's amazement the teacher has made the very same structure he has made without being able to see him make it.

Younger Children

Many younger children are not particularly surprised that their construction has been exactly reproduced by the teacher across from them. This is an indication of their egocentric perspective: they do not realize that the teacher should not have been able to see what they were building. Younger children also tend to be extremely possessive about their side of the space. They do not want their space to spin away from them.

We find that a simpler version of the game works better with younger children. In this version the teacher and child work independently with the material in front of them for a few minutes. When a natural break occurs, the teacher turns the tray 180 degrees. Now what is in front of the child is the teacher's materials. Some younger children are baffled by this switch. Young children tend to take surfaces for granted. They don't anticipate that the surface on which they are constructing a block tower can rotate.

Another way of thinking about this encounter is in terms of figure and ground relationships. Most of us expect that the ground is the stationary part of a perceptual field. It is the figure that normally is dynamic. Spinning Space reverses this relationship. Moving the entire surface shifts the attention to another perspective—that of the whole table top and the lazy Susan covering it—and helps children think about the spatial relationships involved, not just the manipulative objects on the surface.

Some children are irritated at the switch and feel that their side has been taken. Others are not even flustered and just rotate the space back to its original position. A further response illustrates the reciprocal action: some children get up and walk around to the other side of the table and find their materials. (The inverse reversal is to return the space to its original position by spinning it back.)

Older Children

The more complex version of this game, using the mirror, is much more fascinating for older children. Their amazement is genuine. "How could she know what I was doing?" reads the look on their faces. They redouble their efforts to trick the teacher by building more elaborate structures or by building right up under the partition.

Jenny is unable to figure out how Lisa, the teacher, keeps making the same thing that she is making. Finally, she challenges Lisa to switch roles. She tells Lisa that she will be the teacher. She directs Lisa to play for a few minutes with the materials, and she does the same. Then she spins the tray around. She is puzzled when the construction Lisa has made does not match her own. Lisa then asks Jenny if she wants to switch seats. Jenny does, and after a few minutes she notices the mirror on the wall. Now she knows that Lisa has been able to see the other side.

Jenny, through her own explorations, constructed the relation between what she thought Lisa could see and what Lisa apparently was able to see. Jenny discovered the procedure that helped her fill in the *gap* between the apparent versus the real perspective that Lisa held (see CCK, p. 54).

TEACHER IN TROUBLE

Teacher in Trouble is an activity that encourages a child to consider a teacher's predicament. Barbara tied up both her arms in slings. She circulated around the classroom, noting the responses of various children to her plight.

First she goes over to the easel where Hattie, 4½, is painting. She tells Hattie that she wants to paint and asks Hattie how she thinks it can be done. Hattie starts to answer "You can . . ." and then glances at Barbara's arms. She pauses and then says "Oh, they're hurt. You can use your mouth!"

Then Barbara joins Eva in the role-play area. Eva asks Barbara if she wants a drink of water. Barbara responds yes, so Eva fixes a pretend drink. She sets the glass down on the table in front of Barbara and waits. After a while Barbara asks Eva how she can drink it. Eva tells her to pick it up. Then, after looking at the slings, Eva picks up the glass and holds it to Barbara's mouth.

Barbara then observes Aaron's collage making. She tells Aaron that her nose itches. Aaron, 3, is aware of the limitations that the bound-up arms pose for Barbara. He takes her perspective and scratches her nose (see Photo 3.19).

THE "HE'S ME" GAME

Peter, in whiteface, becomes a mirror image during movement time. As you can see in Photo 3.20, he exaggerates and repeats the movements of the child's body in space. The children enjoy this parallel play and imitation. Seeing an adult reproduce their body's form increases their awareness of their own body in space.

The Plexiglas "mirror" (actually transparent) served management needs when used in this game, confining the children to one space. Both Peter and the children used the Plexiglas somewhat differently from a real mirror image, though. With a real mirror, as you move closer to it, the image closes in, too. In the case of the "living mirror," if a child moved closer in, Peter moved back, keeping the distance between him and the child the same. Peter's mistake actually worked well for children this age. He found that, if he did exactly as a real mirror does, the game

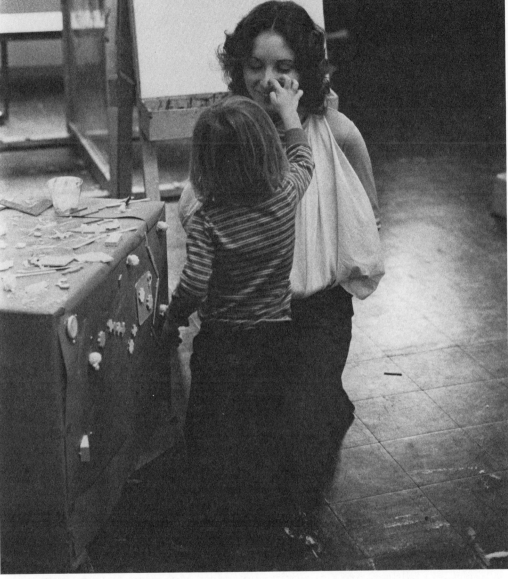

PHOTO 3.19   Aaron responds to Barbara's need to have her nose scratched.

was not as interesting as when he imitated the child's action itself. When Peter initiated an action that moved him closer to the mirror, the child moved back.

The mirror also served to define a plane of motions. Children's movements, especially with their hands, were frequently as if they were softly rubbing an imaginary surface. Because they were not touching the Plexiglas panel, this looked like a pantomime of window washing.

In general, the "He's Me" Game is easier for children to participate in than the "I'm It" Game. "I'm It" involves object imitation. This presents difficulties for two reasons. One, it is hard to find appropriate objects that move at the right speed for children to observe a change in their state. Once we tried watching an inflated plastic tomato collapse as the air whooshed out, but it happened so slowly that everyone lost interest. Even popcorn pops so fast that children more easily imitate the sound than they imitate the action of a single kernel. Second, "He's Me" is easier because

PHOTO 3.20   Peter, in whiteface, mimics everything that Bobby does.

any action will do. Even the most ordinary movement leads to interesting encounters.

Lauren, 3½, is working with Peter. She is in the actor role, and Peter is playing the imitator. Lauren slowly lifts her hands toward her mouth, with Peter following her motions. Just as she is about to reach her mouth, she jerks her hands up to her head. Meanwhile, she is watching Peter carefully to see if she has caught him.

This is an excellent example of a child's thinking about another person's thinking (even though it may be a precocious example). In trying to trick Peter, Lauren illustrated that she knew that Peter was anticipating that she would follow through with her actions to the expected conclusion.

When two children are paired in the "He's Me" Game, they have difficulty agreeing on which one will initiate the actions and which one will imitate. As you might expect, particularly with the younger children, both want to "lead" the encounter.

LEARNING ENCOUNTERS IN THE HOME

Additional self-to-object encounters that focus on a child's position in space relative to some object need not involve elaborate preparation or the purchase of unusual materials. Many common childhood games and pastimes involve self-to-object perspective taking. Parents who observe their children carefully will find numerous moments for appropriate entry during ball games, sports play, dramatic and fantasy play, block building, and everyday conservations. Here are some examples.

Tin Can Alley.   The materials needed for this encounter are a medium-sized ball and tin cans, say coffee cans, or for a quieter game, cardboard or plastic cylindrical containers, say the containers for orange juice concentrate. Indoor or outdoor space will do, but it is important to have a bowling space large enough for the child to experiment with different ways to arrange the containers for bowling and to experiment with different places to stand in order to maximize the number of containers bowled over in one roll of the ball.

Most typically children will arrange their cans in a row perpendicular to their line of bowling. This arrangement of six or seven cans abreast does give the child clear vision of each individual can, but it greatly limits the chances that one can will knock down another in a domino effect that multiples the initial impact of the ball. If the child has sufficient space, she may move to the side of the line of cans, thereby increasing the likelihood that the initial contact between ball and can will set going a chain reaction. Thus the child learns to change her perspective to the set of objects in order to reap more gains from each effort. This game is similar in concept to the spatial relations involved in the Gate Game mentioned earlier.

The parent simply makes declarative statements like, "Each time you bowl you hit only one can." If the child chooses to pick up on the implication that there may be a way to hit two cans at once, the child can do so at her own invention. Or the parent can make the statement, "That time one can knocked over the other." Again the child has the freedom to assimilate the parent's comment to a self-set objective or to not assimilate it. If the parent says something like, "See what happens if you bunch the cans together," this might be too directive. The child could oblige the parent's request, yet not assimilate the change in the arrangement of the cans to the earlier objective of knocking down the cans aligned six or seven abreast. One wants the child to see the new arrangement as a transformation of the old arrangement, therefore it is important that the two arrangements are both assimilated to the same objective, that is, that both arrangements are two means to do the same thing, only one is more efficient.

Note that the child who realizes this has done more than invent a more efficient method of bowling. The child has also begun to think about the double role of an object. The first can in the row can be both the target and the missile. It's the target in relation to the ball, and the missile in relation to the second can in the row. This is pretty tricky two-within-one thinking. Other games that children play at home have this structure and the knowing parent can foster constructive play by providing materials, space, and descriptive comments without overly complicated suggestions.

He Can't Spy. We probably all know the game, "I spy something _____ ." The child says this to another child who is to figure out what the object is that is, say green, that is in the room and within the first child's view. We recommend another form of this perspective-taking game that requires the second child to figure out what a little doll cannot "see" that, given their spatial relations, both children can see. This might even be a good game for children to play while on long automobile trips. The first child positions the doll at one point and then figures out which objects in the area would be obstructed from the doll's line of sight. Then the child, without naming one of these occluded objects, says, "He (the doll) can't see something brown and square (meaning, perhaps, a picture on the other side of the floor lamp).

The staging of this new version of "I spy" will of course require some adult tutoring. But this new set of rules can be given briefly and then the children can either go with it, modify it, or leave it alone. Often it is more educational for children to play a game that breaks down, because then they shift their problem-solving skills to inventing rules that work, thereby teaching themselves just what the value of rules are. So, if the game does not go well, that is all right, and this in itself can be constructive if the children reflect, even momentarily, on what an agreement is and what happens when two people try to play with different rules. This last comment leads us to the other form of perspective taking, self-to-other.

Walkie-Talkie. Many toy stores carry inexpensive, battery operated walkie-talkies. We have observed children play with these toys and find that they present some interesting challenges for taking the other person's perspective. In essence these little toys set up an elegant four-way relation. The first child has to not only press down her button to talk into the phone, but has to indicate to the second child just when her conversation is over so that he will know it is his turn to press down his button to talk and that she will now refrain from pressing her button in order to hear what he has to say. That's some set of social relations! Often children will press and talk indiscriminately without cuing the other child to listen. Eventually children might invent something like the "over" command. In this type of cue the roles are reciprocally reversed: the speaker releases the talk button and becomes the listener, the listener presses the talk button and becomes the speaker. The beauty of the battery operated walkie-talkie is that when the children are out of earshot, there is no way that one child can interrupt the other child without the communication breaking down completely. Thus the walkie-talkie puts such a constraint on communication that cooperation must be learned, just like the cooperative play we discussed in other games such as Co-op Board or Co-op City.

There are numerous ways to stage cooperative play at home that fosters the child's concern for the other child's perspective. A version of twin-line tennis can be set up in the yard using a tree or swing set as an overhead anchor. Stretcher Together can be played at home with just a few extra props in the den or yard. We encourage parents to use their imagination to extend the schoolday activities into the time at home.

SUMMARY: CHANGING PERSPECTIVE

The activities of this chapter all deal with an issue that is central for the child between 2 and 5 years of age. Children in this period are developing in their ability to consider multiple points of view. Initially, they do not consider what things are like beyond what they can literally see. They do not consider that people in different locations perceive things differently. They are rarely aware of other people's feelings as different from their own.

Activities involving changing perspective essentially teach children that what appears to be absolute is really relative to one's perspective. (CCK, pp. 86–91, gives a full discussion of this idea.) Eventually, children learn that their own perspective is limited. In figuring out the limitations of their own perspective, they become more conscious of the relation and interaction between the observer and the observed. They improve their knowledge of the physical and social world by inferring what other perspectives are.

Knowledge of the physical world is improved by expanded perspective taking, or physical decentration. Some of the activities of the Self-to-Object section of this chapter encourage children to think about objects in new ways. Bottomless Bottles, Funny Funnels, Crazy Brushes, and the Buried Body are examples of this type. Other activities involving self-to-object perspective encourage children to think about their own body as an object in space that is in relation to another object. The Gate Game, Video Viewing, Pipe Put Together, and Pendulum Bowling require that the child position his own body in a certain way to achieve the goal of the game.

The other section of the chapter describes activities that require two or more children to cooperate with one another either in a game situation or a dramatic play episode. These self-to-other activities result in increased social knowledge and the development of experiences shared among children. Encounters of this type require the participant to time her actions with another child's actions, negotiate a common goal, and subsume her individual will to group process. Dramatic play episodes allow children the freedom to expand their behaviors beyond an egocentric perspective. When pretending to be a rescue medic, a child develops ideas about another person's activities that are different from his own. He is differentiating himself from that which he is not. The School for Constructive Play has found that these activities are genuinely interesting and appropriate for children 2 to 5 years old. We encourage you to support cooperative social ventures in your classroom.

DEVELOPMENTAL TRENDS

We have once again listed observations about our children that were particularly telling in regard to developmental differences. We realize that many interesting observations that we made cannot be included in these particular categories. But, rather than barrage you with an unorganized list of observations, we have chosen to include only those observations that do fit these categories. Our purpose is to demonstrate common developmental trends that cut across the artificial divisions we have made to define learning encounters.

TWO WITHIN ONE

Cases where one object is both itself and something else:

The younger children would readily accept a plastic jar with its bottom cut out (Bottomless Bottles). They would pour water through the bottom without comment. The older children would comment that the jar did not have a bottom. At least they understood that something was missing. Perhaps a slightly older child would say "This jar is a cup," indicating that the jar was both itself and something else.

Cases where one object is both a whole and several parts:

During the "I'm It" game the older children tried to represent two or more aspects of the object's movement that they were imitating. Younger children usually chose only the most dominant aspect of the action to represent and did not mimic the more subtle and simultaneous parts of the whole action.

Cases where one point has two different references in space simultaneously:

The video camera and monitor confused most of our children. They assumed that they could make themselves appear on the monitor by standing in front of the monitor (as if it were a mirror). They could not infer that, inasmuch as the monitor shows their profile when they are facing it full face, then it could not be the source of the image. In point of fact, the solution of the source of the image requires a child to coordinate three simultaneous points: the camera, the monitor, and himself.

In the Gate Game the younger children had some difficulty coordinating the position of themselves with both the gate and the target on the other side. The older children would take an on-line sighting and then roll the ball when all three points (ball, gate, and target) were lined up.

Cases where one object has two actions simultaneously:

When putting two objects together, as in Pipe Put Together, the younger children had difficulty with the double action necessary to connect the pieces. They jabbed pieces together instead of sticking in and twisting. Older children could accomplish such a double action.

DECENTERING FROM AN EGOCENTRIC PERSPECTIVE

Cases where the child centers on proximal versus distal effects:

In Crazy Brushes the younger children grabbed them close to the brush tip, thereby eliminating the need to adjust to a bent handle. The older children enjoyed the indirectness and the extension of the self when using the bent handles and helmet and belt brushes.

In the Gate Game and Pendulum Bowling younger children knocked down the targets with their hands when they were unable to use the ball successfully. Older children, even when they were unable to achieve the desired end, persisted with the more distal means of knocking over the targets.

Cases where the child centers on a single aspect of an event that has personal relevance versus cases where the child includes the perspective of other objects and persons:

Older children's dramatic play was more thematic than the younger children's play. When playing Cones in the Hole, the older children called the cones "fish" and discussed who was getting a bite on the fish line. At the sand table the older children invented many situations for the little "perspective taking" wooden people. The younger children made the figures hop around in the sand or repeated some other single aspect many times.

Cases where the child centers on the means as if they were an end:

In the Co-op City game the younger children, even when they were obviously trying to reach a particular goal, would start playing "bumper cars" with another child whose car happened to be in the way. The older children would make a brief bump and then begin to negotiate a detour in some other direction.

Cases that involved another person's intentions:

Of course, Chapter Three was full of examples where children differed in their ability to coordinate their own intentions with another child's intentions. The Co-op Board, the Co-op Fire Engine, and Stretcher Together all involve encounters where one child is forced to consider the intentions of another child. The younger children would act as if they were using the material alone and would be surprised when their efforts were thwarted by another child's actions. The 4-year-olds would negotiate a coordinated action between themselves.

It seemed that even the 2-year-olds eventually learned how to coordinate cooperative action in carrying things. They continued to have difficulty on cooperative actions such as the Co-op Board and the Tilt-a-Hole Tray. These later games were more difficult because each child had several actions to do simultaneously.

We hope that these observations will help you to look in a more organized fashion at the actions of young children. In your own work you will no doubt find that some of the 2- and 3-year-olds in your class are more advanced than our summary above might indicate. We expect that. You should look at the summary statements above as developmental trends and not statements about what children do when they are 2 years or 4 years old. Remember, when we say "younger" and "older" we are really referring to developmental differences, not age differences per se.

Chapter Four

Representing Motion

ENCOUNTERS WITH REPRESENTING MOTION

In Chapter One we explained how the form of a motion tells us a great deal. Consider this example: An insurance investigator goes to the scene of an automobile accident. His client has wrecked an expensive car. He looks at the tire tracks left on the pavement. These tracks show that the driver began to brake about 100 feet before the car hit a telephone pole. The tracks also show an abnormally sharp curve. Was this the curve the tires made when the driver tried to avoid hitting a dog, as he says? The investigator reasons that the evidence supports his client's claim. The tire tracks tell the tale.

Many times, the way an object has moved can tell us why things have happened or why things are now the way they are. A tree in the forest is leaning over to the point of falling down. We see a dried-up creek bed and deduce that there must have been great erosion around the base of this tree, loosening its grip on the earth. The creek bed is a trace of the motion of the water, which was the force that caused the tree to lean. These traces of motion are indices of the procedures by which things happen. As we stated in Chapter One, *procedures* are of primary concern for children between the ages of 2 and 5.

Things often happen too fast or took place too long ago for young children to easily figure them out. A pencil falls off the table. The speed of falling is so fast that the child cannot really study the half somersault the pencil does as it falls. A set of wheels on an axle, with one wheel larger than the other, rolls in an arc. But the shape of this arc is so momentary that the child cannot figure out just why he missed his target. If the motions in these two examples left a trace, as the tires did, the children could improve their understanding of what was happening in each case. The activities that follow have been designed with this objective in mind—to freeze the motion of an object with some sort of trace.

We have frozen motion for our children in two ways: in a continuous path or in a discontinuous path. The first we simply call *freezing motion,* meaning that the trace of the motion does not have any breaks. The Morton Salt girl leaves a continuous trail of her walk in the rain as long as the salt in her leaking box is not depleted. The second we call *unitizing motion,* because the movement is broken up into discontinuous units. We do not believe that the child sees these segments as equal units, but she may see them as discontinuous parts of the same continuous motion. For example, the child probably understands that the dashes on the sidewalk made from a wet spot on her tricycle wheel come from the continuous ride of her tricycle across the sidewalk. The dashes on the sidewalk break up a continuous motion into parts, and this event is not too different from what is done in measuring a distance. Unitizing motion is a precursor to measurement. We will touch on other reasons to freeze and unitize motion in the activities that follow.

FREEZING MOTION

SWINGING SAND

Preparing the Environment

For some weeks the children at the School for Constructive Play had been "bowling" with a tether ball attached to the ceiling. (This activity was described completely in the previous chapter as Pendulum Bowling.) We noticed that the children were having difficulty correcting themselves after a miss. They would release the ball, it would miss the pins, and they would grasp it and release it from the same position again. We reasoned that, if they had a better indication of where the ball had traveled on their first attempt, they could correct themselves better. For these reasons the Swinging Sand was invented.

We replaced the tether ball with a plastic ketchup bottle. The bottle had a screw-off cap with a nozzle. The children could take off the top, fill the bottle with sand, replace the top, and swing the bottle on the rope hanging from the ceiling. To facilitate transfer of learning from Pendulum Bowling to this new version, we cut a large hole in a toy plastic bowling ball. We inserted the body of the ketchup bottle into the bowling ball, so the nozzle protruded from the bottom of the ball. Now the game looked a lot like Pendulum Bowling.

Each time the children released the bottle it drained dry sand onto the paper below. If they missed the bowling pin, they could literally see on which side of it the bottle had passed. We hoped that the children would study the "frozen" form of the motion, figure out how that form had been created, and correct their actions in order to make a more accurate release. Although these objectives were somewhat beyond our 2- to 4-year-olds, the game did lead to some useful learning encounters. Six-year-olds would probably be able to see the sand trace as information that has relevance to how one bowls.

Our 2- to 4-year-olds (we had no 5-year-olds at that time) were more interested in the leaking sand than in bowling over the pin. They usually either held the bottle and let the sand drain onto the paper or swung the bottle to see the sand drain out, ignoring the bowling pin. If they did try to knock down the pin, they did not seem to concurrently attend to the sand leaking out of the bottle. Perhaps it was too many things for them to think about at once. Nevertheless, the game was interesting to them, so we set about to modify it in order to maximize the types of encounters the children naturally selected.

We discovered that after five or six passes of the swinging bottle the surface below got so covered with sand that it was difficult to discern individual traces. So we invented a quick and easy way to "erase" the surface. We took two large pieces of ¼-inch plywood, 4 feet by 4 feet. We hinged them together at one end and left them doubled over. We then placed the hinged plywood under the swinging bottle and flat onto one of the 15-inch-high platforms we have in our classroom. After the child had released the swinging bottle for five or six passes, he and the teacher would simply lift the unhinged edge of the top panel upward, making an angle sufficient to cause the sand to slide off the lower end (see Figure 4.1).

The double-panel construction made it easier for the teacher and child to tilt the top panel without its falling off the platform. The sand slid into a trough made out of a cardboard tube split down the middle. This trough could be picked up after it had received the sliding sand and then dumped into a pail for recycling into the ketchup bottle. We also placed runners along the top panel's right and left edges to assure that the sand would not slide off the sides when the panel was tilted. The "ecological cycle" of the sand, passing from ketchup bottle to plywood panel to trough to pail and back to bottle through a funnel, was itself a learning encounter with a closed system of relations.

Entry

Swinging Sand did attract the attention of two to three children at a time. The motion of the swinging bottle itself was interesting, because here was an object that, when pushed away, would come back. The younger children wanted to squeeze the bottle between their two hands, watching the sand drain and pile up below. The older children showed interest in the shape of the paths that the draining sand made. They varied the way they tossed the bottle and watched the change in the pattern of sand traces. The younger children had a tendency to throw the bottle, rather than release it. They seemed to feel the need to impart force to the bottle directly. The older children understood that the weight of the bottle itself would cause it to swing. They held it in one place and released it.

The more direct approach of the younger children, both in terms of squeezing the bottle to make it drain sand and pushing it to make it swing, seems to be part of

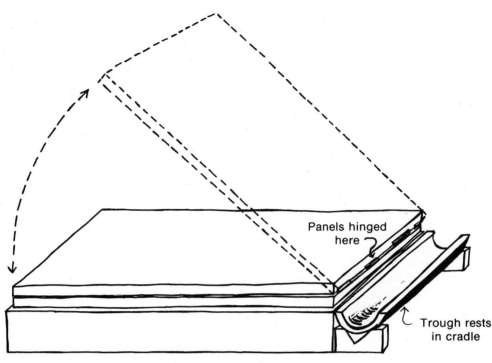

Panels hinged here

Trough rests in cradle

Bottom panel remains flat to stabilize structure during lifting of top panel

FIGURE 4.1   Hinged panel for the Swinging Sand.

the egocentrism of the younger years. They assume that an object moves because of the actions that they themselves impart to it. The notion of "natural motion"—that is, what adults call gravity—is not well formed at this age. To understand that objects sometimes move of their own accord requires a type of decentering from an egocentric view of the world.

Younger Children

Jimmy grasps the bottle in both hands. It slips out and he notices the sand spilling onto the surface below. He recaptures the bottle and holds it about chest high, letting the sand drain between his feet. As it is making a pile, Aaron looks on. Beverly, the teacher, also watches. Jimmy holds the bottle in his hands until all the sand drains out. He holds the translucent bottle up to the window light and sees that there is no more sand in it. He, with slight assistance from Beverly, unscrews the bottle cap and proceeds to funnel in another load of sand.

This turns out to be a favorite activity for Jimmy. Drain and fill, drain and fill. On one round of draining he begins to drain the sand onto the toe of his shoe. The sand splashes down over the shoe onto the plywood surface. When he moves his foot a few minutes later, he is surprised to see a stencil of his foot there in the sand pile. Beverly is quick to expand this learning encounter. She places other objects under the draining sand as Jimmy holds it. After he drains out all of the sand, he or Beverly removes the object to see what sort of "hole" it has made in the spread of sand.

Other children enjoyed this game, too. Some of them drained the sand only on the top surface of the stencil object. They did not quite understand that the hole in the spread would result only if they passed the sand over the outside edges of the object. Consequently, their approach did not leave a clearly defined vacant space in the sand. For these children the game was one of getting the sand to fall on the object.

For Jimmy the game was one of getting the sand to define the outline of the object when the object is removed. Jimmy was, in effect, thinking about the "not-object," the vacant space. At a minimum, he was thinking about where the sand was not going to be. He would deliberately remove the object covered with sand, picking it up gently so as not to scatter the sand that defined the outline of the object. Perhaps this behavior indicated that Jimmy knew, at least in terms of appropriate actions, that the stencil hole was the negation of the sand. Recall our discussion in Chapter One about the level of opposition, in which the child first begins to see one thing as *not* something else.

The nice thing about this whole activity was the way that it evolved. The game had been prepared to let children study the sand trace of the swinging bottle. The teacher, however, did not force that objective on Jimmy. By watching him closely, the teacher expanded the learning encounter that Jimmy set as his own goal. The accident of stenciling his own shoe was expanded into a delightful game for Jimmy and for a lot of children thereafter. Beverly demonstrated good principles of teaching in the way she expanded and facilitated the self-regulated play of the children.

Older Children

The older children did get involved with the shape of the sand trace. In one of our earlier setups, Kevin is holding the bottle in one hand. He then flings it across the black paper that is taped to the floor (see Photo 4.1). Fleet then sweeps the sand away to the side of the paper so that Kevin can try another push and notice the design that it makes.

The setup seen in Photo 4.1 was hard to keep going, because the sweeping took too much time and the sand could not be recycled into the ketchup bottle. That is why we invented the panel of plywood that could be tilted to quickly "erase" the surface. On several occasions we did use a third setup. The sand bottle was suspended over a round table about 5 feet in diameter. With this setup the older children stood around the table and took turns pushing the bottle. Because the string from the ceiling was now shorter, their pushes made very interesting concentric spirals.

The children were used to studying designs on table tops; many of their crafts activities were done there. It seemed that their attention to the sand pattern was heightened when it was left on the table top. No doubt it is a general fact of education that the type of space that supports an activity—be it the floor, a 15-inch platform, or a 3-foot-high table—determines in large measure the quality and form of that activity.

Children up to 4 did not get involved with trying to predict exactly where the sand would be laid down. Nor did they look at the sand trace to figure out where the swinging object had been. They did seem to understand that a straight push would cause straight traces and a wiggle added to a push would cause a scalloped design. They could, in other words, make the correspondence between *their* action and the resultant pattern. They did not show evidence of making a correspondence between the *bottle's* action and the resultant pattern or vice versa.

Some of the very young children would not even move the bottle back and forth. So we decided to see what would happen if we moved the surface under their stationary bottle of draining sand. This idea led to the next activity, the Spinning Sand.

THE SPINNING SAND

Preparing the Environment

At first we tried to put a 3-foot lazy Susan under the swinging bottle of sand. As the bottle made passes back and forth, the children could turn the lazy Susan. The resultant pattern was then the multiplication of the two motions, swinging and spinning. This was too much for our children. They got involved either with the swinging or the spinning, but not both.

PHOTO 4.1   Kevin slaps the Swinging Sand bottle and watches the scalloped patterns of the draining sand.

So we eliminated the string and just gave the children the ketchup bottle filled with dry sand. Now they could hold the bottle stationary, as many of the younger children did anyway, and spin the lazy Susan. The draining sand left circular traces on the flat surface. But the lazy Susan soon filled up with sand, and additional sand that was drained onto the filled surface was completely camouflaged.

Then we noticed that some of the onlookers who did not have ketchup bottles would stick their finger into the layer of sand spinning around. This observation led to the final version of the activity, called the Spinning Sand. We simply filled the lazy Susan with dry sand and let the children make etchings in it by spinning it and putting finger, brush, or some other object to the surface. In Photo 4.2 Juliette slants the scraper so that the edge does not gouge into the sand as she makes a clean etching.

PHOTO 4.2   Juliette turns the lazy Susan with one hand and makes etchings with the other.

Entry

The children were attracted to this activity, as they were to any container filled with sand. The fact that this container turned only increased their interest. Some of the younger children liked to place toy animals in the sand and spin the lazy Susan around. They let it make a few revolutions and then took the animal off. Sometimes, a teacher or another child placed another toy animal on the sand. No matter how long the two animals "chased" each other, they never got closer. An animal placed in the center of the lazy Susan looked as if it were turning around, rather than chasing around. Animals placed on different radii from the center elicited different comments from the children.

The younger children dug in the sand and spun the space as separate acts. Some of them did spin the space and, while it was still spinning, stuck a finger into the sand. Their focus seemed to be more on how the sand would pile up in front of their finger as the lazy Susan turned. The older children liked to vary the diameter of circles and to erase previous etching by smoothing the spinning sand.

Juliette, almost 4, is sitting with Peter, a teacher. Marika sits nearby, looking on. Juliette spins the sand. Peter enters with this question: "Can you make a smaller circle?" Juliette does not understand Peter's question. Some seconds later, when Juliette has her finger in the sand, Peter spins the space. Juliette then begins to see more clearly that the tracks in the sand make a circle. When Peter once again asks Juliette to make a smaller circle, she places her finger in toward the center. She could on most occasions thereafter make a big or a small circle on request. The position of her stationary finger determined the size of the circle.

Tristan brings a fork to the spinning space. He experiments with the different types of marks he can make with it. "I'm making roads!" he exclaims as he looks over the traces in the sand. Peter takes a spatula, presses it into the spinning sand and says "I'm making wide roads." Different objects make different traces as the space moves beneath. Four fingers spread out make a different trace than four fingers close together. The movement of the spinning sand accentuates these differences. Time is added and frozen in the long etches of four fingertips.

Marika joins the game. She is more interested in smoothing the spinning sand down. Tristan makes a mark, and Marika uses her hand to smooth it down. It is not clear that Marika is aware that Tristan might see her actions as undoing his creations. She just likes to smooth down the spinning sand. "Stop it, M'rika," Tristan says. She does stop but probably does not understand why Tristan is upset.

As it turned out, the Spinning Sand was best played with no more than two children; even then, the activity required teacher supervision. With more than two children it was too difficult for a child to keep track, so to speak, of his creations. But then, how many adults would want to work with others on the same potter's wheel? Because the Spinning Sand was so easily constructed, we could have made five or six for individual children. All you need is a Rubbermaid lazy Susan and a larger board of some type glued to it. As long as the board is centered for balance, the surface can be up to 3 feet in diameter. We found other uses for the Rubbermaid lazy Susans, as you will see in the next activity.

THE DRAWING DRIVER

Preparing the Environment

For this activity the floor is covered with white butcher paper. In Photo 4.3 Sydney is bending over to grasp a felt-tip pen attached to a little car. The car itself is attached to a 4-foot wooden dowel that is stuck into a cardboard drum. The drum is attached to a Rubbermaid lazy Susan.

Photo 4.4 is a close-up of the little car, which is actually a single-unit block. We drilled a hole in its side slightly larger than the long wooden dowel, so that the car could slide up and down along the length of the dowel. Wheels were attached to the bottom of the block. A rotating turret was attached to the top of the car, from which extends an 8-inch wooden dowel. The pen is attached to the end of this short dowel by means of a Tinker Toy hub, sectioned slightly and wrapped with duct tape.

The Drawing Driver involves three independent movements: the rotation of the 4-foot dowel around the cardboard drum, the rotation of the 8-inch dowel around the turret on the block, and the back-and-forth excursion of the car along the longer dowel. This means that the child can drive the car to any spot within the largest circumference of the 4-foot dowel and make many embellishing movements with the 8-inch dowel on the turret. As long as the felt-tip pen is moist and the pen maintains a slight pressure on the paper, every move that the car makes will leave a trace of ink. Inside the cardboard drum we placed moist sand in a plastic bag. This gave the drum enough weight to keep the whole setup stabilized. Without the weight in the drum any motion of the car would have caused the lazy Susan to move, thereby destroying the pivot point for marks being made by the pen.

On different days we added different realistic props to the game. Gas station pumps were quite successful, as were little plastic Weebles (which look like people). The children could use these props to create imaginary trips to the gas station or, as one child suggested, a trip to New Hampshire.

Entry

This toy was so novel that it did not attract the children's attention immediately. Usually, a teacher would free-play with the Drawing Driver by herself. One or two children in the large classroom would notice the teacher having fun and come over, asking for a turn. The younger children usually pushed the felt-tip pen itself. The older children invented other ways to make the little car move. They either pushed the long dowel or went to the center and turned the cardboard drum

PHOTO 4.3   Sydney tests the felt-tip pen on the Drawing Driver car.

PHOTO 4.4   The car passes a Weeble (person) on the paper.

like a steering wheel. The younger children were also able to do this, but usually only in response to seeing a teacher or another child do it. Sometimes, instead of rotating the drum to make the car change position, they yanked on the drum to make it slide laterally.

Younger Children

Matthew sees Fredi playing by herself. He comes over to her and wants to play. Fredi has been moving the car on the end of the long dowel by steering from the cardboard drum. Matthew grabs the rim of the drum and turns it. He continues to do this until the dowel comes up behind him and bumps him in the back. He reverses the direction of the motion by rotating the drum in the other direction. Fredi senses that Matthew is not taking his own body into account (self-to-object perspective). "Can you drive your car to the gas station?" she asks. At this suggestion Matthew gets up and holds the car itself, leaving the cardboard drum. He sort of walks the car to the gas station, dragging the whole setup along behind. In other words, he does not try to move the car within the constraints of the three movements defined by the moving parts.

Alex, on another occasion, also played with steering the drum. Unlike Matthew he seemed to notice the action of the car on the end of the dowel 4 feet away. Matthew concentrated more on rotating the drum than on steering the car from afar. As we mentioned in Chapter Two, young children are more interested in proximal effects than distal effects. Alex, however, did seem to be looking at the car as he moved the drum.

Older Children

Loren is driving the car around and around, holding the car itself. Fredi has put a blob of finger paint in the path of the car. Loren says "We got gas in the road." He drives his car through the "gas," and the wheels make tracks on the other side of the "puddle." Loren wants to put more gas in the road. "Why do you want to do that?" Fredi asks. Then Loren explains, in a run-on sentence, that he wants gas on the road so that when he drives through the gas he will get gas on the wheels and so that when he drives farther the gas will come off the wheels and make tracks.

Tristan, about 4 years old, is playing with Aaron, a younger child. Tristan has previously discovered how to change the radius of the car by sliding it along the large dowel. Aaron is driving the car around in circles, holding the car itself. After Aaron has played a few more minutes, Fredi places a small bridge directly in his car's path, saying "Road closed. You have to go around." She expects Aaron to slide the car along the dowel to avoid the obstruction.

Aaron's initial reaction is to move the bridge, but the teacher holds it firm. As Aaron is hesitating, Tristan looks up and says "Make it a little more long. A little more in, a little more in." He gestures by slowly moving his hands closer together in front of himself. Aaron, instead of adjusting the radius of the car, reverses the direction altogether and retraces his path.

Tristan, on another day, is playing with the car himself. The car is on a trip and the gas pump is some feet away. Fredi repositions the gas pumps to a new place and asks Tristan if it is time to fill up his car with gas. He agrees that it is, and so Fredi asks him to drive his car to the pumps. Tristan looks over at the pumps on the other side of the area. His car is about in the middle of the 4-foot dowel. The gas pumps are about 4 feet from the cardboard drum and a half circle away. Tristan then very carefully holds the dowel by its end and rotates it until the dowel is directly in line with the gas pump. Then he grasps the car and slides it up the dowel to the gas pumps.

In other words, Tristan made two discrete movements to reach his destination. First, he rotated the dowel into place; then he slid the car into place. He could have done both at once, sliding the car as he rotated the dowel. We thought it was interesting that Tristan did not use that more advanced strategy.

These encounters gave us some indication that the Drawing Driver did offer some interesting problems for the children to solve. The different combinations of motions made several types of detours possible. The felt-tip pen left an indication of the choice of detours that a child might make. After a child made detours or reached his destination, he could see his choice in the lines on the paper. With children still older than our own you should be able to play more advanced games, such as How Did I Make This Mark? For example, one child called the back and forth wags made by the turret a "rainbow." Other children might want to make more rainbows and could try to figure out how that design was made. You should take your cue from the children and then expand the play gradually.

In Photo 4.5 you can see that Sydney invented a game of push and release. Instead of holding on to the car throughout, she sent it ahead with a sharp shove. The pen on the turret stick wagged behind. Because of the marks on the paper Sydney was better able to anticipate where the Drawing Driver would go when she pushed it forward.

PHOTO 4.5   Sydney gives the Drawing Driver a firm push forward.

Variation—Tire-Tracking Trikes

It is interesting that the creative source of the Drawing Driver was a rain puddle on the sidewalk outside. The children, as usual, were driving their tricycles up and down the sidewalk. On this day their tires left tracks on the dry pavement after they drove through the puddle. Some of the children noticed the tracks. They zipped through the puddle and then looked over their shoulder at their tracks behind.

One 4-year-old is trying to reverse his direction. With the skill of a truck driver he turns the big bars full right, cranks his pedals backwards (passing through the puddle incidentally), whips the bars full left, and cranks his pedals forward. Wow!

He notices that one wheel has made perfect tracks showing both curves of his beautifully executed turnaround. He looks at this track and proclaims to a nearby teacher "I made the letter *Y!*" And indeed he did.

On other days we deliberately wet a spot on the sidewalk with the garden hose. The children thoroughly enjoyed making tracks and looking at how they diminished as the wetness wore off the wheels. The tracks were a fun way to freeze motion and study the shape of it. The tricycle's tracking also made such a vivid impression on the children that games played inside in miniature could draw on the real tracking outside. You may recall Loren at the Drawing Driver explaining why he had to have more "gas" that he could drive through.

THE WATER PENCIL

Preparing the Environment

During one staff meeting the teachers were remarking on the failures of the day. We had wanted our children to add water to dry paint so they could understand the transformation from dry to wet. The children dumped in huge quantities of water to the dry ingredients, making a memorable mess. We even tried tiny cups of water to slow down the transformation. Our children had used their free access to the bathroom to bring back to the easel a bucket of water. During this staff meeting someone said "We need a steady supply of a small quantity of water." Perhaps one of us thought about a leaky faucet, and then Lisa said "How about an IV [intravenous] tube from the hospital!" We instantly knew that this was the perfect solution to our problem. From then on the Water Pencil, as we christened it, has been standard equipment at the School for Constructive Play.

We got several IV tubes from the university infirmary. We took a gallon-size plastic milk carton and cut out its bottom. This was to be the water reservoir. We hung it upside down from the ceiling and inserted an IV tube in its mouth, using a rubber stopper and duct tape to make this connection leakproof. We hung the milk carton with a plant hanger (see p. 222 in CCK). The children could hold the nozzle end of the tube. Just above the nozzle was a thumb screw that regulated the flow of the water. The children could easily change the flow from a continuous stream to a steady drip to no flow at all.

The Water Pencil can be used most anywhere that you can find a place to suspend the reservoir. We use it over the sand table and the work tables. When it is placed over the sand table, the Water Pencil is a good means to freeze motion. The children can set the flow on a continuous stream and make designs in the dry sand. Food coloring can be added to the water so the children can see it better. Two Water Pencils at the sand table are enough. Sometimes sand gets trapped in the thumb screw. When this happens, a nearby teacher simply uses one Water Pencil to clean the other. The children can usually wait the few seconds that this takes.

Children using the Water Pencil over the work tables can make designs on construction paper or waxed paper. We will discuss some of these activities again in the section later in this chapter on unitizing motion. Set to drip steadily, the Water Pencil is an excellent means to break a continuous movement into parts. As the child moves his Water Pencil across waxed paper, the motion leaves a "unitized" trace in the tiny beads of water spaced at regular intervals.

Entry

When we placed the Water Pencils over the sand table, the children came to this area anyway. The teacher modeled for a few minutes, and the children quickly took the nozzle and began to drop the water stream into the sand. We started the activity with the stream very slow, so the sand would not get saturated before the focused-activity period was over. We left the usual sort of play implements in the sand table, such as a few cups, shovels, and shifters.

PHOTO 4.6   David and Hattie play with the Water Pencil. Water reservoir is hanging from ceiling (out of picture).

The younger children either held the stream of water in one place, making a puddle, or held it over their other hand to feel the water. The older children moved the stream of water around more. Sometimes, they made patterns; other times, they used the water stream to wash off miniature objects such as toy trucks. All children were able to see how the dry sand was gradually changing into a heavier, wetter, and more easily modeled substance. We had given the children control over the transformation in such a way that the change could be understood.

Younger Children

Amy is playing with the Water Pencil in the sand table. She directs the water back and forth from her palm to the sand. The water has slowed down to a steady drip. She wants it to flow faster, having seen it do that before. She squeezes the nozzle tip, as if this will bring more water. Even after she sees the teacher move the thumb screw, she still squeezes the nozzle whenever the flow is too slow. This is an example of how young children concentrate on the more proximal of two possible causes.

Amy continues to direct the water to the sand. The flow is dripping again. Amy studies this dripping momentarily and then begins to poke the nozzle into the sand. The holes that she makes with the physical contact of nozzle to sand look like the dots made by the water drops.

It is not unreasonable to conclude that Amy, by poking the nozzle into the sand, was duplicating the effect of the drops of water. She, perhaps, was trying to understand how the drops make the dots in the sand. She did this by "concretizing" the experience—that is, by using a more direct, proximal, and physical method of making the dots herself. Perhaps then she could assimilate the action and effect of the water drops to her own direct action of poking the sand. We noticed that this same scheme of poking was used on innumerable occasions by many of the children.

Older Children

Jenny is making long, slow passes with the Water Pencil over the dry sand in the table. The water leaves a clear, dark trace in the sand. Jenny first smoothes down an area, making a "tablet" to write on. Then she makes loops and curls with the Water Pencil.

Tristan's Water Pencil is shut off. He opens the thumb screw all the way. The teacher asks "Can you make it go half as fast?" Tristan gets the idea that the teacher wants the water to come out more slowly, so he closes the thumb screw down. But he overshoots the halfway point, and now the stream has been cut off altogether. The teacher says "Oops. Now it's not going at all. Can you open it just a little?" Tristan rolls the thumb screw forward until it reaches its physical terminus. The water is flowing at its fastest again. Most of our children had difficulty stopping the thumb screw midway.

The child's tendency to make changes go to their full limit is quite general at this age. They want to empty all the water from a glass, all the sand from a container. They want the marble to roll all the way down the ramp, not halfway. Recall the example we used in Chapter One in the section of the level of opposition. Tristan could not push the marble down the ramp with just enough force to make it stop in the middle portion of the ramp. We see here again, with the thumb screw on the Water Pencil, that Tristan is having difficulty with the concept of *degrees* (see Chapter One's discussion of discrete degrees). However, it was Tristan who said about the Drawing Driver "Make it a little more long, a little more in." In some activities, evidently, he could think about degrees of change, not just the opposite extremes of a change.

The Water Pencil can also be placed near the easel so children can trickle water down the paper. Colored water on white or yellow construction paper works nicely. We used paint powder and dusted the moistened surface of our huge Plexiglas easel. Then the children trickled and dripped the water to see how the powder would change to liquid paint. (Recall that this was the origin of the idea for the Water Pencil.)

We even used the Water Pencil with play dough. We put the dough inside an empty water table, and the children could make channels of water and lakes, sculpting the pretend terrain as they liked. Unfortunately, the play dough crumbled or dissolved after a period of time. Potter's clay or modeling clay would have worked better. Wherever we needed a steady and easily controlled supply of water, we used the Water Pencil.

THE REVOLVING EASELS

Preparing the Environment

This activity was a natural extension of the Spinning Sand, in which the child can keep her brush stationary and turn the lazy Susan to make marks in the sand. At a Revolving Easel the child can again hold her brush stationary and make marks on the paper as it turns under the brush. Using large cardboard drums, we constructed both a horizontal and a vertical Revolving Easel.

In Photo 4.7 Marya is making the papered drum revolve away from her while she holds a felt-tip pen to the paper. In Photo 4.8 Fleet helps Marya undo the paper from the drum so they can look at her marks flattened out. This horizontal version takes about an hour to make. Just cut two pieces of plywood the size of the drum's diameter and screw them into the ends. Bore a hole in the center of each end piece, stick a large wooden dowel through both holes to create an axle, and then mount the ends of the axle on some type of scaffolding. We used two shelf braces screwed into a plywood base.

The vertical version can be made in about five minutes. Take a cardboard drum and duct-tape the bottom end onto a lazy Susan (see Figure 4.2). The drum is heavy enough as it is to resist the lateral pressure children make on the sides when they make marks. You can attach sheets of construction paper to the outside surface with clothespins.

Entry

On the vertical drum the children began by making vertical marks with their felt-tip pens and crayons. The tallness of the drum may have suggested the vertical strokes. Also, by making a vertical stroke the children did not have to cope with the curved surface. They made a few marks, turned the drum, and made a few more marks. Only after several days of experience with the vertical drum did they begin to make horizontal strokes. When they did this, the teacher slowly turned the drum to give them the idea that they could make even longer marks without getting up from their seats.

Lilly and Jessica played a game at the vertical Revolving Easel. Lilly made a mark and turned the easel. Jessica laughed as she saw the marks that Lilly had made. The game was cut short by a distraction in the room, but it could have a lot of potential for future days. The Revolving Easel makes it very easy for children to exchange spaces, add marks to each other's work, and create a cooperative composite.

The horizontal easel did not lend itself as well to these cooperative games. But it was the preferred easel for freezing motion. The children could make all sorts of zigzag lines on the freely spinning drum by simply moving their pen back and forth from left to right. They seemed amazed that simple actions led to such interesting patterns on the flattened sheet taken off of the drum.

We also put black and white paper on these easels, half and half. A black crayon would make marks on the white paper but not the black half; a white crayon (or chalk) would make marks on the black paper but not the white half. The children liked to experiment with these opposites by turning the drum to different positions.

PLEXI-PAINTING

Preparing the Environment

All of the activities that follow in this section use our large Plexiglas panels. These are two ¼-inch-thick panels of Plexiglas about 5 feet by 3 feet, mounted in wooden frames. The frames are hinged together at one end. The panels can be stood up in easel-like fashion (see Figure 4.3). They can also be folded or spread out

PHOTO 4.7   Marya pushes the Revolving Easel with her right hand and makes marks on the paper with her left hand.

124   PHOTO 4.8   Marya and Fleet look at the marks that Marya has made.

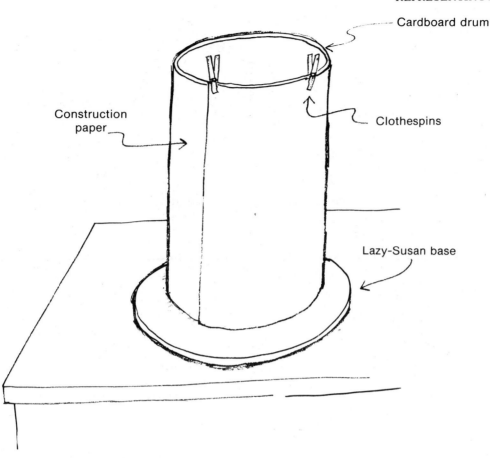

Cardboard drum

Construction paper

Clothespins

Lazy-Susan base

FIGURE 4.2   Vertical Revolving Easel.

horizontally and placed on saw horses; this makes a Plexiglas table. Or they can be placed on the floor in an L formation on two long sides; this makes two perfectly vertical surfaces on which children can stand and draw. Finally, they can be placed with one panel a horizontal ceiling and the other panel a vertical wall, as we did in the shadow play described in Chapter Two. In this arrangement the children can look at objects from an underneath perspective through the ceiling of Plexiglas (see p. 165 in CCK).

Plexiglas easels can also be easily made with two cardboard drums. Stand them on end, cut a vertical slit in each, and insert the right and left sides of a Plexiglas sheet into the drums. Children can stand on opposite sides and trace each other. In Photo 4.9 Hattie is painting Tom's face, beard and all. Tom is lying down in the loft of our climber, and the panel is built into its railing.

In keeping with our emphasis on movement, we decided to make things move behind a vertical Plexiglas panel. The children were given felt-tip pens (with washable ink) and asked to copy the motion of the things that moved. We called this version of Plexi-Painting *Kinetic Drawing*. In Photo 4.10 Katie has just seen Fleet pull back toward her and then release a plastic spool attached to an elastic band. The spool makes a rapid vibration at the top of the elastic before it falls straight down. The elastic is stretched taut between two points on the tiny scaffold and passes freely through a hole in the spool. In the photo you can still see the spool vibrating slightly as it descends. Katie makes her "copy" as Marya looks on. We will describe several different learning encounters with this setup.

Entry: Kinetic Drawing

The children initially drew the static features of an object. But with some encouragement they drew the motion of objects, such as the trajectory of a falling feather or the vibration of the spool on the elastic band. The slower the action and

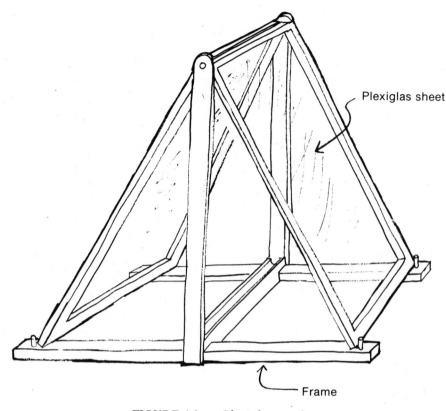

Plexiglas sheet

Frame

FIGURE 4.3   Plexiglas easel.

the more gracefully undulating the fall, the easier it was for the children to reconstruct the motion.

Younger Children

Katie, at 2½ years of age (she is about 4 in Photo 4.10), is watching Lisa drop a feather from about 5 feet above the table. Lisa asks "Can you draw how the feather falls?" Katie makes a 4-inch mark and crosses it with three perpendicular lines. Evidently, Katie is trying to draw the feather itself, as it looks when it is motionless. Lisa drops it again and says "Draw how it is falling." Katie again draws the static feather. On the third attempt she begins with a shaft and three perpendiculars but then draws a long trailing line downward, with abbreviated dips here and there. The trailing line looks like the trajectory of the feather's fall. Now she is thinking about the movement. The fourth time that Lisa drops the feather, Katie brings her pen down hard on the drawing surface. She smiles, looks at the feather, and crashes her pen down again.

It seemed that Katie's pen had become the embodiment of the feather. She had shifted from a graphic representation of the feather's falling to a physical (or gestural) form of representation. Perhaps the graphic representation did not express all the information that Katie wanted to represent. The pen-as-feather could express the actual contact that the feather made with the table. Young children seem to be very attentive to the point of contact between objects.

Older Children

Clayton watches Lisa drop the feather. He waits for it to fall all the way, and then he makes a single downward line on the Plexiglas. He does this several times. Lisa feels that the feather is falling too straight. So, she throws it aloft with a sharp movement of her hand. Clayton, interestingly enough, makes a sharp upward motion with his pen.

PHOTO 4.9   Hattie paints Tom's face on the Plexiglas panel in the climber/loft.

PHOTO 4.10   Katie makes lines on the Plexiglas to represent the action of the spool on the elastic band.

127

Clayton had apparently shifted from representing the fall of the feather to representing the sharp rise of Lisa's hand. Actually, what Clayton did seems natural, because Lisa's hand is more like Clayton's pen-holding hand than is the feather. The correspondence between his hand and Lisa's hand could be the reason he changed to making a physical (gestural) representation of action.

When Lisa drew back and released the spool on the elastic band, Clayton made a diagonal mark from top right to left and then made the mark drop straight down. His drawing indicated that he had thought about both the horizontal vibration of the spool and its subsequent drop. Or his drawing might have represented the initial position of the spool when Lisa had it drawn back, ready to release, and then the subsequent drop. He made a similar set of marks on a second trial, but the orientation of the two marks was rotated 90 degrees. Clayton was thinking about some aspects of the movements but had not quite worked out their relation to the bottom of the table. The game was brand new for Clayton, and with time he would probably think more about the motion itself.

Kinetic Drawing is quite unlike any other activities that we are familiar with as early-childhood teachers. Our culture teaches young children to draw a house, a tree, or a person. These are static objects. We teachers make the assumption that children cannot draw the shape of a motion. Yet these small successes that we had at the School for Constructive Play made us believe that Kinetic Drawing is both possible and enjoyable for young children. On top of all this, it may be good pedagogy if it serves to give the child a more dynamic world view, a view of how things change.

We thought that the kinetic aspect of objects could be more easily studied by children if they watched moving shadows. The shadow can be cast directly on paper, using the rear-projection technique that we have already described. The child can make marks directly on the moving "object." In point of fact, we should have invented Kinetic Drawing with shadows first, because it is easier than the drawing on clear Plexiglas. The following encounters describe the children playing with kinetic shadows.

Entry: Kinetic Shadow Drawing

We used two versions of Kinetic Shadow Drawing. For one version the shadows were cast on a vertical panel. The children marked on the paper on one side, and the teacher moved an object in front of a light source on the other side. Objects with slow, undulating movements elicited the most attempts to draw action. One of the best was the Wonderful Waterfuls, a commercial game that consists of small, plastic rings in an enclosed, clear-plastic reservoir of water. By pressing a button that created a water jet inside the reservoir, the teacher could make the little rings shoot upward in the water and gracefully float and tumble down. The rings made the most captivating shadows seen from the child's side of the papered Plexiglas panel. Marika, for example, would make long, comma-type marks inside the shadow of the reservoir. When the teacher removed the Wonderful Waterfuls from the light source, Marika could clearly see her marks. The marks had frozen the motion or, at least, Marika's understanding of the motion.

For a second version of Kinetic Shadow Drawing we placed the Plexiglas panels horizontal on saw horses. The children could trace moving shadows or a moving light on paper. We found that small penlights worked better than regular flashlights. They were easier to move around, and the children did not have the tendency to color in the surface area of light. With a small point of light the children got more involved with movement. They kept their crayon on the point of light wherever it went. When the teacher turned off the light, the children could look at their marks. The marks were, as one child said, "where the light went."

All of the activities in this section have dealt with freezing motion. Children eventually construct the relation between the object in motion and the trace left behind. Once they construct that correspondence, the traces present information about motion that is otherwise lost with the passage of time. We now shift to freezing motion in a different way. The trace left behind is a discontinuous representation of a continuous action. The motion is broken into "units."

UNITIZING MOTION

In the activities on unitizing motion we take an action with continuous motion that the child can easily see, such as a rolling ball, and add to this some trace of the action. But the trace is discontinuous. Through these activities, we hope, young children will get the idea that a continuous motion can be broken up into parts, or segments. Many skills, such as telling time from a clock, measuring off a distance, and calculating the rate of rise or fall of a moving object—all things that the child will do at an older age—involve the simple notion that a single motion can be broken into segments. We have no illusion that our children will regard these segments as equal or not equal, but we do sense that they are intrigued with the discontinuity of the traces within the continuity of the motion.

The discontinuity is not always frozen in a trace. Sometimes, we use the physical starting and stopping of the moving object itself, such as a spool rolling down an incline and hitting speed bumps every 12 inches or so. The continuous downward motion of the spool is unitized by the punctuation of the bumps as the spool rolls. The child, in this case, makes a mental representation of the discontinuity, rather than seeing the physical representation of a paint trace or water mark. That is, the child sees the second bumping action, relates that to the first, and gets some sense of the discontinuity of the motion. To think about the discontinuity, the child must remember the whole roll.

THE BLIP SPOOL

Preparing the Environment
The Blip Spool is so named because, as it rolls down a papered incline, it leaves a spot of paint twice every revolution. The children called these spots "blips." In Photo 4.11 Seth has just released the spool down a narrow table that we had jacked up at one end to make an incline. The spool is rolling toward a target made out of Tinker Toy parts. If Seth has aimed correctly, the spool will hit the center Tinker Toy stick and spin it on its goal post axle. The table is covered with butcher paper, which is changed after every four or five trials. The more enterprising of you might construct a holder at one end of the table so that the exchange can be a simple matter of rolling paper out and tearing the old sheet off.

The spool itself came from a recycling center. It was probably used for electrical wire. We took two little sponges and epoxied them to the center shaft of the spool, one on each side. Before each roll the teacher dabbed a little finger paint on both sponges. The paint was thick enough to leave on the paper an easily discerned spot without the splatter that thinner paint would cause.

To make the game easier for the younger children, we tacked 3-inch cardboard retaining walls on the sides of the table. The walls also discouraged waiting children from interrupting the roll of the spool.

Entry
Our children at the School for Constructive Play were quite familiar with rolling games. They enjoyed them and knew how to manage them. Even without modeling the children would place the spool at the higher end of the table and release it. The teacher did have to structure the game somewhat in order to apply the paint to the sponges. The marks on the paper were a new experience. It seemed

PHOTO 4.11   Seth releases the Blip Spool toward the target. The spool leaves traces of paint as it rolls down the incline.

that the onlooking children noticed the blips before the child who had released the spool noticed them. But after a few runs—particularly after a few misses—the child who had released the spool would look at the blips.

On a larger table the teacher can reposition the target. Her role is to create a slightly different problem for the child. A whole variety of challenges can be posed by changing the position of the target, changing the slant of the incline, and changing the number of sponges moistened with paint. If the table is unevenly elevated at one end, with one leg higher than the other, the sponges make glancing blows to the paper as the spool both rolls and slides. (This last variation depends on the friction of the paper to the spool and does not always work.) The aim of the activity, as always, is to start the children off but then fade out and see how they begin to explore the possible changes.

We wanted to invent a spool on which the position of the sponges could be changed. This would be more in keeping with our emphasis on *change without exchange*. The blip marks would then be closer together or farther apart depending on how the child spaced the sponges on the circumference of the spool. In general, a spool works better than a ball. Balls roll in so many different ways that the sponge infrequently comes into contact with the paper.

If the children do not comment on the marks, do not force their attention to it. Casual comments every now and then should be enough. At first, the children will be much more involved in the rolling than the marks. They begin to notice the marks incidentally at first, but more deliberately later. As we said, the marks are a novel experience, and it may take some time before the children assimilate the marks as relevant to the motion.

HOLELY STROKES

Preparing the Environment

In Photo 4.12 Hattie has been painting at our Plexiglas easel. We had prepared the easel beforehand by duct-taping four rubber sheets, filled with holes, onto the panel. The children could make brush strokes across the sheets—thus the name of this activity. Then, when they lifted one, as the teacher is doing in Photo 4.12, the children could see that they had made circles on the Plexiglas. The rubber sheets came from a recycling center in Boston, the duct tape came from the hardware store, and the idea came from our objective of unitizing motion. The continuous movement of the paintbrush is broken into parts, the separate circles made on the Plexiglas panel.

PHOTO 4.12   Hattie looks at the discontinuous circles left under the rubber sheet.

Entry

The younger children liked to fill in each individual hole one at a time. The older children, with a wide-bristled brush, made a single swath across a row of holes and then looked at the pattern left underneath the rubber sheet. With the sheet of larger holes, however, even the older children enjoyed filling in individual holes with paint. The large holes seemed to suggest individual spaces that should be filled.

Younger Children

Matthew stands at the easel, holding the brush almost all the way up the back of the handle. He repeatedly jabs paint into the rubber holes and twists the brush. After he has filled several adjacent holes, a whole area appears blacked out. At this point a teacher raises the rubber sheet. Matthew looks at the same area now. It no longer appears blacked out. He has made some globby circles, some connected because of the excess of paint he used to fill in the holes. He laughs at this and, when the teacher lowers the sheet, he begins to paint again in the same manner. He begins to anticipate that the teacher will, after a while, raise the rubber sheet. Now he uses less paint per hole and shifts to a new hole more frequently. Perhaps he is thinking about how the blacked out-area (continuous color) will look when the rubber sheet is raised (discontinuous color).

Older Children

Eva is painting over the rubber holes. Aaron is on the inside of the easel with a paintbrush. Wherever Eva makes a circle of paint by painting across the holes, Aaron adds a dot over it from the inside. "I'm painting yours," Aaron says to Eva. Eva doesn't say anything. About five minutes later, after Aaron has left, Eva gets inside the easel. She starts to paint the other side of the circles she has made, just as Aaron painted her circles. From the underside of the easel it appears that the circles are on top of the rubber sheet, an interesting reversal of perspective (see Chapter Three).

Hattie is making swaths of paint across a row of holes. She knows to dip her brush deep into the paint in order to have enough to cover more than a few holes. When the teacher lifts the rubber sheet, Hattie laughs. Before the teacher lowers the sheet, Hattie dips her brush into the paint again and connects the individual circles with a single stroke. This behavior could indicate that Hattie has assimilated the row of separate holes to the scheme she used to create them, a single stroke of the brush. She has converted, in effect, the discontinuous circles back into a continuous swath of paint!

After we watched children explore the rubber stencils at the easel, we decided to use them on the overhead projector. The effects were enlarged on the projector. Children found this variation quite exciting, except that the younger ones had difficulty making the correspondence between the painting surface and the image on the wall. We also used finger paint by itself on the overhead projector. Here the children could both freeze continuous motion or unitize motion, depending on the implements they used. The swirls and texture of the finger paint projected on the walls were extremely beautiful. We also liked the fact that the dynamic aspect of finger painting, the motion, was so conspicuous.

ROLLED-OUT PLAY DOUGH

Preparing the Environment

We described the preparations for this activity, in part, in Chapter Two. The teachers prepared a large batch of play dough and rolled out a ¼-inch layer over a large surface of the table. The children could use this layer as an etching tablet. They could freeze continuous motion by rolling a toy car over the dough. Or they could freeze motion with a discontinuous trace by using a sprocketed wheel such as a pizza cutter or a plastic gear. In Photo 4.13 Lauren is rolling a plastic gear through

PHOTO 4.13   Lauren rotates the plastic gear through the play dough and leaves a unitized representation of her motion.

the play dough. Look closely, and you will see the track that the gear leaves in the dough—a discontinuous row of teeth marks.

Some implements work better than others to make these unitized traces of motion. The difficulty with a plastic gear is that the child cannot make its marks go any farther than a half revolution before her hand gets in the way. The pizza cutter works better. It is on an axle, which is attached to a handle. The cutter wheel turns as the child extends her arm across the play dough.

The pizza cutter, however, has very small sprockets. It does not leave in the dough marks that are clearly separate. So we made our own pie cutter with Tinker Toy parts. Two wheels on an axle, with the axle on a handle, turned out to be the ideal implement for unitizing the forward motion of the cutter. We placed shortened dowels in the holes around the rim, as you can see in Figure 4.4. The children could change the pattern of the teeth prints in the dough by adding or subtracting teeth or by simply twisting one of the wheels on the axle without twisting the other.

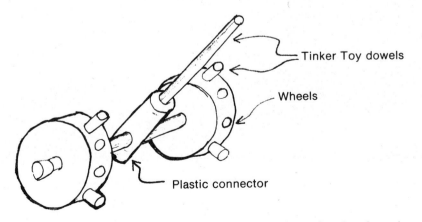

FIGURE 4.4   Wheels for unitizing motion in play dough.

Entry

The children named these little prints everything from "the broken wheel" to "footprints in the snow." The younger children sometimes tried to gouge up the play dough with the sprocketed wheel. The older ones were quite fascinated with the row of holes that the wheel left behind. For these older children, we might venture to say, this encounter was a precursory experience with measurement. After all, measurement involves marking off a total distance into parts. In fact, something quite like our sprocketed wheel is used to measure athletic fields. We will not push this analogy too far, but we do think the children are at least intrigued with the discontinuity (the row of holes) within continuity (the smooth action they use to make the holes).

SPEED BUMPS

Preparing the Environment

In the next few activities the child encounters a motion that is punctuated by a bump or a jerk. There is no trace left behind, but the child can change the motion back and forth between smooth and jerky, smooth and bumpy. In this fashion he may begin to understand that one continuous motion can be divided into units. In Photo 4.14 Kevin is rolling two cardboard wheels down an incline. The teacher has placed three cardboard rods across it. As the wheels hit the rods, they bump in a rhythm determined by the spacing of the rods. Kevin can either change the spacing of the rods or remove them altogether.

The wheels are "pipe sections" sawed from a larger cardboard tube. The

PHOTO 4.14   When Kevin releases two wheels down the incline, their roll is unitized by the speed bumps.

incline is actually a slide from an indoor climbing gym. We propped it up on one end with a wooden step-block. The "speed bumps" are cardboard tubing taken from coat hangers. They can be cut to specification, so that they will stay firm between the edges of the slide but can also be moved to make the wheel bump in different rhythms.

Entry

The teacher does little more than facilitate the children's explorations and help them take turns. At times, a speed bump will bend beyond repair, and the teacher can give the child a replacement. The speed bumps do not always stay in place, and a teacher can help cut them to improve their fit. If your school has the resources, you can improve this activity by routing out grooves along the side walls of the incline within which the cardboard rods can slide but not lift up.

The younger children have a tendency to push the wheels down the incline. The older children, as you see Kevin doing in the photo, place and release the wheels. The release works better, of course, because a vigorous shove is likely to cause the wheels to skip and even fall out of the alley.

We constructed a more advanced variation of the Speed Bumps by using a plastic spool. The spool was of the same type used in the Blip Spool activity. In this instance we cut a notch in both sides of the spool, as you see in Figure 4.5. The notches were cut deep enough so that, whenever they rolled directly over a speed

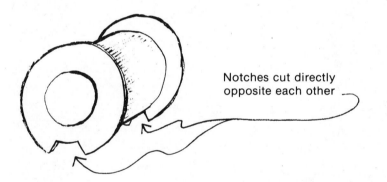

Notches cut directly
opposite each other

FIGURE 4.5   Notched spool for Speed Bumps.

bump, the spool would not bump. There was an arrangement of the speed bumps that made it possible to roll the spool down the incline without a single bump! The speed bumps were stationed apart at intervals equal to the circumference of the wheel's rim. It was then simply a matter of starting the release with the notches placed on the first speed bump. Our children did notice the differences in the way the spool behaved, sometimes bumping, sometimes not. But none of our 4- or 5-year-olds could figure out how the bumpless rolls occurred.

Part of the problem was mechanical. The construction of the speed bumps made exploration of their various positions difficult. The cardboard rods would either bend or fail to stick properly. The teacher had to help too often. Part of the problem also could have been the child's level of understanding about a motion within a motion. To understand the bumpless roll, the child would have had to think about the rotation of the notch around the center axis of the wheel (one motion) and at the same time think about the forward motion of the spool down the incline (another motion). As we have discussed before, children between 2 and 5 have difficulty thinking about two simultaneous functions (two within one). This more advanced version of the speed bumps, however, might be an interesting problem for 6- and 7-year-olds to solve.

SLATTED ROLLWAY

Preparing the Environment

We solved most of the "human-factor" problems of the Speed Bumps by using some long boards and hardwood blocks to make the Slatted Rollway. First we placed a saw horse on one of our 15-inch platforms. On it we propped two parallel 10-foot seesaws, resting their opposite ends on another saw horse on the floor.

We commandeered about three dozen double-unit and six-unit blocks from the block area. We lined the double-unit blocks all along the crack between the two parallel boards, creating a "Slatted Rollway" (see Photo 4.15). The slats were held in place with six-unit blocks, placed on edge and duct-taped together to create a retaining wall for objects to be rolled down the slats. The retaining wall was itself held in place by more six-units blocks duct-taped flat to the seesaw boards. The child could

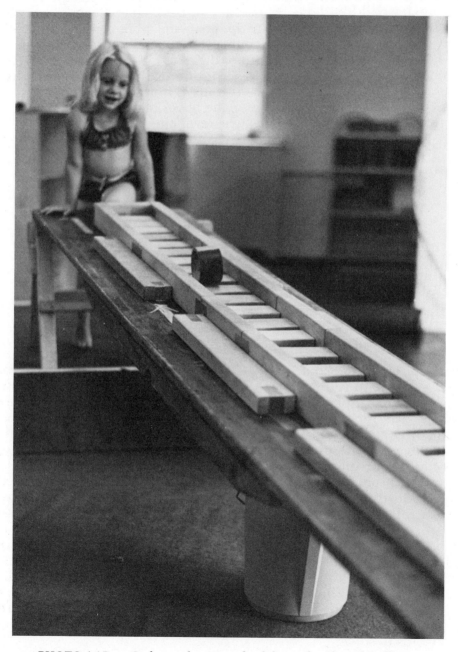

PHOTO 4.15   Sydney releases a wheel down the Slatted Rollway.

make holes and gaps anywhere along the Slatted Rollway. In Photo 4.16 a cardboard cylinder falls through the end of the rollway into a bucket below.

The whole setup was like a big xylophone. As the wheel rolled down the rollway, it would make a clackity-clack of rhythms determined by the spacing between the slats. That is, the motion of the rolling wheel could by unitized in different ways. The children had easy control over these transformations.

The children had several options for changing the Slatted Rollway. They could move individual slats (the double-unit blocks) or many at the same time. They could move the retaining wall as a unit without moving the slats. The retaining wall of six-unit blocks was securely duct-taped together as an enclosed box, 8 feet long and 1 foot wide. Finally, children could either remove or add blocks to make the rollway either less or more continuous.

We also discovered that the double-unit wooden cylinders produced interesting effects when rolled down the rollway. These cylinders would exactly fit within the sides of the retaining walls, roll down to a large gap in the slats, and come to rest on the inside edges of the parallel seesaw boards without falling through. On some occasions we substituted these wooden cylinders for most of the slats and let the children explore the functional properties of a rollway made with two or three dozen cylinders. We will also discuss other variations of this activity, which turned out to be one of our most versatile and popular games.

Entry

Most of our children, both younger and older, became fascinated with the "moving hole." By pushing the slats together, they could make one large hole in the rollway. They preferred to make the hole all the way at the bottom of the incline. This way, when they released the wheel at the top, it would roll the maximum distance before it fell through the hole into the bucket below. After whoever was playing the game had made the wheel roll the complete distance, the teacher created a small problem for the child to solve. The teacher pushed the slats and opened a hole at the middle of the rollway. Children of different ages had different strategies for solving this problem.

PHOTO 4.16   The wheel drops through a hole in the rollway into a bucket below.

Younger Children

Alex, a 2½-year-old, is rolling the wheel down the rollway. Gary, a student teacher, is nearby. Each time Alex rolls the wheel, it falls into the bucket. He retrieves the wheel from the bucket and returns to the top of the incline to roll it again. Just before Alex rolls the wheel, Gary changes the position of the hole, so that it is no longer over the bucket. Apparently understanding the implication of this change, Alex repositions the blocks, one at a time, until the hole is again directly over the bucket. After a few more rolls, Gary moves the bucket instead of moving the hole. Alex has a choice. He can either move the bucket back where it was (the inverse of Gary's transformation) or move the hole to be over the bucket (the reciprocal of Gary's transformation). Alex chooses to move the hole by pushing the slats down one at a time.

Although the reciprocal is usually a more difficult compensation for a child to make, in this case, perhaps, it was easier. After all, moving the slats was what Alex had done the last time the hole was not over the bucket. We did not ever see Alex move many blocks at once, which could be done by grasping and sliding a block several slats away from the current position of the hole. The younger children approached the problem with a one-at-a-time strategy.

Perhaps this strategy is another indication of the younger children's focus on the most proximal site of an effect. They could grasp and push a block that was next to the hole to move the hole over one space. But to grasp a block several slats away from the hole did not occur to them, because this latter strategy would require thinking about an effect some distance from the site of action. It would also require an understanding that pushing one block can cause other blocks, not directly touched, to move. We have seen the same thing with toy trains. A young child will pull a train by grasping the locomotive and pulling the other cars along incidentally, but he will seldom grasp the caboose and push the other cars ahead deliberately. The idea of force's being communicated through a series of connected objects does not occur to 2-year-olds as easily as it might to older children.

Older Children

Loren has been rolling several wheels down the Slatted Rollway at the same time. The hole in the slats is at the bottom of the incline. As he approaches the top of the incline holding a wheel in his hand, Gary opens a hole in the middle of the rollway by pushing many of the slats at once. When Loren gets to the top of the incline, he notices that the hole is in the middle. He walks back toward the lower end of the incline past the hole in the middle. He grabs the bottom end of the retaining-wall box made of the six-unit blocks. With a firm, steady tug he draws all of the slats inside the box together and recreates the hole at the bottom of the rollway! Loren has discovered a very interesting way (a reciprocal reversal) to undo the change that Gary made.

After several more rolls, Loren is again challenged by a hole in the middle of the rollway. This time Loren presses a flat palm on a slat about eight slats below the hole and slides that slat and the other seven upward, creating a hole closer to the bottom of the incline. He repeats this strategy one more time, and the hole opens up at the bottom of the rollway.

Not only did Loren understand that he could push many blocks ahead of the one he touched, he also knew that a hole would open up behind (not ahead) of his direction of push. He did all this with the certainty of a craftsman who knows his tools intimately.

After the Slatted Rollway had been in the classroom for about two weeks, we modified it slightly by making it possible for the children to change the incline. We did this by screwing cross-boards between the parallel seesaw boards so that both boards could tilt as a single unit. Then we placed the rollway on a single saw horse at the midpoint.

Tristan invented a new game with this setup. Placing a small doll on one of the slats, he tilts the incline so that the slats start to move down. "Give the baby a ride," he says. The doll rides down the incline on the slat. "Look, they took the baby away," Tristan comments. Gary facilitates this game by taking out more of the slats so that the doll will have a longer ride. Other children get interested and find their own objects to put on the slats. The game becomes a sort of conveyor belt. "Can you send me some coffee?" Gary asks Aaron. Aaron puts a coffee pot on one of the slats and then tilts the incline down toward Gary. The coffee pot slides down the incline on the slat.

We even added seats on each end of the rollway so that two children could make the seesaw version change inclines the way all seesaws do. We placed a mixture of double-unit blocks and double-unit cylinders in the retaining-wall box. As the children seesawed, the cylinders rolled first to one end, then to the other, creating holes at the top of each change of incline. The children were fascinated with the back-and-forth motion of these blocks. Heretofore, a seesaw had meant an up-and-down motion. Perhaps the Slatted Rollway, in this version, gave expression to a type of motion, back and forth, that the children had never considered.

Variations

The school semester ended before we could make other modifications to the Slatted Rollway. We considered many possibilities. For one, it seemed that we could not use the gaps themselves to unitize motion. The children preferred to roll the objects into a wide gap rather than across a slight gap. We plan to try different types of slats. A slat slightly higher than the others could make a speed bump that the children could easily move around. Several of these slightly raised slats could be spaced regularly among the others in order to unitize the motion of rolling objects. The rollway could even be set up so that the retaining walls converged slightly. Then the slats would have to be seriated to fit inside. The Slatted Rollway should be considered a general-purpose activity.

In the fall of 1978 we did try an activity that evolved from the Slatted Rollway but was different enough to have its own name, the Domino Row. This activity was field tested by Susan Kowal. Rectangular double-unit blocks were stood on end in the familiar row, regularly spaced so that they would knock one another down when the first was pushed over. We modified the activity to fit the ability of our 3-year-olds, who had trouble arranging the blocks in a straight line. We made a long channel by taping two 8-foot boards (2 inches by 4 inches) parallel on the floor. Each block for the row was hinged to a single-unit block with a piece of duct tape. The upright double then had a nice pedestal that would slide freely inside the long channel. All the children had to do was stand the blocks up and slide them back and forth within the channel. By reducing the need to make a straight line, we invented a unitizing-motion game within the ability of the younger children.

CASCADING WATER

Preparing the Environment

The Cascading Water was designed to give children encounters with a unitized flow. We placed the water table on one of our platforms. Then we built a set of steps up to the table, using our large step-blocks from the block area. On top of each step we placed a split section of cardboard tubing about 5 inches wide. These split tubes functioned as troughs for the water, a set of tiers down which it could cascade. The troughs were lined with tinfoil to make them waterproof (see Photo 4.17).

Entry

This activity is one of our most successful in terms of extended play by a variety of children. Both the younger and the older children enter the Cascading Water area and stay there at play for 30 minutes or more. Because they are familiar

PHOTO 4.17   Jessica pours water down the Cascading Water in order to wash a bead down the tiers. A bucket is out of the picture at the bottom.

with water and because this setup gives them control over many different types of effects, the children enjoy the Cascading Water immensely.

Younger Children

The younger children like to watch the effect made by pouring water down the cascade. They put their hand under the lip of one of the troughs and let the water run over it. On one occasion we had put the Water Pencil at the head of the cascade, trickling water continuously down the tiered troughs. Debby, a student teacher, added a teaspoon of blue paint powder to the top trough. The powder colored a segment of the water, which then snaked down the troughs. The effect was quite spectacular. The clear water took on life and motion that was not visible before. The younger children showed the most interest in adding the paint. Matthew would put a bit of powder in the water stream and gaze in rapt concentration as the blue trickled down each silver trough and then disappeared.

Older Children
The older children invent games using solid objects such as beads. One day, Nauman places a bead at the foot of each of the five troughs while the water is not flowing. He shouts "Ready, set, go!" and washes all of the beads down with a dump of water at the head of the cascade. If any beads pile up at one of the troughs, he dumps a glass of water directly on the bottleneck and says "Down you go."

Jessica and Tristan play a similar game. Jessica, in Photo 4.17, dumps water at the head of the cascade to wash a single bead down. Each time the bead begins to fall over the bottom edge of a trough, she says "Vrooom." As the bead drops off the last trough into the bucket, Tristan says "Splash." They repeat this game for some minutes, giving four "vroooms" and a "splash" at the appropriate points in time. We felt that Jessica and Tristan were punctuating the motion of the bead with these noises; that is, they were breaking a continuous motion into punctuated points of discontinuity.

We never, as much as we wanted to, had an outdoor version of the Cascading Water. Outdoors, we could have had more troughs, branching right and left, stopping here and there. We could also have constructed the troughs so that they swiveled, sending water to a left trough or a right branch below. Such an outdoor version could give children more variables to explore—and less concern about spilled water.

Variation—The Snake Shoot
We did use the cardboard troughs in other ways to unitize motion. In Photo 4.18 Chris has just released a ball down the Snake Shoot. One end is attached to the

PHOTO 4.18   Chris releases a tennis ball down the Snake Shoot.

railing of the loft, the other to a low table. The Snake Shoot is a series of split cardboard tubes wired together end to end. The front end of each trough is wired on top of the back end of each preceding one. This long trough can be attached in many different parts of the room. We used it in the loft, in the block area, and outside. The ball makes discontinuous bumps as it rolls down the entire length of the Snake Shoot. We did not solve the problem of how to give the children more control over the intervals between each section. Perhaps you could.

JUMPING PEAK TO PEAK

On the outdoor playground we arranged a row of step-blocks. The row alternated high, low, high, low for a distance of about 15 blocks. The children could either step on the top of each successive block or jump from "peak to peak."

We noticed that Marc began this latter strategy by jumping and making a long pause before his next jump. After some practice he was better able to anticipate each successive jump. He jumped from one block and landed on another in such a way that his transfer of weight made it easier to jump immediately to a third block. That is, Marc seemed to be thinking about his next jump at the same time that he was making his landing. This made his movement more continuous in spite of the discontinuity of the gaps between the peaks. At the level of sensorimotor schemes Marc was having an encounter with unitizing motion.

IMAGINING MOTION

In the previous two categories of transforming motion, the children could see the entire motion. Even in the activities concerned with unitizing motion, the children could see the continuous motion of the object. In the activities that follow, the motion of the object itself is discontinuous; that is, the children cannot see its entire path. The children encounter gaps in motion that they are asked to fill. They do this by imagining the segment of motion that they did not see.

These types of encounters occur many times during an average day. Seth accidentally drops a wallet-size photograph behind the bulletin board hanging on the wall. It does not fall out. He curls his fingers under the bottom of the bulletin board directly in a line below where the photo disappeared at the top. He assumes, correctly in this case, that the motion continued in a vertical and downward path, even though he did not see the motion.

Katie runs in the back entrance of the climber. Nauman, standing on the other side of the room, sees her enter. He runs to the front entrance of the climber and waits. When Katie emerges, he yells "Boo" in a mock ambush. Nauman assumes, perhaps with more certainty than was merited in this case, that Katie will continue to move in a line and out the front entrance. These were both invisible displacements, and the children imagined the path of the motion that they did not actually see.

Many of these encounters occur spontaneously without special preparation of the environment. Others—the ones that we will describe in this section—occur because some activity is planned. Sometimes these activities require that the child reconstruct a motion recently completed, such as the example of Seth's trying to find the photo behind the bulletin board. At other times the child is asked to predict the path of a motion that has not yet happened, such as trying to predict where a marble will emerge from a maze. The Confusion Box is such a marble maze.

THE CONFUSION BOX

Preparing the Environment

Clara, one of our teachers, cut holes and slits in a cracker box, as you see in Figure 4.6. With the box lid closed, the children would drop a marble into the hole in the top. The marble would hit a cardboard partition inside and roll down it. Clara

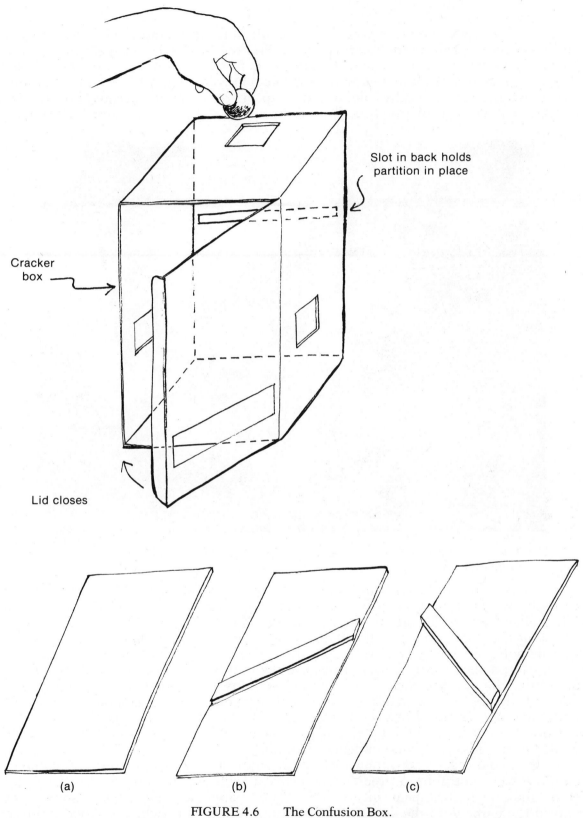

Slot in back holds
partition in place

Cracker
box

Lid closes

(a)　　　　　　(b)　　　　　　(c)

FIGURE 4.6   The Confusion Box.

had made three of these partitions, which could be exchanged. Their structure
determined where the marble would come out. The plain partition caused the marble to come out the front slit. The other partitions, with raised, slanting runners,
made the marble come out the holes in the sides of the box.

Entry

Clara drops the marble down the top hole, and it flies out the left side. David and Hattie see her do it and want to try. In Photo 4.19 Hattie has just released the marble through the top hole, and David has his hand ready to catch the marble on the side. (This was the hole where the marble had rolled out when Clara first modeled the game.) Both children know some aspects of the game already, but neither has had to make a prediction based on the structure of the partition inside the box.

PHOTO 4.19   Hattie drops a marble down the hole in the Confusion Box. David catches it as Clara watches.

Clara then opens the "front door" (lid) of the Confusion Box so that David and Hattie can see the partition. Clara lifts this partition out and inserts another one, which will make the marble roll out the hole in the opposite side of the box. Clara says "Look at this. I'm going to put this piece in the box. Can you figure out where the marble will go the next time we drop it down the hole?" David and Hattie look into the box, and then Clara slowly closes the door to the box. David, without saying anything, changes his position so that he can cup his hand under the hole in the opposite side of the box. Without any difficulty he has figured out where the marble will come out. Hattie drops the marble, and David's expectation is confirmed. He catches the marble, and then with one hand he drops it himself through the top hole while he cups his other hand under the exit hole.

Both the older and younger children enjoyed this little game. The younger children were not able to predict where the marble would roll out. But they did enjoy making it disappear into the box and reappear. The teachers sometimes played the game with the door open for these younger children. The older children were amazingly adept at predicting where the marble would reappear. Even when the teacher rotated the entire box just after shutting the door, they could still predict where the marble would come out.

Variations of this game can be made with tubes inside the box. With tubes the children can try to predict which color marble will come out first. This is a game of reconstructing the order. If the exit hole has a stop gate, the teacher can delay the marbles long enough for the child to recall, out loud, which color will come out first. The tubes ensure that the marbles don't get bumped out of sequence. So often the child will say that the color most recently inserted in the top hole will be the first to reappear. Note that this game should be embedded in a more naturalistic context. Perhaps the tube version could be set up as a tunnel on a miniature train track, and the marbles could be exchanged for train cars of three different colors. We leave it to your creativity to adapt these encounters with invisible motion and invisible changes to the setting of your school.

THE SHELL GAME

Preparing the Environment

This game goes back many centuries—but not, perhaps, using tennis balls and berry cartons, as we described it in Chapter One. Only a few specialized items are necessary: a small table with a hole cut directly in the center, three berry cartons, a tennis ball, and a supple pillow. Place the pillow on the floor, under the hole, before the children arrive. The child's objective is to find the tennis ball. As the child watches, the teacher covers the tennis ball with one of the cartons and then moves the cartons around. The child watches closely and makes a guess when the teacher stops moving the cartons.

Entry

Children love to find hidden objects, so the Shell Game is a natural. Finding the ball on one guess becomes their incentive to search for it again the next time. For younger children, keep the movements simple. Move one carton at a time. Let the child find the ball under a carton a few times before you pass the covered ball over the hole in the center of the table. Once you do let the ball drop, you will probably notice that the younger children look under all three berry cartons before they look under the table. The older children will understand the meaning of the hole. Once the carton that covers the tennis ball passes directly over the hole, the older child will stop looking at the movements of the cartons and will look under the table for the ball.

There is no need to conceal the hole to make this game a challenge. The hole should be clearly visible. The problem for the younger children is not their failure to *attend* to the hole; it is their failure to *understand* the hole. Be sure to mix your moves. Do not end a series of moves with the ball always under, say, the carton on the right. This would give the child a very simple way to find the ball. For older children, moving two cartons at once in opposite directions increases the challenge and interest of the game. Or the table can have several holes, all of which open into deep cloth sacks, like pool-table pockets. Any number of variations can be made to increase the challenge and interest of the game.

It is also possible that two children will pair off and play this game between them. Their method of reconstructing the rules reveals just what they understand about the order and timing of the component parts of the game. We noticed that one of our younger children would move the cartons around and then—quickly, before his playmate had a chance—grab and lift the carton hiding the tennis ball. The older children better understood the two different roles of presenter and guesser.

THE SEE-THRU NOK-OUT BENCH

Preparing the Environment

For this activity we modified a commercially available toy, the Nok-Out Bench by Playskool. This toy is a small, wooden cobbler's bench with a toy hammer. The child drives 2-inch wooden pegs into a hole in the top of the bench. The pegs go into a channel inside the bench that curves to the horizontal so that, after five pegs have been driven into the hole, one peg pops out the side of the bench. In the commercial version the children cannot see the channel inside the bench. In Figure 4.7 you can see that we have modified the Nok-Out Bench by removing the side panel of wood and replacing it with a sheet of Plexiglas. Clear acetate will do as well.

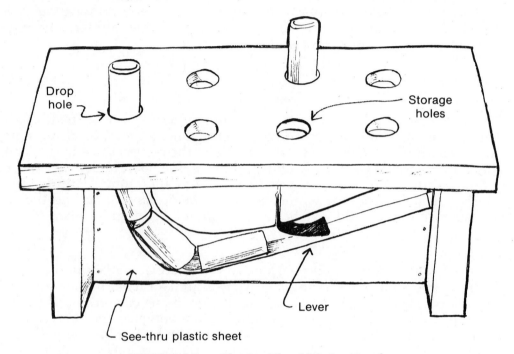

FIGURE 4.7   The See-Thru Nok-Out Bench.

There are six recessed holes on the top of the cobbler's bench. These holes were designed as storage receptacles, so that the child could have pegs easily accessible. It was amazing how many children intently hammered a peg in one of these recesses, thinking that the peg would go through.

Entry
The teacher had available one of the Nok-Out Benches with the plastic side panel and another one without this modification. We found that even with the plastic side panel children would not think to bend down and look at the channel. To increase the probability that the children would see the side of the bench, the teacher had placed a long mirror on the platform where the children were banging away.

Younger Children
Amy puts a peg into the hole, hits it, and, because the channel is already full, a peg shoots out the side of the bench. She takes that peg, places it in one of the recesses, and begins to hammer it. She hammers a bit and looks out to the side, where the peg shot out a few seconds before. The teacher asks "Will it come out?" Amy nods her head and continues to hammer. "Where will it come out?" the teacher asks. "Down there," Amy says, pointing to the floor beside the bench. She continues her futile hammering on the peg in the recessed hole. "Is it working?" the teacher asks. Amy nods and says "It's going down, a little." It is interesting how young children will assimilate the physical facts to their own desires (not unlike adults, we might add).

Marya hammers a peg through the real hole. It displaces a peg into a metal dish that the teacher has placed at the side.

"How did the peg get into the dish?" the teacher asks.

"It jumped off the top," Marya answers.

Marya evidently thought that the peg that had emptied into the dish was the same one that she had been hammering. If she held this belief constant, then her answer was, in a sense, logical. She did not, of course, see the peg jump off the top, but that is the only "logical" way she could account for the invisible motion of one and the same peg. Here we see a beautiful example of how young children use inference to cope with invisible motion.

Older Children

Hattie has been hammering pegs in and watching them come out the side. She studies the channel through the Plexiglas panel. She seems delighted that a peg of one color hammered in causes a peg of another color to come out. She then points to the metal lever inside the channel: "See this? This keeps the pegs from falling out."

Somehow, Hattie knew that without this metal lever the weight of the pegs in the vertical portion of the channel would force out those pegs in the horizontal portion. She was truly seeing the pegs lined up in the channel as a system of potential movements—not, more simply, a static line of objects.

David has already hammered pegs through the channel several times, watching their displacement through the Plexiglas panel. Then he does a most inventive thing. He lines up five pegs, end to end, on the carpet of the platform riser where he is working. He takes the hammer, hits the left end of the line and watches the pegs separate!

David perhaps thought that he could duplicate the action of the pegs inside the cobbler's bench. But because he had no resistance on the last peg, analogous to the metal clip in the bench, his pegs separated uniformly. Nevertheless, David's attempt to reconstruct these effects on his own, outside the bench, bore witness to a remarkable attitude. David felt that he could more clearly understand the effects of this chain reaction if he constructed the setup himself. His attitude was not unlike that of the scientist trying to understand nature by simulating it.

Once the children had had sufficient experience with the see-through version of the cobbler's bench, the teacher asked them to consider what was happening inside the bench with the opaque panel. The questions varied from "Where is the peg now?" to "What color will come out next?" The one drawback of this particular toy was the fact that the shape and direction of the channel could not be changed. We have since constructed variations on the Nok-Out Bench in which the pegs go into flexible tubing. The children and the teacher can rearrange and redirect the tubing so that the game of guessing where a peg will come out is more challenging.

Many other variations are possible. We used cardboard tubes, marble rollways, and covered mazes to engage the children in encounters with invisible motion. They had to imagine the path of an object by studying the structure of boundaries and barriers. These games were fun for the children, and we felt that they gave them good experience in imagining motion that was not visible. Our greatest pleasure came during those moments when several children played these games independently in small groups.

LEARNING ENCOUNTERS FOR THE HOME

Certain items and situations more common to the home environment serve well the purposes of this chapter. In fact, the example of tricycles driving through water puddles as a means to freeze the motion of the tricycle is a frequent occurrence at home when Mom or Dad is washing the car on the concrete driveway. It takes just a moment to make a comment such as "I can see where you have driven your tricycle," just after the child passes through the puddle. And children are universally intrigued with making an etching in the dirt along the path that they walk. It takes only a prepared mind for a parent to say, "We can find our way home by following the marks in the dirt." These are instances of freezing motion and are embedded in the everyday experience of the child.

Home versions of the activities mentioned for the classroom setting can also be easily made. It is a simple matter to screw a lazy Susan to a three-foot-diameter wooden, circular board so that the child can experiment with the paths that crayons make when the board is papered and spun around. Even a version of the Drawing Driver can be made if you have a suitable sidewalk or driveway. Chalk can be securely fastened to wheeled toys so that they leave chalk traces of their movements here and yonder. The sidewalk soon becomes a record of traffic congestion or traffic flow and affords many opportunities for young children to read implications from these representations of past actions.

Moving shadows can be traced in the same way that we used the rear projection on papered plexiglas. Nail a large piece of homosote to a wooden frame (indoors) or a garage wall (outdoors). This provides a convenient surface to tack paper to so that your child can draw the action of shadows on it. A light passed through a fishbowl with fish makes interesting moving shadows on the paper. The child can have a great deal of fun trying to keep his or her marker on the shadow of the fish and then looking at the directions of this mark after the light is extinguished. A hanging mobile can also make interesting moving shadows and provides welcome relief to the fish. Anything that has an interesting, somewhat regular movement with moderate speed can be tracked by the child. However, tracking a shadow made by an object placed between the child's hand and the light source will make the encounter more difficult than the rear projection technique because the child will have to discount the shadow of his or her own hand. A plexiglas panel with rear projection is better, as we discussed earlier, but may not be completely necessary for the child who knows how to minimize the interference from his or her own hand. If you have an aquarium with a flat side, the rear projection system can be used by papering the front of the aquarium and shining the light through the rear, thereby casting the shadow of the moving fish on the backside of the translucent paper on which the child draws the motion. Even brief encounters like this can give the child a new appreciation of the shape of the fish's motion, sort of a time study of where the fish spends his time. If the refraction of the water presents a problem in creating a sharp-edged shadow, and empty aquarium with a moth or cricket could be used instead. An inchworm might work for the more patient child.

Home versions of unitizing motion also abound. The stoop in the front or side of the house might be an appropriate site. The child could set up three short troughs, one on each step, each at a slight incline. Then the child could either roll a tennis ball down the stoop in the troughs, as in the Snake Shoot, or flood the top trough with water as in the Cascading Water. Three steps or four steps would probably be enough and would make it easier and safer for the child to repeatedly put things at the top of this unitized incline. The neighborhood sidewalk often provides its own source of speed bumps in the form of expansion cracks or heaves. But these permanent cracks do not allow the child to experiment with the rhythm of the clickity clack of the tricycle wheels. The child cannot rearrange the distances between the cracks. But the child might at least experiment with the change in the beat of this clickity clack as he or she drives a Big Wheel more quickly or more slowly over the sidewalk cracks. A fence with missing pickets also provides another opportunity for the child to predict a rhythm when a stick is dragged along the fence on a walk. And we have all seen the joy on a young child's face when peddling a bicycle with a cardboard flap slapping repeatedly on the spokes of the wheel.

Dominoes aligned in a row, as we have already mentioned, give the child many interesting minutes of playing with unitized motion. The advantage of doing this at home rests on the somewhat greater chance of protecting the child's work from one day to the next. A child intent on making a long row to knock over can take time to do this if the space is reserved from one day to the next. But for the three- or four-year-old such long range plans are not so common. For the younger child a parent might want to attach a set of dominoes to a cloth ribbon in a manner similar to what we did in the classroom. This reduces the decisions the child has to make, yet still gives the child an opportunity to experiment with the chain reaction effect. Just staple each domino on its end to a common ribbon about an inch and a half apart. The child can still make straight and curved rows by standing up the dominoes on end. If dominoes are too small and require too much dexterity, use larger blocks with the same proportions as a domino.

An advanced game can be played in the backyard or playground with a little demonstration from the parent. The game needs to be motivated by some fantasy play, like "Don't let the alligators bite." The objective is to get from one side of the yard to the other without stepping on the grass. All the child has is two small pieces of carpet or cardboard. The child learns to place one carpet in front, step to it, turn around to lift the piece recently left, and place that piece in front. The game involves a great deal of forethought about how far to place the pieces and how each piece has the dual role of being now a place to go and now a place behind. This is truly a thinking game that leads the child to encounter concepts of unitizing motion and dealing with two purposes within one object.

SUMMARY: REPRESENTING MOTION

The overall objective of these activities was to stage encounters for the children with the shape and rhythm of motion. Our activities in this chapter involved freezing motion with a continuous trace, freezing motion with a discontinuous trace, punctuating continuous motion with bumps and pauses, and having the children imagine the motion of an object that they did not see. If a child can figure out the shape of a motion, she can often understand how an event happened. Our success for these objectives was mixed.

The younger children did not seem to grasp the correspondence between the trace of a motion and the motion of the object. For example, in the Swinging Sand the younger children were interested in how fast the sand drained from the bottle but not in how the swinging bottle could be pushed in different ways to create different effects. The older children did vary their own actions to create different patterns of sand traces, but they did not look at the sand and retrospectively figure out how the bottle had moved.

We had a little more success in the play dough. The children could look at a track in the layer of dough and figure out at least what object had made the track. But this is not the same as figuring out what particular type of movement made the track. A few of our older children, however, were able to look at a track that the teacher had made and then duplicate that track themselves. At the level of sensorimotor schemes, these children could understand the correspondence between a frozen motion and the means by which that frozen motion was produced.

In the activities involving discontinuous traces—unitized motion—the children showed varying levels of understanding. The Blip Spool was perhaps our most successful activity. The children called the spots of paint "foot marks" and would walk beside the incline, tracing with an extended finger the path that the Blip Spool had taken. The children did understand that the discontinuous paint spots were the remains of a continuous motion. The homemade version of the pizza cutter also worked quite well. The children could change the spacing of the sprockets and explore the change in the effects as they rolled the wheels across the play dough. We consider this an ideal material, because the children can make changes within an object rather than exchanging that object for a different one.

The invisible-motion activities caused the children to imagine those segments of motion that they did not see. The Confusion Box and Nok-Out Bench are good examples of small-scale games. We also had large-scale games outside, such as tunnels and sheets used to hide the movements of one child while a nearby child watched. Both types of encounter have their advantages. The small-scale encounters give the child faster and more direct control over the transformations. The large-scale encounters give the activity more interest and more personal relevance to the everyday world of getting around or—perhaps we should say—of figuring out how others have gotten around.

For the younger children we did not have too much success in staging encounters with predicting a motion before it occurred. For example, they could not look at the slats in the Confusion Box and figure out where the marble would come out. But in other ways the children were quite adept at predicting a motion, particularly if it was a continuation of something already in progress. For example, the 2- and 3-year-olds could anticipate whether a ball was on its way toward knocking over something. That portion of the trajectory from the ball to the target had not yet happened, but the younger children could imagine that portion. However, this is an encounter with a point-to-point contact and does not clearly involve the *shape* of a motion. The child could accurately predict whether a ball was about to hit a target simply by confusing line of sight with line of action. Give this child a curved path, and he would have more difficulty.

Now let us review some of the differences between the older and younger children. We do this just to help you maintain a developmental perspective on learning encounters. The strategies used by the younger children are, we think, necessary precursors to the more advanced strategies used by the older children. We ask that you protect the younger child's space and time so that these precursors can run their natural course.

DEVELOPMENTAL TRENDS

TWO WITHIN ONE

Cases where one object is both a whole and several parts:

The younger children would try to gouge the rolled-out play dough with the Tinker Toy pizza cutter. The older children would roll it lightly to make tiny holes. This seems to represent a general tendency for the younger children to think about objects as *solid wholes*, whereas the older children can think about objects as *a system of movable parts*.

Cases where one object has two actions simultaneously:

The younger children could perform one or another action but not two actions at once. They would, in the Spinning Sand and the Rotating Easels, move their brush *or* spin the laxy Susan, but they had great difficulty doing both. The older children had more or less difficulty depending on the nature of the two actions involved—for example, their similarity, location, and so on.

Cases where two (or more) discontinuous actions create one continuous action:

Of course, all of our games that involved unitizing motion could potentially place the child in an encounter with the continuity of one action across the discontinuity of several component actions. The Slatted Rollway, Domino Row, and Blip Spool are all good examples. We will cite one observation from the activity Jumping Peak to Peak. Younger children would jump from the first peak to the second and then pause for a few seconds to get new footing before jumping ahead to the third peak. The more advanced children could land on the second peak in such a way that they were at the same time prepared for the departure to the third peak. The two discontinuous actions of landing and departing were smoothly integrated into one continuous action.

DECENTERING FROM AN EGOCENTRIC PERSPECTIVE

Cases where the child centers on proximal versus distal effects:

With the Drawing Driver the younger children wanted to have direct contact with the felt-tip pen. The older children enjoyed making the pen move from afar by steering the cardboard drum at the center.

Cases where one point has two references in space simultaneously:

With the Drawing Driver the younger children would sometimes forget that their own body was in the way of the rotation of the wooden dowel. They could consider the relation between the dowel and the pen, but they forgot the relation between the dowel and their own body.

Cases where the body itself represents the event:

Our children, in various contexts, did things to "concretize" an event. Amy poked the tip of her Water Pencil into the sand to make holes just like the holes the water drips were making. Hattie connected the separate circles on the Plexiglas easel that she had made by brushing a single stroke of paint across the top of the stencil a few moments before. Perhaps she was "concretizing" that single stroke, now represented in the connected circles. Katie smashed her pen to the drawing surface as she saw the feather falling. She "concretized" the witnessed action of the feather by making her pen the physical embodiment of the feather. David lined up a row of pegs to reconstruct the chain reaction he had witnessed inside the See-Thru Nok-Out Bench. All of these examples seem to be the child's attempt to understand an event by reconstructing it in a more concrete form. The younger children such as Amy and Katie do this very directly, using the same object in two ways—first as a means to represent an action (marks with the pen and the Water Pencil) and then as the physical subject of the action itself (crashing the pen and poking with the Water Pencil). The older children do this in more indirect ways, such as David's using a line of objects to reconstruct the chain reaction outside the Nok-Out Bench.

Cases where the child centers on the teacher's body rather than on the object the teacher is manipulating:

Clayton seemed to imitate the action of Lisa's hand, rather than the action of the feather, during Kinetic Drawing. Making a correspondence between his hand and Lisa's hand is somewhat more egocentric than making a correspondence between his ink mark and the action of the feather. However, he did do the latter on several occasions.

SEEING THE DYNAMIC WITHIN THE STATIC

Cases where action is constrained by static structure:

The younger children could anticipate where a moving object would go if they had seen that same action some moments before. For example, the children could predict where the Drawing Driver, Swinging Sand, and Tire-Tracking Trikes would go, based on recent experience with these objects. The older children could look at the static structure of a channel or path, as in the Confusion Box, and figure out in advance where a ball rolling down this path would end its journey. However, even the younger children, when given the opportunity to change the boundaries and barriers, showed a sensori-motor understanding of motions that had not yet occurred. Their skill, of course, depended on the complexity of the boundaries. They were much better in predicting all-or-none barriers than more subtle deflections and channel-izations of motion.

FROM OPPOSITE EXTREMES TO MIDDLE DEGREES

Cases where the child has difficulty constructing the middle term:

At times, children did not seem to be able to construct the middle condition, even when they seemed to desire it. Tristan had great difficulty making the thumb screw on the Water Pencil stop midway between fully open and fully shut. He also had difficulty making the marble roll just partway to the end of the rollway. But he could tell a friend to move the Drawing Driver "a little more in." It takes time for children to construct the notion of a continuum between two extremes, as we mentioned in Chapter One.

With the Slatted Rollway the children wanted to keep the hole at the bottom of the incline. They resisted attempts to have the hole in the middle. It seems, in many contexts, that children prefer the "terminal condition." This preference may be due, in part, to the difficulty of constructing the middle term. This tendency varies with age. As children grow older, they probably see the middle condition as interesting *because* it is not at the ter-minal condition.

Cases where the child does not consider how one action could lead to an opposite effect:

With the Swinging Sand the younger children wanted to cover stencils with sand. The older children understood that covering the stencils was a means to making a negative space, the hole in the sand after the stencil was removed. The negative space, of course, is opposite to the filled space. The older children were able to think about the absence of the stencil even when it was present; the younger children could not. These encounters with constructing opposites prepare the way for thinking about the variations between opposites (see Chapter One).

We have greatly generalized from a few observations. But our familiarity with the research literature (see CCK, Chapter Four) makes us believe that these observations are consonant with general principles of cognitive development. Therefore, we feel comfortable that teachers might use these summary statements to guide their own observations of children. When a teacher has a few anchor points, such as these summary statements, it becomes easier to interpret the developmental significance of a child's free play. And the ability to see the significance of a child's free play helps the teacher to facilitate free play.

Chapter Five

Making
Functional
Relations

ENCOUNTERS WITH THE RELATION BETWEEN TWO VARIABLES

Tristan tilts the seesaw up. The wooden bead in the Plexiglas tube taped to the seesaw rolls down quickly. On the next occasion Tristan tilts the seesaw up only slightly. The bead now rolls very gently. Tristan seems to be exploring how the change in the slant changes the speed at which the bead rolls. He is exploring the relation between two variations: the different pitches of the incline and the different speeds of the rolling bead. Two variations that are causally related, as these two are, we call a *functional relation*.

But a *function*, as we are using the word, is more than a simple event-to-event relation, such as you see in Figure 5.1. The occurrence of one event (*A*) can often be followed by another event (*B*). For example, pushing down on one end of a seesaw causes an object on the other end to fly up.

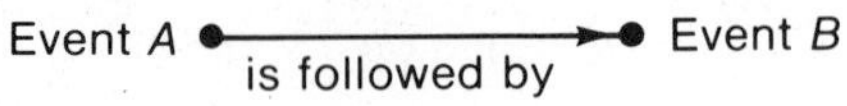

Event *A* ●——————————▶● Event *B*
is followed by

FIGURE 5.1   Simple cause and effect.

A functional relation, however, holds between two sets of events, such as you see in Figure 5.2. It involves the coordination of two *variables*, which is more difficult than coordinating two *events*. Functional relations come in two varieties, the direct function and the inverse function.

In Figure 5.2a we have represented the direct function. An increase along variable *A* leads to an increase along variable *B*. For example, an increase in the force that Seth uses to push down the seesaw (the left-hand vertical line in the figure) causes an increase in the height to which the object on the other end flies (the right-hand vertical line). If Seth understands this direct functional relation, he can adjust the height of the object by adjusting the force with which he pushes the seesaw.

In Figure 5.2b we have represented the inverse function. An increase along variable *A* leads to a decrease along variable *B*. For example, an increase in the weight of the object placed on the end of the seesaw leads to a decrease in the height

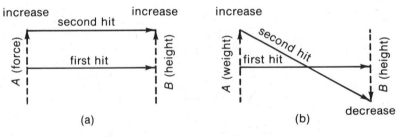

(a)   (b)

FIGURE 5.2   Direct and inverse function.

to which it flies (provided, of course, that Seth pushes his end with the same force for all objects tested). If Seth understands this inverse functional relation, he can adjust the height to which the object flies by adjusting the weight of the object. In this case Seth knows more than what to do to make the object fly upward (Event *A* leads to Event *B*); he also knows how to change one variable to make a predictable change in another variable (changing *A* changes *B*).

CHANGING DIRECTIONS

One of the simplest forms of functional relations involves the direction of a movement. The child can vary the position of, say, a pea shooter on a pivot, and this changes the direction that the pea travels when shot. By moving his end to the left, he makes the pea travel more to the right. Hitting a wall straight on with a ball makes the ball bounce back directly to the thrower; hitting the wall at an angle from the left makes the ball bounce off to the right. The activities that follow fall into this category of changing the position of one object to change the direction of movement in another object.

FOOLING WITH PULLEYING

Preparing the Environment

A double clothesline pulley presents some interesting problems for young children. Pull the right-hand rope, and a basket attached to the left rope moves away. Push the right-hand rope, and a basket attached to the left rope moves nearer. The direction of the action of the hand is opposite to the action of the basket. Ordinarily, when a child pulls a rope, she expects that the thing attached to it will come nearer. Children enjoy exploring the novel effects of clothesline pulleys.

We strung an 8-foot loop of rope between two nylon pulleys about 5 inches in diameter. One pulley was attached to the railing of the loft; the other was attached to a jungle-gym tower 8 feet away. In Photo 5.1 Chris is in the jungle-gym tower and Loren is in the loft. Loren is sending Chris a basket with a little doll inside by pulling the top of the rope. The basket is attached to the rope with a clothespin. This means that a teacher standing on the floor underneath the clothesline can switch the basket from rope to rope. The children can also do this from their respective perches.

Entry

Once the clothesline pulleys were set up and the basket attached, the children invented their own games. For example, on Saint Valentine's Day the children decided to send valentines to each other. At other times, it was enough to send and

PHOTO 5.1   Loren pulls the rope to make a basket go to Chris.

receive an empty basket. The younger children would grab one of the ropes and move it back and forth, watching the basket move back and forth. Eventually, they would discover that they could move the basket an ever increasing distance by repeatedly grabbing, pushing, and releasing, using one hand. It was uncommon to see our youngest children use a hand-over-hand strategy to keep the movement of the basket continuous. This alternating-hand strategy was more common in the older children.

Younger Children

Aaron pushes the top rope to send the basket to Marika over in the tower. He is using the one-handed strategy. The basket is attached to the top rope. Peter, from the floor, switches the basket from the top rope to the lower rope. Aaron continues to push the top rope away, but he stops when he sees that the basket is making a return toward him. He hesitates, and then he grabs the lower rope and begins to push it away.[1] Now the basket is once again moving in the desired direction, toward Marika.

Loren, an older child, climbs into the tower just as Aaron's basket arrives. Loren sends it back to Aaron by pulling the top rope. Peter intercepts the basket about midway and transfers it to the top rope. Now the basket is moving toward Loren. Loren does not like this, so he immediately grabs the lower rope and pulls it. Now the basket resumes its passage back to Aaron.

Older Children

Chris drops a block into the basket so that he can send it over to Lauren. He pushes the top rope away, but this makes the basket back up toward him. On observing this unexpected event, Chris tests each rope in turn. He grasps the bottom rope and gives it an abbreviated back-and-forth test; then he grasps the top rope and gives it the same test. From these tests he figures out that he should either push the bottom rope or pull the top rope to make the basket travel to Lauren. By the time the basket gets to the other side, Lauren has climbed down from the tower. Chris, undaunted, immediately shifts from pulling the top rope to pulling the bottom rope. This makes the basket come back to him.

We have seen younger children, when the basket reaches the other end, continue to pull on the top rope. They presume that the basket is temporarily stuck and that a few hard yanks will free it so it can come back to them. It takes some forethought on the child's part to figure out how to reverse the action of the basket once it reaches the other side.

Variations

The clothesline pulleys can be used in a variety of places. We used them outside, and the children transported sand from one sandbox to another in a small bucket. Sometimes, we had a bucket attached to each rope. As one bucket was leaving, the other was arriving. Once, we attached two paintbrushes to the clotheslines. As one brush dragged over a papered table in one direction, the other dragged over the paper from the other direction. One child could make two brush strokes at once. A favorite version looked more like a ski-lift gondola. The children on the floor could lift objects in the basket up to the children in the climber. The variations are limited only by the need to be able to sink a hook for the pulley.

The clothesline pulley is easy because it is not a true functional relation. The child only needs to relate the position of his grasp (top or bottom rope) to the direction of his movement (push or pull). The encounter is simplified because there are only two choices to make on each "variable." These are not continuous variables, so perhaps the clothesline pulley makes a good introduction to functional relations. Variables with more degrees can be introduced later.

---

[1] Here we see a vivid example of how a teacher can pose a problem without disrupting the child's self-set goals. See the discussion of Teacher as Troublemaker on pp. 113–114 in CCK.

TEETER-TOTTER TUBE

Preparing the Environment

We taped a Plexiglas tube about 7 feet long along the top of a seesaw. Through it the children can roll beads, marbles, and pegs back and forth to each other (see Photo 5.2). They soon learn that the position of one end of the seesaw determines the direction in which the bead travels. If they want to change the direction, they must change the position of the end. Unlike the clothesline pulleys, which have only two positions to choose from, the Teeter-Totter Tube has an infinite number of end positions between all the way up and all the way to the floor. But there are only two choices in the second variable. Either the bead rolls to the right or to the left. Of course, the speed of the bead has an infinite number of degrees, but for the moment we will discuss change of direction.

PHOTO 5.2   Katie releases a bead through the Teeter-Totter Tube. Marya is ready to catch it.

The child should have on hand several types of objects that she can roll or slide down the tube. Round beads roll easily. Cylinders slide, but require a greater slant. You might have a little basket to catch the beads as they come out, just in case a child wants to play the game by herself. The children like to put several beads in their end of the tube at once before they tilt the tube. This way, they can see the beads "chase" each other as they travel down the incline. We also used a version with two parallel tubes, in which the children could see two beads running neck and neck down the incline.

Entry

This activity requires a brief amount of modeling. The setup looks like a seesaw, so the children are sometimes confused. If they do mount the ends and start seesawing, this can be turned to great advantage. Simply place a bead in the tube. The two children will see the bead roll in the tube as they ride up and down. This is a great way for the children to learn about the function of inclines by using their whole body to change an incline.

They will also want to dismount and play with the bead as they stand on the floor next to the seesaw. Interestingly enough, the children who play with the Teeter-Totter Tube as a tilting incline for the bead refuse to call it a seesaw anymore. The identity of a seesaw is tied to its use, and because this thing before the child is designed to roll beads, it cannot at the same time be a seesaw. Actually, the teaching staff tried to encourage a more flexible attitude toward what things are or can be, as you recall from our discussion of identity in Chapter Two.

The younger children knew that something could be done to make the beads roll through the tube. Their most common mistake was their failure to consider the slant of the tube. They would stick the bead into the hole at their end even when the tube was slanting downward toward them. The older children would lift the tube up above the horizontal position before inserting a bead. The younger children's failure is a good example of *centration*, focusing on a single point when a broader view is required. The older children also discovered a means to prevent the bead from changing direction at all. They would put the bead in one hole and then immediately move the tube to the horizontal position.

Younger Children

Howie, about 2½, puts a bead in the hole at his end of the Teeter-Totter Tube. It rolls slowly away from him. As he stoops down to get another bead—still holding onto the tube with his left hand—the tube slants toward him, and the bead rolls out at his feet. He picks this bead up and inserts it into the tube. This time it drops out immediately, so Howie grabs it again, sticks it in the tube and crams it inside a few inches with his finger. It still drops out. He looks into the tube, standing up as he does so and, fortuitously, raising his end of the tube. He tries the bead once again, and this time it rolls slowly away.

Kevin catches a glimpse of the rolling bead from where he is playing in the block corner. He runs over to the Teeter-Totter Tube and grabs at the bead through the Plexiglas! Gary, a student teacher, catches the bead at the end opposite Howie, puts it back in, and tilts the tube to make the bead roll back to Howie. Kevin watches the bead speed toward Howie and once again makes a dash to catch it, grabbing at the bead through the Plexiglas tube.

These children play for 10 or 15 minutes, and then Nuffy comes along. Nuffy tries to put a marble in the "down" end of the tube. Taneka sees Nuffy's problem and walks over to Nuffy's end of the tube. She lifts the seesaw up on Nuffy's end and says "You can do it here." Nuffy leaves his end, runs to the opposite end of the tube that is tilted down, grabs it, lifts it up all the way, and puts his marble into the tube, sending it down toward Taneka.

Older Children

Tristan approaches the game and is immediately able to make the bead go in the direction he wants. He even begins to experiment with the degree of tilt. When he lifts the seesaw up high, the bead shoots out the other end; when he lifts the seesaw slightly above the horizon, the bead barely drops out the other end. Gary says "You made it go fast" or "You made it go slow" at the appropriate times. Tristan uses these words also, but his uses are not perfectly appropriate to what he is doing at the time.

Tristan tries a cylinder in the tube. Because of its increased surface area in contact with the tube, it offers more friction than the round beads and therefore requires a greater slant before it will move at all. He very adeptly pushes the seesaw end up all the way.

Tristan also invented a game of trying to knock down little targets on the floor. Watching him play this game gave us the idea that the distance the bead rolls is a direct function of the height of the high end of the seesaw. This observation led to a variation on the Teeter-Totter Tube that fits the next section of this chapter, which deals with changing speed and distance. For convenience we will discuss it here.

Variations

You can place masking-tape marks on the floor, parallel to each other and perpendicular to the end of the tube. Then the children can try to make the wooden bead go particular distances by changing the height at which they hold the end of the seesaw. Little targets or small boxes give the children an incentive to make the bead go particular distances.

Some of our more ingenious children invented a way to make the bead fly upward. They would release it down the tube and, just as it came out of the end onto the plank, they would push down on the "up" end, launching the bead through the air for some distance. The timing was difficult and the seesaw a little too big, so these attempts did not often work. A smaller seesaw and shorter tube might have made this variation easier.

Sometimes, the children set up different types of backstops for the bead to hit as it rolled out of the tube. Marc might ask Jenny not to catch the bead so it would hit the backstop and make a resonant clunk. On other days the children used curved backstops, which made the bead roll around and almost return to where they were standing. Without the backstops, however, the Teeter-Totter Tube encourages cooperative play. The activity is almost a dialogue in action, as the children send beads back and forth to each other. We like the cooperative structure of this activity.

SEESAW WATER PIPE

Preparing the Environment

What can be done with discrete material, such as wooden beads, can usually be done with continuous material, such as water. We used a combination of nylon tubes (Pipe Put Together) and plastic scaffolding (Girders) to make a version of the Teeter-Totter Tube for the water table. There are surely many other ways to make a water pipe that pivots. We simply used what we had available in the classroom.

As shown in Photos 5.3 and 5.4, the scaffolding is supported inside a small pan placed inside the water table. The pan is filled with sand, which supports the fulcrum of the scaffolding. The nylon tubes are duct-taped to the crossbeam of the scaffolding.

Given the materials that we used, this activity had a variety of options for the child. He could choose which hole to pour water through, which way to slant the pipe, and which direction to twist the joints on each end.

Entry

Jenny and Marc are playing cooperatively with the Seesaw Water Pipe. Kevin is engaged in parallel play at the other end of the water table. Jenny and Marc pour water down the center hole. Because so much is poured, the water comes out both ends of the pipe, even though the pipe has a slight slant down to the right. Jenny decides to pour water from the left end of the pipe. She raises it appropriately, but the elbow joint is twisted the wrong way. "Hold it," she says to Marc, which means either to wait a minute or hold the pipe steady. Marc pauses. Jenny fiddles with the joint but does not relinquish her grip on the jar she has been using to pour water. Then she puts the jar into the water table, holds the pipe in one hand, and twists the joint with the other.

Meanwhile, Kevin grabs the jar. "Hey, that's mine," Jenny yells at Kevin. Rather than have Jenny diverted too long from experiencing success at fixing the elbow joint, a teacher intervenes and asks Kevin to return the jar to Jenny. The teacher gives Kevin a substitute jar. Jenny then completes her objective by pouring water through the upturned elbow joint. The water pours through the pipe and out the other end. Marc catches this water with his jar and then dumps its contents into the center hole. Jenny and Marc continue playing in this fashion for several minutes, recycling water through various holes, various tilts, and various twists of the elbow joints.

PHOTO 5.3   Jenny and Marc pour water through the middle hole
of the Seesaw Water Pipe.

PHOTO 5.4   Jenny tilts her end of the pipe up to make the water
flow out the opposite end.

Variations

On some days we attached Styrofoam cups to each end of the pipe. The cups dangled by string like balance pans on a scale. We tightened the screws in the scaffolding slightly, so that the pivot arm would move only with pressure. Then the children could discover that, the more water drained into one of the cups, the lower that cup would sink toward the water table. We had created, in effect, a water balance. The children enjoyed pouring water through the center hole and directly into either cup. Once the lower cup had started the pipe tilting, all subsequent water that was poured through the center hole would flow to that same cup. After the cup had lowered all the way, the children would dump it, set the pipe horizontal, and begin again, wondering which cup would build up with water this time.

THE SOLOMON SWING

Preparing the Environment

Karen and Cathy, two of our student teachers, told the staff one day about King Solomon, who supposedly measured the worth of his subjects by placing them in a balance and matching their weight with gold. Despite the fact that we unanimously doubted the truth of this tale, Karen and Cathy designed the Solomon Swing. They screwed two heavy-duty hooks into a ceiling beam and attached a pulley to each. They then threaded the pulleys with a strong nylon rope, attaching each end of the rope to a little "buddy seat," as you can see in Photo 5.5. (The main rope was attached to each seat by another set of ropes, which forked to either side of it. The fork was held apart by a wooden crosspiece.)

Jenny has made Marc go up because he weighs less than she. She can also make Marc go down by pushing off with her feet. For children smaller than Jenny and Marc we placed a low, carpeted step-block on the floor directly under each seat. This way, if a child inadvertently lowered a playmate too quickly, the step-block would stop the seat and prevent the lowered child from getting his feet caught under it. For the 2- and 3-year-olds it was necessary to have a teacher supervise the play, especially when there were two children at play. The buddy seats are better than flat seats, because the seat back keeps the children from sliding out the back and the cushioned bottom prevents them from sliding out the front.

The children could play alone with the Solomon Swings as well as in pairs. Some children liked to lift one swing by pulling down on the other. Also, they could hoist weights that we had made. The weights, about 5 pounds each, were made by filling plastic containers for computer tape disks with sand. We duct-taped the sides so the sand would not spill out. These weights were easy to handle and fit into the buddy seat well (see Photo 5.6).

Entry

The empty swings attracted immediate attention. The idea of indoor swings added to the allure. On the first day we had two teachers at the Solomon Swing. This is advisable as a precaution until you get a feel for the range of skill that your own group of children exhibit.

We have already described Aaron's entry into the activity (see Chapter Two, Creative Problem Solving). Recall that Aaron tried to make both seats go down at the same time by placing a hand on each seat. He had some difficulty figuring out that, the more one seat moved down, the more the other seat moved up. That is, he did not understand the connection between the two seats. He treated them as two separate swings. He may have understood that both swings could vary their respective positions, but he had not integrated these two variables into a functional relation. This general difficulty with the functional relation between the two seats was common for our younger children.

The older children made some mistakes initially, but they quickly learned the functional relation between the two seats. They also liked to add and subtract the

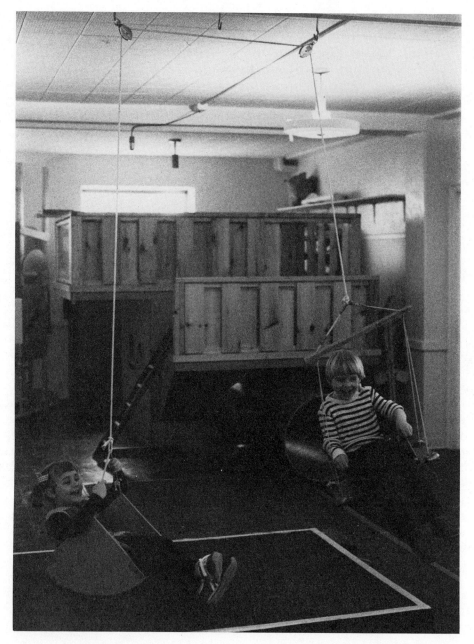

PHOTO 5.5   Jenny pulls Marc up in the Solomon Swing.

5-pound weights. For some of our 4-year-olds this was something of a motor ritual rather than an attempt to counterweight the opposite seat or child. But through these motor rituals children eventually understand the significance of what they are doing. Let's now drop in on some of our children at play.

Younger Children

Taneka sits in one of the swing seats, call it Seat *A*. The teacher pushes down on Seat *B*, raising Taneka; lowers her; and repeats. After several seconds of being at rest, Taneka jiggles in her seat in an attempt to make it go up. She obviously knows that her own seat is "not up." But Taneka's attempt to undo the "downness" of her seat does not work. So she stands up, turns to her seat and commands it with an emphatic "Up! Up!" Her verbal command works no better than her jiggle.

A slightly heavier girl named Jake wants to play. The teacher places Jake in Seat *B*. Now Taneka goes up, and Jake remains on the carpeted step-block. Jake looks enviously at Taneka swinging freely. Jake gets out of her seat and Taneka

PHOTO 5.6   Marc adds weights to the empty seat in order to unweight Jenny.

drops to the carpeted step-block below. Jake then issues a command to Taneka: "I want the up swing."

Jake evidently understood that Seat *A* was variable but did not understand the functional relation between the two seats. Jake tried to undo the "downness" of her own seat by exchanging seats with Taneka. Here we see another example of how young children try to *exchange* their object for another, instead of trying to *change* the object they already have.

Older Children

Loren sits down in Seat *A*. Taneka remains in Seat *B*. Because Loren is heavier, Taneka goes up. Loren immediately looks up at the ceiling, inspecting the rope and pulleys. He looks at Taneka and gives her little jiggles by alternately straightening and relaxing his legs with feet planted on the floor. Then he stands up slowly in order to lower Taneka gently to her carpeted step-block. Some minutes later, Taneka leaves. Loren continues to play with the swing set by himself. He hoists Seat *B* all the way to the ceiling by pulling his rope hand over hand. When that seat meets resistance with the pulley, he unreels the rope hand over hand to lower the seat to the floor. (We noticed that Alex, a much younger child, tried to get a tether ball down from a ceiling pulley by continuing to pull, instead of unreeling.) Through these actions Loren demonstrated his understanding of the functional relation between the two seats.

PULLEY PENDULUM BALL

Preparing the Environment

This activity is a variation on Pendulum Bowling, which we described in Chapter Three. Instead of using a single length of rope, we looped a longer cord over a pulley attached to the ceiling. We attached a tennis ball to one end and a small metal ring to the other. Perhaps the best way to describe the setup is to walk you through the action portrayed in Photos 5.7, 5.8, and 5.9.

PHOTO 5.7   Lauren draws her target for the Pulley Pendulum Ball.

PHOTO 5.8   Lauren lowers the position of the ring on the rope to raise the tennis ball.

PHOTO 5.9   Lauren releases the ball, just missing the target.

Lauren is drawing a circle on a free-standing blackboard. This circle will be her target (Photo 5.7). You can see the pendulum ball hanging behind her in the foreground. Because she has drawn her target fairly high on the blackboard, she realizes that she must change the height of the ball. She does this in Photo 5.8 by lowering the opposite end of the pulley rope and attaching the ring to a cup hook on the free-standing room divider. There are four hooks in a vertical row at various distances from the floor. After Lauren attaches the ring securely, she takes the ball on the other end of the cord, draws it back, and releases it. As you can see in Photo 5.9, the ball is about to hit just to the right of her target, but the height of the ball is correct. On a second release she hits the target dead center. The tennis ball, having previously been dusted with chalk, makes a spot to prove it.

Entry
The younger children like to play with the ball directly. They enjoy watching it go up when they pull down on the rope. And, as we have mentioned in the Pendulum Bowling description and elsewhere, they are more likely to push the ball than release it. Older children know, in a practical way, that they can reduce "error variance" if they let the ball swing freely.

Those young children who do try to adjust the height of the ball usually put the ring on a low hook when they want the ball to be low. They center on the cup hook and do not look over their shoulder at the ball. Or they look at the ball and the target and try to place the ball, in its resting position, at the same height as the target. This, of course, would cause the ball to swing above the target. They fail to account for the upward arc of the swing as the ball travels beyond its lowest point. The older children do not ordinarily figure this out in advance, but they can make the necessary adjustments in height after one or two misses.

We have varied the activity by changing the type of target for the younger children. We used a single cymbal from the musical instrument box. We mounted it with a chemist clamp on a vertical metal rod so the children could raise and lower it. This proved to be easier than drawing a circle on the blackboard and was more fun to hear.

THE HUGE HANGING HOOP

Preparing the Environment

The Huge Hanging Hoop was one of our most bizarre pieces of equipment. Someone found the hoop up in the attic of the Home Economics Building. It looked like the rim to a giant bass drum, something like 7 feet in diameter, made of wood. The thing turned out to be a pain to keep in the room. No shelf was big enough, and it kept rolling out of closets, almost as if it were saying "Use me." Use it we did, and the children loved it.

We decided to stretch clear polyethylene over the hoop. We stapled the plastic, pulling it tight. This created what looked like a huge tambourine or perhaps one of those round fire fighter's nets used to catch people as they jump from flaming windows. This huge hoop was just too heavy for the children to manipulate. So we suspended it from the ceiling with nylon string. Two double strands of string were attached at 12, 3, 6, and 9 o'clock around the circumference of the rim and fed upward to a common ring in the ceiling. The Huge Hanging Hoop floated gracefully, horizontal to the floor, about waist high to the children (see Figure 5.3). We chose

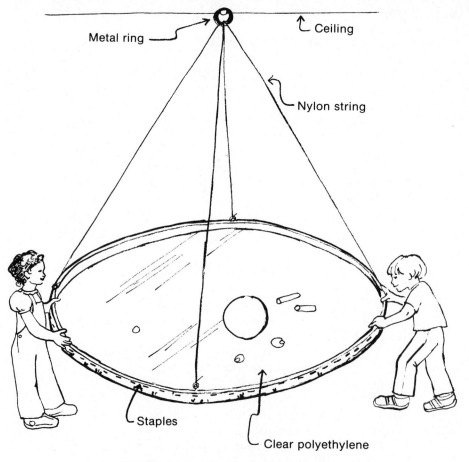

FIGURE 5.3   The Huge Hanging Hoop.

the bay window alcove as the place to suspend the hoop. The windows surrounded the hoop, and the light of a sunny day would make beautiful refractions through the colored plastic beads that we placed on the plastic sheet.

We designed the equipment as a new type of incline, one that could be tilted in any direction around its 360 degrees. The strings that held up the hoop were actually two loops that passed through a ring on the ceiling. The strings could slide within the ring, allowing the hoop to be tilted in any direction. We soon learned from the children that the hoop had more potential than we had imagined.

Entry

To the delight of all of our children, this huge object would move at the slightest touch. Jake pushes down on one end, and the whole plane raises on the other side. Fredi puts a Nerf ball in the center. As the children tilt the hoop, the ball rolls back and forth, around and around. Nathaniel pushes way down on the rim; the huge hoop arcs upward and begins to turn on its vertical axis. Nathaniel grabs the lower rim with both hands and walks in a large circle, looking at the sunlight through the stretched plastic. From the other side of the room George sees Nathaniel doing this. Since he cannot see the strings from that distance, it appears to him that Nathaniel is performing a graceful dance of balance with an object far out of proportion to his wee size, like an ant waltzing with a butterfly's wing. The joy in Nathaniel's face expresses this same sense of mastery over the huge hoop.

Matthew, 2½, Lillian, 2½, and Donna, a student teacher, put gym mats on the floor under the hoop and lie on the mats in order to look up through the plastic surface. Tristan, Marika, and others roll colored plastic beads across the surface of the plastic. Sometimes, they spin the hoop, making the objects collect in a slight depression; at other times, they tilt the hoop, making the objects roll and slide to each child.

Marika throws a giant copper penny into the center of the plastic. It sluggishly slides as a Nerf ball goes speeding by. "It's too flat," she says, apparently comparing it with the round ball. The weight of the giant penny makes the plastic surface somewhat concave. When the hoop is not tilted, the round objects roll to the penny. Tristan notices the influence of the penny and slides it here and there in order to see the herd of round objects migrate to it.

Loren comes and wants to spin the hoop. This time the children spin it so fast that the objects spin with it, and some spin out. The children release their grip on the rim to retrieve the objects, and the hoop begins to unwind its twisted strings. Matthew, Lillian, and Donna, looking up from the floor below, watch the remaining objects on the plastic turn as the hoop unwinds. Lillian lifts her foot to poke at a wooden ring turning in the center of the plastic. Matthew follows her suggestion, and the two children begin to poke and make the objects on the plastic sheet bounce.

Jessica throws a couple of wooden tiles onto the plastic while looking directly at Matthew through the sheet. She and Matthew smile at each other. The objects tossed to Matthew were stopped in midair, so to speak, by this invisible protective shield. The children continued to play with the hoop for the remainder of the focused-activity period, floating in and out of the activity as they chose.

Variations

After the children had grown familiar with the Huge Hanging Hoop, we made some changes. First we added colored sand and glitter to the plastic. This proved to be a little messy, as the sand would spill out over the rim. To solve that problem, we stapled another sheet of polyethylene over the top, making a double layer with a space in between. But the condensation made the colored sand stick, destroying the beauty of patterns made when the sand was dry. Kosher salt added to the fine sand made a good desiccator.

We hung the hoop in the smaller room, put a single spotlight in the ceiling above it, and turned off all the other lights. The children were invited two or three at a time to come in to see the new hoop. They would lie on their backs under it and tilt it with their feet. The patterns of the blue, white, and silver granules looked like swirls of surf and cross sections of the earth. The spotlight accentuated the whole effect, particularly where the granules were thinly distributed. Here the light made the patterns glow with a vibrant translucency. To quote Tristan, "They're flying dots." Interestingly enough, this whole experience of lying on their backs in a semidark room and making patterns with the huge hoop had a quieting effect on the children. They enjoyed this activity but approached it with an abstraction that we had not expected.

CHANGING DISTANCE, FORCE, WEIGHT, AND SPEED

The activities in the previous section gave the child a reason to change the direction of a motion. Tilting the Huge Hanging Hoop, the Seesaw Water Pipe, and the Teeter-Totter Tube caused solids or fluids to change their direction. The functional relation for these encounters was between a change of position and a change of direction. In the activities in this section the child deals with a functional relation between changes in position that create changes in distance or speed; changes in weight that create changes in force; changes in force that create changes in distance and speed; and other combinations of these factors.

The activities in the previous section were not too difficult. Usually, the relation between position and direction did not truly involve two variables. For example, with the clothesline pulley it would be an overstatement to call the position where the child grasped the rope a variable. He had only two choices, the top rope or the bottom rope. There was no continuum of positions, no *variable.* The same was true of direction. The basket on the clothesline pulley would go either forward or backward but would not travel in other directions. We had, in effect, reduced the "degrees of freedom" to make the activities easier for the younger children. (See p. 190 in CCK for a discussion of "degrees of freedom.") The most the child had to do was coordinate the two possible positions with the two possible directions.

Several of the activities involving changing direction did have a true variable on at least one factor. The Teeter-Totter Tube, for example, had a true variable on position. The child could hold the seesaw in any position between down on the floor and the highest point in the air. But as long as the child's objective was to regulate the direction of the wooden bead, these variations did not matter. Any position below the horizon made the bead roll backward; any position above the horizon made it roll forward. Now, if the child were trying to regulate the speed of the bead, this would be a true encounter with two variables. Both the position of the seesaw and the speed of the bead have many possible degrees between the two extremes of high/low and fast/slow, respectively. In this section we will describe activities that generate encounters with a true functional relation between two variables.

WEIGHT YOUR TURN

Preparing the Environment

The basic materials for this activity were a hollow plastic ball and bowling pins. Sand could be put into the ball and the pins. If the bowling ball was too light to knock over a pin filled with sand, the child could either empty sand from the pin or add sand to the ball (see Chapter One). The balls were clear plastic so the child could see what was inside.

The ball in Photo 5.10 is actually a hamster cage we bought at a local pet shop. Jenny is adding tennis balls for weight. The hamster-cage ball has the advantage of having a big hole and a lid that is round. Unfortunately, the plastic is

PHOTO 5.10   Jenny adds weight (tennis balls) to the Weight Your Turn bowling ball.

somewhat brittle and will crack if repeatedly dropped on the floor. We also bought a Flutter Ball (Playskool) because it was made of nonbreakable, clear plastic. We bored a hole, about 2 inches wide, in it and removed the cardboard butterfly that the manufacturers had placed inside. Then we had a hollow ball with a hole in it. The children could pour sand, dice, and other small objects in through the hole and close it with a patch of duct tape.

Using sand in the ball did not work too well; the ball would make a few lopping moves when tossed and then stop dead. We found that filling the ball with cotton and then adding or subtracting plastic dice from our recycle closet worked much better. The cotton prevented the dice from collecting at the bottom of the ball, and the 40 to 50 dice added sufficient weight to change the impact force of the ball when tossed at a bowling pin.

Using tennis balls in the hamster cage also prevented the problem of the lopping ball. They would roll inside the cage, and there were enough of them that the weight was more evenly distributed. For the bowling pins we just bored a 1-inch hole in the neck of the pin and patched it with duct tape. The children could funnel in or dump out sand as they wished.

Sometimes we set the bowling alley up indoors, sometimes outdoors on the sidewalk. We laid two 10-foot seesaw boards parallel to create an alley. At the end of the alley we placed one or two pins, with a free-standing chrome mirror behind them. The mirror served as a backstop and gave the children a reflection of themselves in action. Photo 5.11 shows the whole setup. Jenny has just knocked over the pin after adding weight to the ball. Marc, Katie, and Marya look on, ready to "weight their turn."

PHOTO 5.11   Jenny's ball was heavy enough to knock over the pin filled with sand.

Entry

Aaron, 3, Eva, 4, and Seth, 4½, are playing with the weighted bowling ball and pins outside. Seth bowls the ball toward a pin set up in the alley. The ball, because some of the dice inside have settled, does not roll all the way to the pen. "What can we do?" Lisa (a teacher) asks. Seth rolls it again with more vigor, but the ball stops just as it touches the pin. "The ball stopped," Lisa says in a matter-of-fact voice. Seth exclaims "What's that stuff inside? Take it out. The ball's too heavy." Seth and Lisa sit together to work on the ball. Lisa holds a plastic dish and Seth, after taking off the duct-tape patch, begins to shake out the dice into the dish.

"Is that enough?" Lisa asks Seth.

"No," he says, continuing to shake out the dice.

"How many do you think you should take out?"

"All of 'em."

After several minutes of work Seth has emptied out all of the dice. Only the cotton remains. With the lightened ball he goes back to the sidewalk, makes a big backswing, and bowls the ball with both hands. Now the ball is so light that, when it hits a bump in the sidewalk, it jumps off course and rolls onto the grass. Seth retrieves the ball just before Aaron gets to it. Seth, perhaps realizing that he is going to be asked to give Aaron a turn, walks within 3 feet of the pin and throws that ball overhand, hitting and knocking over the pin.

Aaron gets the ball. He takes it to the head of the alley, backs up about 10 feet for a running start, runs full speed toward the alley, and throws the ball underhand with both hands just as he gets to the head of the alley. The ball rolls, ricochets off the alley wall and hits the pin. Since the pin is filled with sand and the ball has been emptied of dice, the impact of the ball is not sufficient to knock over the pin. "What can we do?" Lisa asks Aaron.

Eva says to Lisa "The knock-over thing [meaning the pin] is stuck." She picks the pin up. With the sand inside, the pin weighs a good 3 pounds, quite a conspicuous weight to a child trying to lift it with one hand. She uses both hands now, and, as she lifts it higher, she notices the shadow of the sand level through the translucent plastic: "Ugh, it's heavy."

Aaron takes it to feel how heavy it is. "Get another," he says to nobody in particular. (Here we have Aaron trying to exchange objects to solve the problem rather than changing the object he has.) Lisa, sensitive to our desire to have children encounter within-object transformations, asks Aaron "Can we do anything to make this pin lighter?" Marya (a 2½-year-old who has joined the group) pipes up: "Make it lighter. It's too dark. Too dark."

Aaron does not know what to do to make the pin lighter. Eva, however, says "There's sand in there. I saw you do it [meaning add the sand]." Lisa makes a decision to take off the duct-tape patch, but she leaves the sand in. "Let me do it," Aaron says. He holds the pin in both hands and begins to drain the sand. It is not clear that he understands the relation between draining the sand and bowling over the pin. For the moment he seems intent on draining out all of the sand. Eva, in contrast, is watching and is able to get a broader perspective on the interrelations of the component act: untaping, draining, and bowling. Lisa asks Aaron "How much do you need to let out?" Aaron: "All of it." Like Seth, Aaron does not think about the change from full to less-full as a continuum. The pin is either full or empty (Chapter One). Also, when Lisa asks him how much he needs to remove, he is probably not thinking about the amount needed to have the pin fall over when hit. Eva says "Bowl it now." Perhaps she knows that the pin is sufficiently lightened, even though it is not completely empty. Or perhaps she is impatient for her own turn.

Aaron shakes out the last grain of sand with an air of finality. Lisa sets the pin up for Aaron, who takes a 10-foot running start and throws the ball down the alley. It smacks the pin dead center, and the pin makes a clean fall to the carpet. Aaron throws both arms up above his head with joy.

THE DRUM DROP

Preparing the Environment

Tissue paper, an embroidery hoop, a tennis ball, and a cardboard tube are all you need for the Drum Drop. Fit the tissue paper over the open end of the tube, and hold it in place with the embroidery hoop, as shown in Figure 5.4. The teacher and the child can set different objectives, such as trying to make the ball break through the paper or trying to add enough layers so the dropped ball will not pierce them.

The functional relations exist between the number of tissue sheets, the height from which the ball is dropped, the force with which the ball is thrown (if not dropped), and the nature of the material used to cover the drum. Sometimes we used a sheet of rubber. The higher the level from which the ball was released, the higher the ball would bounce.

Variations on this game can be constructed by anchoring the drum securely so that, when the rubber head is hit, the drum will not slide. Then the children can attempt to make a tennis ball bounce into yogurt containers nailed on a vertical board, like basketball hoops, at different heights. This gives the children a reason to discover the functional relation between the force of a downward throw and the height of the upward bounce.

Entry

David, 4½, and Tom, a teacher, are sitting on the edge of a carpeted riser playing Drum Drop. Tom holds the drum steady, and David drops the ball into the center of the tissue paper. It immediately breaks through. "Let's see if you can make the paper *not* break," Tom suggests. David and Tom together add the amount of tissue paper that David selects, about five sheets. Tom secures the embroidery hoop,

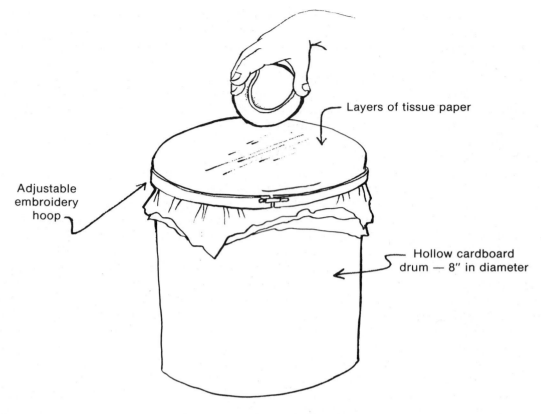

Layers of tissue paper

Adjustable
embroidery
hoop

Hollow cardboard
drum — 8″ in diameter

FIGURE 5.4   The Drum Drop.

and David drops the ball again from about the same height. The paper breaks. David looks at Tom and says "We need more paper. It's not thick enough." David selects what he thinks is more than the last attempt, but is really the same amount. The ball breaks through again. "Still not enough," David concludes. This time he gets conspicuously more, about eight sheets. Tom forces the embroidery hoop over this stack of tissue and David raises the ball. Now when David drops the ball from approximately the same height as before, the tissue holds firm. The ball plops to a rest on the tissue paper.

David seemed to know that he was testing the tissue paper. He did not change the height at which he dropped the ball. Compare David's play with that of Kevin, age 3. Kevin drops the ball on the eight sheets of tissue, and it does not break through. "How can we make the ball break through, Kevin?" Tom asks. Kevin throws the ball down hard at the stretched tissue. The force of his throw causes the tissue to be pulled from under the embroidery hoop, but it does not break. "See if you can break the paper, but drop the ball." Tom is trying to set some limits on the game, consciously taking the risk that Kevin might not like this limit. Kevin stands up and holds the ball waist high. Tom has reset the eight sheets of tissue. Kevin drops the ball, but it does not break a hole in the tissue. "What can we do to make a hole with the ball?" Tom asks again. Kevin starts to poke his finger through the tissue. "Wait a minute, Kevin, maybe there is another way. Let's take off some of the paper." Tom has decided to use a more directive approach just out of his own curiosity about Kevin's reaction. Kevin helps, and together they stretch about five sheets over the drum rim. This time Kevin holds his hand very high and throws the ball down, breaking a hole in the layers of tissue paper. "I did it!" he exclaims.

Unlike David, Kevin did not seem to be testing the thickness of the tissue. His objective was to make a hole in the tissue by any means he could think of, including poking with his finger. David, on the other hand, kept to the single dimension of the tissue's thickness. He did not vary the height of his release or the force of a throw. We do not think that David had clearly separated the variables, as this would require a level of thinking uncommon in 4- and 5-year-olds. But he did see the game as a test of the strength of the tissue. This approach itself is an advance over the more general goal of Kevin to make a hole in the tissue. David was thinking about the means to an end, testing variations of those means. Kevin was thinking about the end and trying all means possible.

We also noticed that we had some difficulty trying to set the goal for the younger children of *not* breaking a hole. Whenever the younger children did not break through the paper, they were displeased. The effect of *not* breaking is more conceptual than physical. The effect of breaking makes a great sound with a clear physical result.

Note that this version of the Drum Drop (breaking a hole in the tissue) was not a functional relation between *two* variables. David could vary the number of sheets, but the hole was either made or not made. The hole did not show any variations between its presence and absence. In contrast, bouncing the ball into yogurt cups at varying heights was a true functional relation between two variables. The child could vary the force of a throw and his choice of which cup to aim for. Consequently, the game of trying to make a ball bounce into different cups on different occasions has a structure more difficult than trying to make an all-or-none effect, such as ripping a hole in the tissue.

THE TEETER-TOTTER TUBE

We have already discussed the Teeter-Totter Tube in the previous section. But the children had several learning encounters with this activity that deal with a functional relation between two variables. For example, Tristan found that, if he increased the length of the pegs that he fit into the tube, he would have to increase the height of his end of the seesaw to make it slide down the tube. Short pegs would go down easily; longer pegs required more slant. He also discovered that the speed of a rolling bead was directly correlated to the slant of the tube. The greater the slant, the faster the bead.

Loren and Lauren discovered that, the greater the slant, the farther a bead would roll across the floor. They could either make the bead drop out the end of an almost horizontal tube, or they could make the bead roll to the wall by slanting the tube all the way.

We must point out that, even with the activities that allowed for degrees of variations between two extremes, our children would usually fixate on the opposite extremes. When they did consider degrees of variation in the midrange, it was usually in the variable over which they had direct control—that is, the cause. They would regulate their own behavior (slanting the Teeter-Totter Tube) in order to get a single desired effect (the bead's hitting the wall). It happened infrequently that our children—even the 5-year-olds—would systematically vary both their own behavior and the effect desired.

For example, children will vary the force of their throw to make the ball bounce into the yogurt cup, but they will designate one cup as the correct cup. If the ball lands in any other cup, the children treat that as an accident. Even when the rules are structured—as when a teacher asks the child to make the ball bounce into the top cup first, the second topmost second, and so forth—the 4- and 5-year-olds find that difficult to do, even when they understand the instructions. Our guess is that the difficulty arises because the corrective information gained from a successful throw cannot be applied to the next throw if the goal keeps changing after every success. The older the children are, however, the better they become in coordinating changes that occur with regard to both the means (throwing) and the goals (the position of the cup).

CHANGING LIMITS

These activities give the children a reason to experiment with the probability of an event. The child can limit the number of ways some event can happen. That is why we call this section Changing Limits. We could have called it Changing Probabilities or Changing the Range of Possibilities just as well. In Chapter One we mentioned the first activity to be discussed here, the Weighted Wheels. The child can move a counterweight on the wheel so that the wheel will always roll to a stop in the same position. The child also has the option to set the counterweight so that the wheel's position cannot be predetermined. The child, in effect, is changing the limits, from zero to infinity.

THE WEIGHTED WHEELS

Preparing the Environment

Photo 5.12 is a close-up of three Weighted Wheels. The wheel itself is a section cut from a cardboard tube about 5 inches in diameter. We drilled two holes opposite each other in the wheel so we could insert a Tinker Toy dowel. We pushed the dowel through one of the holes and then put a weighted bead on the dowel and continued pushing until the dowel was secured by the opposite hole. The bead by itself was not heavy enough, so we duct-taped a metal nut onto it. This additional weight assured that the position of the wheel when it came to rest would be determined by the position of the bead. The top half of the wheel was painted light green and the bottom half, brown. With the weighted bead pushed behind the green half, the wheel would always roll to a stop with the brown section up (left-hand wheel in Photo 5.12). With the bead behind the brown half, the wheel would come up green (middle wheel). With the bead placed directly in the center of the dowel, the position

PHOTO 5.12   Three Weighted Wheels with the sliding bead on each in a different position.

at which the wheel rolled to rest could be anything. (It just happens to be brown in the right-hand wheel.)

Entry

Ideally, the children will be amazed that the wheels always stop in the same position (given that the weighted bead is pushed flush to the inside of the rim). They might notice that on some occasions the wheel even rocks backwards just before it comes to a full stop. You should let the children discover the odd motion of these wheels on their own and then see if they can figure out why these wheels do not work like other wheels.

Younger Children

Younger children are not likely to be amazed at all. For one thing, they do not wait for a rolled wheel to come to a natural stop. A rolling wheel to a 2- or 3-year-old means *catch*. Even with a teacher there to add constraints, the younger children do not comment on the way the wheels rock backward sometimes or how the wheel always comes up green. To see the consistency as unusual, a person has to know a great deal about wheels already. For instance, a round wheel is round everywhere; therefore, there is no way to explain the consistency of these wheels by their shape. Could a 2- or 3-year-old know that much about wheels? Probably not. Therefore, they see nothing unusual in the Weighted Wheels.

Perhaps, too, the children cannot remember from one roll to the next what color has just come up. We thought about this possibility and then gave the children several wheels to roll at once. We thought they might be more surprised if they saw three wheels roll to a stop on the same color at about the same time. The younger children still did not look at these events as something that needed explaining. They just did not look at the wheel roll as being *overdetermined*. The notion that some action is more determined than what one would expect comes later in development than age 2 or 3.

Older Children

Our 4- and 5-year-olds were not overly surprised either. But they did get the idea that the bead could be moved and could determine the position of the wheel. Katie, age 4, adjusts the bead on the dowel (Photo 5.13). She adjusts all three wheels, then she rolls them one at a time across the carpeted platform, noticing how they stop (Photo 5.14). Katie seemed to understand in some general way that the position of the bead affected the position of the wheel when it stopped, but she did not understand that the weight of the bead "pulled" the wheel into a particular position. The notion of an object's having weight disproportionately distributed within it does not occur to the 4-year-old. Objects are heavy or light as wholes, not as parts within wholes.

We did not field test the Weighted Wheels with kindergarten-age children, but we imagine that that age range would be more suited to the subtlety of these wheels. The children could keep track of how a wheel turned up each time by marking either a green tally or a brown tally. Then they could begin to see that they had made tally marks of only one color. The teacher might risk asking "Why do you think it never comes up brown?" But in general it is better to wait for the child to think of this question. The teacher can have two children working together, one with a wheel counterweighted for brown and the other with a wheel counterweighted for green. Perhaps the discrepancy between the two children's wheels will cause them to question why. Or the teacher might surreptitiously change the position of the bead after a child had rolled the wheel five or six times.

Does the child eventually understand that everything within a moving object contributes to its weight and therefore contributes to the way it rolls to a stop? Perhaps 5- and 6-year-olds could discover on their own how to set limits on where the wheel will stop. After that, keep them away from the roulette wheel lest they rig it in their favor!

PHOTO 5.13   Katie adjusts the sliding bead on one of the Weighted Wheels.

PHOTO 5.14   Katie rolls the Weighted Wheels to see how they will stop.

THE MOVING GROOVES

Preparing the Environment

The idea for this activity came from some research by Piaget on tilting marbles back and forth in a tray. The research task began with a row consisting of four black marbles and four yellow marbles against one of the sides of a shallow tray. The color groups were separated by a short rim perpendicular to the side of the tray. As the experimenter rocked the tray back and forth, the marbles began to mix. After about a dozen rockings there were as many marbles of one color as another on either side of the short rim. Many of the children, ages 4 to 7 years, thought that the marbles would return to their original positions in a few more rocks. On one occasion the marbles had divided into three blacks on the right and four yellows and a black on the left. A 4-year-old thought that on the very next rock of the tray only the black marble would change sides, thereby reestablishing the original division of colors, four and four! The children did not understand the random nature of the mixing.[2] This understanding did not appear until after age 7.

So, of course, we did not expect that our children would be able to predict that tilting the trays would keep the marbles mixed. But we did want to give our children a means to set limits on just how mixed the marbles got. We wondered if they could at least understand that mixing was a function of an "open field" within the tray. If the tray had grooves, the marbles would not mix. If the children could move the grooves, they could control the degree to which the marbles mixed.

In Photo 5.15 David and Jenny are tilting their trays back and forth, watching the marbles roll and come to rest at either side. David has placed a set of grooves into his tray. When his marbles roll, they do not mix. Jenny has an "open field"; her marbles roll and mix.

PHOTO 5.15   David moves a tray with grooves. Jenny's tray has an "open field" for her marbles.

[2] See J. Piaget and B. Inhelder, *The Origin of the Idea of Chance in Children* (New York: Norton, 1975, p. 5).

The trays are actually lids from plastic storage drawers. The grooves are made of heavy cardboard. Balsa wood works better, because the child can move them apart or together, making grooves big enough for one marble or more than one. He can even push them all to the side or remove them to make an "open field."

Entry

George (a teacher) and Bobby are sitting at the table, playing Moving Grooves. George has a tray without any grooves; Bobby has one with the balsa wood slats spaced equidistantly. Bobby has three "redheaded people" (painted wooden beads) in the first three grooves and three "yellowheaded people" in the last three grooves. George begins to roll his beads around in a circular fashion. "My little people are chasing each other," he says. Bobby makes similar circular motions, but his beads stay within the grooves. (We had added a sheet of Plexiglas to these trays to prevent the beads from spilling out.) "Mine don't do it. They stay in the roads," Bobby remarks.

George: "Yes, yours aren't mixing up."

Bobby rocks his tray back and forth. Then he tilts it from side to side. "Lemme play with yours," Bobby asks George.

"You want your little people to visit each other, the reds and the yellows," George reflects to Bobby.

"Yeah," Bobby replies. "They're trapped."

"What can we do with yours?" George asks.

Bobby rocks the tray back and forth a few times and then says "Take out the roads so they can move around."

Bobby had seen George add the slats, so he figured that they could be removed. With a little prompting from George, Bobby shifted from seeking a goal via an object *exchange* ("Lemme play with yours") to seeking a goal via an object *change* ("Take out the roads").

Bobby, with a little help from George, slides out the Plexiglas sheet. He wants to take all of the roads out. George allows this, knowing that the first strategies children use with new games are generally all-or-none changes (level of opposition). They reinsert the Plexiglas, and Bobby rocks and tilts his tray, content with the increase in the freedom of movement.

Meanwhile, George has added a single slat up the middle of his tray, with all the redheads on the left and all the yellowheads on the right. As George tilts and rocks his tray, the little people chase each other but do not mix. George puts his tray down and watches Bobby for a while, anticipating that Bobby will want to play with the abandoned tray. He does. As he rocks and tilts the tray with one middle slat, George asks "Can you make the little redhead people visit the yellowheads?"

"Wait a minute!" Bobby says, a little annoyed. He tilts and rocks. The beads mix on either side of the slat, but of course the colors do not mix. "I can't do it. They hit the wall," Bobby says, as he tilts his tray on the long axis, making a tier of yellows on line above a tier of reds. But Bobby seems content to tilt and rock as it is. George does not push the objective further at this point. Perhaps Bobby vaguely knew why the beads did not mix, but he was not interested in changing the slat.

Variations

The activity can be varied in a number of ways. You can make slats of different shapes, such as H-shaped ones. The children can invent their own mazes and use a single bead, trying to get their little person from the top of the tray to the bottom by tilting and rocking appropriately. The maze slats will have to have little doorways cut into them, but this is an easy matter with balsa wood. The beauty of the homemade mazes is that the child himself has control over how he sets limits on the movement of the beads. He can vary the limits from an open field to a completely determined single track. All varieties of branching paths come between these two extremes. Give the child control over these variations and, we feel, he will be more likely to learn the functional relation between the structure of the slats and the limits set on the motion of the beads. As we said in Chapter One, the child needs to understand the *procedures* by which things happen. To this end, teachers should give the child control over the procedures by which things are constructed.

THE WHEEL OF CHANGING CHANCE

Preparing the Environment

The Wheel of Changing Chance shares aspects with the Weighted Wheels and the Moving Grooves. In all three of these activities the child is given a procedure by which she can change the range of possible outcomes. In the Wheel of Changing Chance the child can change the probability that a spinning pointer will stop on a particular color. The wheel (see Photo 5.16) is made of heavy posterboard. The

PHOTO 5.16   Marya moves the yellow sector on her Wheel of Changing Chance. Katie thumps the pointer to make it spin.

colored sectors are mounted in layers on the black backing in such a way that they can be independently turned. Because they overlap, the sectors can be turned to expose different-sized areas of color. Marya (on the left) is bringing more of the yellow sector into view from under the blue sector. Fleet (behind Marya) has placed a yellow bead on the black backing. Marya is trying to maximize the chances that the spinner will land on yellow, matching the color of the bead. Other beads lie nearby. These beads are blue and red, the colors of the other sectors. Katie, to the right, is just about to flick the pointer. But her color sectors are all glued down to the black backing. There is no way for her to maximize the chances for the spinner to land on a particular color. She, too, has a set of yellow, blue, and red beads nearby.

Entry

This activity has certain rules. Therefore, it requires at least an initial phase of teacher direction. The younger children like to spin the pointer but are not too concerned about where it lands. At first they are delighted that their thump causes the pointer to move so quickly. They may announce ahead of time where the pointer will land; if it doesn't, they just keep spinning until it does. The older children seem to know that the wheel with the movable sectors is better for predicting than the wheel with the fixed sectors. Here are some observations on our children at the School for Constructive Play.

Younger Children

Katie flicks the pointer of the wheel with movable sections. It lands on red. Lisa asks Katie "Can you make it land on blue?" The blue sector is a little smaller than the red sector. Katie does not move the sectors in order to increase the surface area of blue. She spins the pointer once, and it lands on red again; spins again, yellow; spins again, yellow again. She seems to quicken her pace each time the pointer does not land on blue. Then, on the last attempt, she simply pushes the pointer to blue directly. Lisa, wisely, does not tell Katie that what she did was cheating. Not only would that be a put-down, but from Katie's point of view moving the pointer directly to blue by pushing it is a better means to reach her goal. "There!" Katie says to Lisa. "OK," Lisa responds, and then she changes the sectors while Katie watches. Lisa makes the blue area bigger by moving the yellow sector partially under it. "Now see if you can make it [the pointer] stop on blue." This time Katie has more "success." The pointer lands on the blue on the second spin. "It's on blue," Katie announces to Lisa.

Lisa had hoped that Katie would begin to experiment at this point with the relation between the surface area of one color and the probability that a spin would land on that color. Katie would sometimes move the sectors before she spun the pointer, but it was not apparent just what relation the sector changing and the pointer spinning had with each other. One observer did think that Katie understood that she could eliminate the chances of a particular color by reducing the size of that color to nothing (level of opposition). But the observation was not clear-cut.

Older Children

Eva and Lisa are playing with both wheels, the one with movable sectors and the one without. Each time Eva spins the pointer, she takes a crayon of the corresponding color and makes a mark in one of three columns on a sheet of paper. At this point Eva has about five yellow marks and two reds. No blues. This reflects the fact that blue is only a sliver of a sector, with red not much bigger. "My goodness, most of your marks are yellow, Eva," Lisa says.

"One, two, three, four, five," Eva counts. "I got five."

"How can you get more red marks?"

Eva moves the red sector, but because it is moving farther and farther behind the yellow sector, she has, in effect, decreased it. She has, however, inadvertently increased the blue area. She spins and makes her marks several more times. On one of the spins, she gets a blue. "I got a blue!" she says with pleasure.

Eva evidently knew that she had not gotten blues before. This means that she understood that her marks indicated the past positions of the pointer. Not all children who were able to make the correct mark after a spin could then look at the frequency of the marks as an indication of the pointer's past performance. Also note that, when Lisa asked "How can you get more red marks?" Eva did not just add more red marks directly to the paper. We did see this more-direct strategy with some of the younger children.

"How can you get no blues?" asks Lisa, thinking that a complete opposite might be easier than a change in degrees. Eva spins the pointer several times in a row without marking. On about the third spin the pointer stops on blue. "I got it again," she says. Lisa's question is probably ill timed. Eva has just gotten her first blue, and Lisa is asking her to get no blues. Lisa senses her mistake and just watches for a while. Eva continues to spin the pointer and has lost interest in making the marks on the paper.

Lisa turns her attention to another child nearby for a few minutes and then returns her attention to Eva. Eva spins a few times and moves one of the sectors. She has grown familiar with the way the sectors and the pointer move. She has also learned that she can get a better spin out of the pointer if she flicks it close to the tip rather than toward the center. The red sector is fully exposed (about three-quarters of the wheel), and reds are coming up fairly frequently. But because Eva is not keeping a running record of her spins, she is probably less aware of the red frequency.

Lisa gets an idea, based on knowledge that Eva likes the color blue. "Which color do you like best, Eva?"

"Blue."

"Well, what can we do to make it land on blue more? How about making it so the arm never lands on red?"

"Yeah, let's get rid of the red." At this she rotates the sectors until, by trial and error, she completely covers up the red sector. Then she spins the pointer with some certainty that at least she will not get red.

It is not at all certain to us that she also knew that, by reducing the amount of red, she had conversely increased the amount of blue and yellow. This actually was not Lisa's intention. Lisa only wanted to give Eva a reason to think about how to change the chance of red to zero. This latter concept Eva seemed to understand. Further note that the elimination of one color altogether does not at all require an understanding of the relative areas of these color sectors. The functional relation between varying amounts of two colors was beyond the level of these children. However, they were having some good learning encounters on setting limits in an all-or-none fashion. And as we said in Chapter One, the level of opposition (blue versus no blue) is a precursor to the level of functions (a gain in blue is functionally related to a loss in red).

THE WHEELS AND WEDGES

Preparing the Environment

This activity uses a set of Tinker Toy wheels on a common axle and two triangular blocks from the block area. The blocks are made by cutting a four-unit rectangular block along the diagonal. The wheels can be from either the standard Tinker Toy set or the larger set called Connector Blocks (see Appendix). The children can align the two wedges and roll the wheel assembly down them, as in Photo 5.17. Little wooden objects can be targets.

The child can either increase or decrease the possible movements of the wheels. When using wheels that do not slide on the axle, the child does not worry about adjusting the distance between the wheels. He worries only about the distance between the two wedges, matching that distance to the distance between the two fixed wheels. The child can also use one big wheel and one little one. If he elects to do that, he has to worry about the right/left orientation of the wheels when he aims at a target.

After a period of free play with these materials, children learn how to set limits on the alternative actions of the wheels; that is, they learn to reduce the degrees of freedom. Of course, the presence of several degrees of freedom makes the game interesting, and children also enjoy trying to cope with these options.

The structure of this activity is quite elegant from a mathematical point of view. The wheels will roll down the wedges only if the distance between the wheels is the same as the distance between the wedges. If the wheels are closer together

PHOTO 5.17   Seth rolls the wheels down the wedges to knock over the little figures.

than the wedges, the child can compensate by doing one of two things. She can either move the wheels farther apart or move the wedges closer together. The one is the perfect reciprocal of the other. In addition to the reciprocity between the distance of the wheels and the wedges, the game presents the geometrical problem of making two objects parallel. If the wedges are spaced apart more at one end than at the other, the wheels will not track properly. When you watch young children trying to adjust the wedges, you realize that making two linear objects parallel is no easy task.

In this, the last activity reported in the book, we will try to bring into focus many of the things we mentioned in Chapter One. We have, in this sense, saved the best for last.

Entry

All of our children found the game interesting. The 2-year-olds as well as the 5-year-olds understood that the goal was to roll the wheels down the wedges. The 2-year-olds would push the wedges flat together more often than not. The idea that the wedges should be apart in order to support the wheels just did not occur to them very often. We saw here the same thing that most nursery school teachers know about a child trying to build a bridge with three blocks. They push the two lower blocks together in order to support the top block. Perhaps they think that a gap between the two support blocks means that the third block will necessarily fall through. They have to "concretize" support by filling in the gap. Or perhaps it just means that, when you give young children two blocks, they will push them all the way together—another case of children's preferring the terminal condition.

Children around 2 and 3 also showed an interesting strategy: they separated the two wedges to accommodate the wheels, but only at the top end of the incline. That is, they centered on the distance between the wedges at the top end, matching it to the distance between the wheels, but failed to decenter from the top and construct the same distance all the way down the length of the wedges.

Another strategy was characteristic of the younger children. If the teacher slipped in some change, such as pushing the wedges closer, the younger children would typically engage the inverse reversal instead of the reciprocal reversal. That is, they would push back the wedge the teacher had moved until that wedge was where it had been, rather than adjust the wheels to fit the new distance between the wedges. The reciprocal reversal seems to be more advanced than the inverse.

Younger Children

Derrick and Trina are sitting on the floor in the block corner. Lisa, the teacher, is a few feet away. Derrick has the wheels in his hands; Trina has a little wooden person. "Roll 'em," Trina commands Derrick. Oblivious to Trina's urgency, Derrick puts one wheel on the wedges, which are flush. When he lets go, the wheels get hung up, with one wheel on and the other off. Derrick gets the idea that the other wheel needs some support, too, so he expands the wedges at the top. The wedges make a V structure. Now when Derrick releases the wheels from the top of the inclined wedges, they go an inch or two and fall off, straddling the wedges. "Do it right, Derrick," Trina barks in a mock bossiness uncannily like that of an exasperated parent.

Lisa senses that Trina is getting impatient, so she includes her in the game: "Trina, why don't you put your little person down there [pointing to the lower end of the inclined wedges] so that Derrick can knock it over with his wheels." (We suggest you use bowling pins in order to eliminate the pretend homicide.) Trina places the little person directly at the foot, touching one of the wedges.

We found this interesting, because Trina could have put the little person anywhere between the two separated ends of the wedges. (Derrick had inadvertently made the wedges more-or-less parallel.) Perhaps Trina thought that the person had to be hit by the wheel and not the axle. And perhaps Trina had to put the little person touching the lower end of the wedge, instead of several inches back, because she did not like the gap between the wedge and the little person. Here may be another case of a child's "concretizing" an event by eliminating the gap.

Derrick rolls the wheels down the parallel wedges. The left wheel knocks down the little person, and Trina takes the wheels. Derrick politely allows Trina to have a turn. Lisa picks up the wedges and passes them, flat together, to Trina. The wheels are at their full extension. Trina has no trouble setting up the wedges. She turns them with the tapered ends facing Derrick and spreads them apart until they are parallel. She makes one placement with the wheels to the wedges and notices that the wheels are too far apart. She grasps the left wedge in the middle and moves it in such a way that the parallelism is preserved. She then successfully rolls the wheels down the wedges toward Derrick.

Lisa asks Derrick to return the wheels to Trina, at the same time pushing the left wedge in. Trina takes the wheels and puts them onto the wedges just slightly, noticing that the wedges do not match the wheels. She moves her hand toward the right wedge, apparently with an intention to move it, but she stops and instead moves the left wedge back where it was. After all, this was the wedge that Lisa had changed.

We think that Trina's decision not to move the right wedge could have meant that she realized that the right wedge was not the one Lisa had moved. Trina wanted to undo, in the most direct way, what Lisa had done. In fact, would she have understood that she should move the right wedge out, instead of in? Moving the right wedge out is the reciprocal to Lisa's moving the left wedge in. It could have been Trina's uncertainty regarding what to do that led her to move the left wedge.

Older Children

Seth and Clayton are playing with the wheels and wedges. Fleet has a set of off-sized wheels. The two boys have a set of regular wheels. So far, they have solved the problems of making the wedges parallel, as well as the problems of changing either the distance between the wedges or the distance between the wheels. They can push the wheels in when Fleet pushes in the wedges and push the wedges out when the wheels are given to them fully extended. The off-sized wheels present a greater challenge.

Fleet gives Clayton the off-sized wheels. "Where should we put the blocks so that you can knock them down?" Fleet asks. "I'll do it," Clayton answers. He places the blocks directly in front of the wedges, about 8 inches away. He then rolls the off-sized wheels and, as you see in Photo 5.18, they arc off to the left. "What hap-

PHOTO 5.18   Clayton misses his target on the Wheels and Wedges because the off-sized wheels roll in an arc.

pened?" Fleet asks. "They missed," Clayton replies, giving a literal answer to Fleet's question. He tries again, using the same right/left orientation for the wheels. Once again they arc away from the target. "Why do the wheels do that?" Fleet asks. She is addressing the air of concentration around Clayton more than posing a direct question to him. "The big one makes it go crooked," Clayton says, referring to the larger wheel.

This was a rather interesting construction of the problem, because the arc was no less a function of the small wheel. But children at 4 years of age have difficulty understanding a pure relation—that is, the difference itself. Clayton placed the cause within a single wheel rather than in the relation between the two wheels. A wheel is concrete, a difference is abstract. Nevertheless, Clayton eventually learned how to orient the wheels so that they made an arc in the other direction. He never did learn how to move the target to be either right or left of a direct line coming off the inclined wedges. The idea that you should put something off center to hit it may have violated too many of his previous experiences. Perhaps you can remember the first time you tried to hit a moving target with a stone, arrow, or rifle. You had to lead the target by a few inches so that the path of the missile and the path of the target would intersect at the same time. The tendency to shoot directly at the moving target is hard to suppress. Rolling off-sized wheels presents a similar problem for children.

LEARNING ENCOUNTERS IN THE HOME

Children can experiment with functional relations in any active situation that allows them to vary either the cause, the effect, or both. The bathroom faucet, a light switch dimmer, the volume control on the TV, all are cases where a change in the position of a knob changes an effect. While we might not enjoy a child experimenting with these household accessories, perhaps we could provide the child with other opportunities around the house for constructive play with functional relations.

Video games can be one source of play with functional relations. We prefer the non-aggressive games like Street Racer (by Atari) and Helicopter Rescue (by Odyssey). These games require the child to discover the functional relation between the position of the paddle control and the moving image on the TV screen. The problem is one of fine tuning the sense of a small change in one with a small change in the other. The video game also adds an element of timing. For example, in Street Racer the child has to avoid obstacles in the race track as they appear on the TV screen. If the child oversteers, then the racer crashes into the rail. If the child understeers, then the car crashes into another car. (This game is psychologically non-aggressive since the objective is to miss the other vehicles, not to blow them up as in other space games.)

Atari also has an interesting inversion of Street Racer, called Number Cruncher. Here the objective is to hit the numbers on a moving track, but the numbers are not personified as evil space ships or enemy troops. By having both games, Street Racer (to avoid images) and Number Cruncher (to make contact with images) the child develops a fuller sense of functional relations. A function depends not only on the physical movements, but also on the general objective. The contrast between Street Racer and Number Cruncher should remind you of the Drum Drop's two objectives (to tear the paper or to make the paper strong) and the Tilt-a-Hole Tray's two objectives (to maneuver the ball into the hole or to maneuver the ball away from the hole—see Photo 3.16). Thus the child must learn more than the mechanical relation between paddle and image, but also keep in mind which effect is more desirable from the perspective of a game rule.

The strategy of functional relations is even more obvious in a video game called Super Breakout (by Atari). The game has some features of a Ping Pong match, but the objective is to knock a ball repeatedly into a brick wall in order to knock a hole into the wall, and eventually to knock down the entire wall. The paddle control moves a horizontal dash right and left (the Ping Pong paddle, so to speak). The moving dot bounces off this dash if the child positions the dash in the path of the moving ball. Additionally, if the ball strikes the dash more to one end, the ball bounces off at a greater angle than it would have it struck the very center of the dash. In this game the child learns to anticipate just what type of angle is needed to knock out the bricks and then to execute the position of the dash appropriately. So the game involves more than hand-eye coordination, but also some thinking about best strategy. Furthermore, the length of the dash shrinks as the game progresses, adding one more degree of difficulty for the child. Fortunately there are many varieties of this game and each has its own range of difficulty. Children usually know which ones are fun and optimally challenging for themselves. Just ask.

We hope that many of the activities mentioned for classroom activities will find their way into homes. Clothesline pulleys, teeter-totter tubes, pulley pendulum balls, bowling balls and pins that can be weighted, wheels and wedges—these are all materials that are fairly easy to find and set up for the child in a play space. Sometimes it is appropriate for the adult to give a momentary demonstration of a new set-up, just to prompt the child a bit. For example, the function of a plexiglas tube taped to the see-saw may not be immediately apparent, so the adult casually puts a bead in one end just before two children start the see-saw moving. That's it. The child will either take it from there or leave it. Yet even if they leave it, our experience has been that within the next few days, they spontaneously try the bead in the tube for themselves.

Many children today have Match Box cars with plastic tracks, sometimes called Hot Wheels. These little toys with their changeable tracks give the young child at home a marvelous experimental kit for functional relations. The slope of the track determines the speed of the car. The degree of the curve sets limits on how fast the car can travel without spinning out. The inventive child will also construct jumps, such that the car hurdles through the air for a distance that is a function of the upward pitch of the end of the jump as well as the downward pitch of the beginning of the track. The timing of two cars arriving at an intersection is a function of their speed, or if their speed is the same, a function of the length of their respective tracks. The experimentation in play goes on and on, mainly because the tracks can be re-arranged. This is what makes this toy so suited to our emphasis on transformations.

Children like to play board games at home perhaps even more than at school. But some board games are rather complicated for 3, 4, and 5 year olds because of the number of arbitrary rules that have to be accepted, just as part of the challenge. As we mentioned in the Wheel of Changing Chance, the child feels "Why shouldn't I put the spinner directly on the red sector, why should I let the spinner come to a natural stop? Isn't the objective to get the spinner to end up on the red sector?" The social contract between players is actually part of what it means to learn to play a board game, and this deals more with those things we mentioned in the chapter on perspective taking. But there are perhaps some games that are useful for learning encounters with the functional relations that change the probability of an event.

In the game Spill the Beans (by Schapper), the probability of the bean pot tilting over increases as the number of beans placed on top increases. Does the child show greater care in placing the later beans? In pick-up sticks, the probability of moving an adjacent stick is highest in the beginning of the game rather than the end. Does the child show an appreciation of this fact? In a card game, the probability of my having a certain card decreases with the number of times that card has been played in previous turns. Does the child realize this relation and therefore make guesses on the basis of past plays of the cards? The parent can be sensitive to this quality of board games and parlor games, and that some games encourage children to determine the functional relation between the frequency of two events or between the frequency of one event as determined by the variation (size, amount) in another. As we stated before, functional relations are everywhere and can be found and encouraged if you know what they look like.

SUMMARY: MAKING FUNCTIONAL RELATIONS

Functional relations involve the coordination of two variables. A variable is either a cause or an effect that has a whole range of possible values. A cause or effect that has only two possible values is not properly called a variable. For example, breaking a hole in the tissue paper on the Drum Drop is an all-or-none effect. It either happens or does not happen. Because breaking the hole has only two possible values, it is not a true variable.

The activities in this chapter involved various combinations between variable and two-choice causes and variable and two-choice effects. The clothesline pulley is an example of a two-choice cause (two ropes) and a two-choice effect (two directions). The Pulley Pendulum Ball is an example of a variable cause (many heights of the ring on the cup hooks) and a variable effect (correlated height of the swinging tether ball). The Teeter-Totter Tube is an example of a variable cause (many heights of the seesaw possible) and a two-choice effect (the right or left direction that the bead rolls). The Teeter-Totter Tube can also elicit encounters with a variable cause (the height of the seesaw) and a variable effect (the speed of the bead).

It seemed that our children, when confronted with a functional relation with one or two variables, would convert the variable into a two-choice affair. For example, children frequently liked to make the bead go fast or slow in the Teeter-Totter Tube, but they did not experiment with the degrees in between. The physical structure of the activity did not preclude such exploration. The children themselves chose to constrain their explorations to the opposite extremes. This tendency is consonant with Piaget's theory of development, which predicts that children will explore opposites before they explore gradations (degrees) between opposites (see Chapter One).

We also found that, when children did explore variation per se rather than opposites, they more often commented on the variable under their direct control. If they changed the position of the ring on the Pulley Pendulum Ball, they would comment on the different heights of the ring more often than the height of the tether ball. They would note if the ball was a hit or a miss, but they did not remark very frequently on the fact that the ball's height had been *changed*. Perhaps change, from the child's point of view, is a case of personal action, such as "I pumped up the tire." Change, by this reasoning, is not a case of a difference between two external events—for example, "The tire is now inflated," which compares the tire as it is now to the tire as it was earlier, when it was flat. We consider these trends as suggestive, not conclusive, but worthy of future research.

DEVELOPMENTAL TRENDS

TWO WITHIN ONE

Cases where two (or more) discontinuous actions create one continuous action:

The younger children would pull the pulley rope with one hand. The older children could use a hand-over-hand action that kept the rope moving in a continuous fashion even though the hand actions were discontinuous.

Cases where both sight and touch appear possible but are not:

The younger children would try to grab a bead moving within the Plexiglas tube by grabbing "through" the tube. The older children evidently realized that the tube not only guided the path of the bead but also prevented direct touching of the bead (two aspects of the same tube).

The younger children were afraid that a crayfish in a goldfish bowl would bite them. The older children were not afraid, evidently because they realized that, if the bowl held back the water (one aspect), it would also hold back the crayfish (the other aspect).

Cases where the body itself represents the event:

DECENTERING FROM AN EGOCENTRIC PERSPECTIVE

The younger children would use the Teeter-Totter Tube like a seesaw, making the bead go back and forth (as well as up and down) with their own body. The older children enjoyed the game as well just as a tube on a movable incline.

Cases where the child centers on proximal versus distal effects:

The younger children would put the bead into a hole in the downward end of the Teeter-Totter Tube, failing to consider the slant of the whole tube. Older children could decenter and consider the entire slant, thus anticipating the need to have the entrance hole in the upward position.

Cases where the child centers on means as if the means were an end:

The younger children would try any means to reach their goal in the Drum Drop. Throwing the ball harder and poking a finger through the tissue paper were both acceptable to them. The older children seemed to understand the difference between testing the limits of a given means by varying its limits and the simpler task of reaching the goal by any means. That is, the older children could decenter from the goal itself in order to test the limits of a given means.

Similar to the play with the Drum Drop, the younger children playing with the Wheel of Changing Chance would do anything to reach their goal. They would physically move the pointer to the color of their choice. The older children would explore the various means to make the pointer come to a stop on a particular color. They did not receive satisfaction from just getting the pointer on the color by any means, such as physically moving the pointer to that color.

SEEING THE DYNAMIC WITHIN THE STATIC

Cases where action is constrained by the amount of space:

In the Wheel of Changing Chance, the final resting position of the spinning pointer was constrained by the amount of a given color exposed: the less the color area, the less the probability that the pointer would stop on that color. The older children had some success in discovering this relationship. The younger children simply enjoyed flipping the pointer and making it spin for the longest possible time.

Cases where action is constrained by static structure:

Most of our children had trouble adjusting the height of the Pulley Pendulum Ball, even those who knew that putting the ring on a low hook made the ball swing higher (an inverse relation). They would make the ball the same height as the target on the blackboard, disallowing the arc made by the constraints of the pendulum rope.

Cases where action is constrained by the static position of weight:

In the Weighted Wheels game the heavy bead constrains the final resting position of the rolling wheel. The younger children were not particularly amazed when the Weighted Wheels always came up the same color. They did not see this series of events as "over-determined"; that is, they did not search for the constraints that determined these nonrandom events. The older children were not particularly amazed either, but they did get the general idea that the position of the bead was related to the final position of the rolling wheel. However, they could not predict in advance which color would be up at the end of a roll.

Cases where action is constrained by the relative difference in size:

Even our older children thought that the off-sized wheels, in the Wheels and Wedges game, made an arc because of *one* of the wheels—usually they said the larger one—instead of the difference between the two wheels. (This observation is also a case of *two within one*.)

FROM OPPOSITE EXTREMES TO MIDDLE DEGREES

Cases where the child has difficulty constructing the middle term:

On the Wheel of Changing Chance the probability of the pointer's landing on a particular color was directly proportional to the amount of area showing for that color. Even our older children had difficulty increasing the probability by degrees. But they did understand how to eliminate all chances for a "hit" on a particular color. In other words, they could construct the opposites (hit versus no hit) but had more difficulty constructing the middle terms—that is, the degrees between these extremes.

On the Solomon Swing one of our youngest children tried to push both seats down at once. Also, one of our 3-year-olds thought that one of the two seats, in some absolute sense, was the "up" seat. These errors indicate that the younger children had difficulty understanding that each seat was a variation on the other, because of the rope in the middle between them. Our older children understood that the two seats were connected in an inverse functional relation.

Most of our children wanted to empty all of the sand from the bowling ball or from the pin in the Weight Your Turn game. This is a classic example of young children's concern for all-or-none effects (opposites) before their consideration of gradual changes (degrees). We might say that for the young child it is not clear that *some* (as in "some sand") is embedded within and is a subpart of *all* (as in "all the sand"). That is, *some* is midway between *none* and *all*.

Cases where the child does not consider how one action could lead to an opposite effect:

On the Drum Drop the younger children rejected the teacher's suggestions to make the ball *not* break a hole in the tissue paper. They preferred to make the obvious effect of a hole. The older children were able to explore means to prevent the hole. Perhaps making a "not-hole" is more conceptual than physical. This would explain the younger children's preference for the real hole.

The younger children would pull on the rope when the basket reached the opposite end of the pulley rope, thinking that a pull would unstick the basket. The older children knew to reverse their pull. Here we have a classic "detour" problem.

The younger the child playing Wheels and Wedges, the more likely she was to use the inverse transformation, rather than the recriprocal transformation, to undo a change made by the teacher. In other words, she could not surmise that moving the wheels inward would make the wheels *not* fall off, given that the teacher had moved the wedges closer together.

Chapter Six

Your Children

The activities described in this handbook were probably strange to you. The purpose of this last chapter is to suggest ways that you can create similar activities in your setting, thereby reducing the strangeness. Yet we do not want you to make these activities so "unstrange," so familiar, that they lose their newness. Toward the end of preserving the newness, we are including, in the final section of this chapter, a brief discussion of what we see as the purpose of early-childhood education in general, something we call *interactive consciousness*. So, as the title of this chapter implies, we are going to cover two topics: applications of our approach to *your children* and the nature of *children as a whole*. As we discuss how you can extend the contents of this book to your school, we hope to do so in a way that places these suggestions in the appropriate context. That context is the whole child, using his or her intelligence to make sense of both a social and physical world through constructive play.

CHILDREN AT SCHOOL

How can you apply the contents of this book in your school? We do not believe that you need to get a new building, a bigger budget, or a larger staff. (Hooks on the ceiling, however, would be great for new types of activities.) We feel that our approach is primarily a method of observing young children and thereby knowing when and why to enter their spontaneous play. There are things you can do to improve your observations of children and your entry into their play.

Take Notes

We carried little "hipbooks" in a holster on our belt. When we saw something interesting, we jotted it down the first chance we got. For example, Karen was busy supervising the Solomon Swing and heard Jake's comment "I want the up swing." Five minutes later, as one child was leaving and another child was entering the area, Karen whipped out her hipbook and wrote "Up swing bit, Jake to Taneka." Later that day, after the children had gone, Karen took about three minutes to flesh out the episode on a sheet of paper that we put in a file. After two months we had over a hundred such sheets, a growing pool of observations from which to make judgments about what was working and what was not.

Evaluate in Process

In-process evaluation can come primarily from the written observations. We also used two other methods. One was rather conventional. We would play the same game with every child and see how each performed. We often played the game individually in a smaller room, not a testing room but a quiet room across the foyer from the large classroom. For example, we had spent two weeks on the concepts *physical balance* and *esthetic balance*, such as symmetry. The children had been playing with all types of balancing things—movement games, play dough balanced on the edge of the table, teeter-totter boards, water balances, and hanging hoops—a real "balance blitz," as we called it. Halfway through these two weeks we had each child come into the quiet room to play with a small balance beam, to balance on a one-person teeter-totter, to reconstruct an arch by leaning two blocks together, and to do other similar activities. We were interested in finding out, in some more systematic way, what *balance* meant to our children.

This we found out. For the younger children it seemed to mean "arms straight out to the sides." This was a rather static notion of balance. The older children understood that balance is a dynamic state of equilibrium, which could go off-balance at any minute. Be that as it may, the systematic observations in the small room gave us information that we then used to help the children understand that balance can refer to symmetrical forces as well as to symmetrical posture. For example, we found ways to accentuate the fact that falling was more likely if the arms were positioned asymmetrically.

Our other technique for evaluation was to use big words. These were called *probe words*. We would first determine if the child had ever used or been exposed (relatively speaking) to a given word (such as *opposite*) by talking with parents and our staff. Then we would begin to use this word in the classroom. For example, we set up an obstacle course. When the children entered a dead end in their little push wagons, we would say "Oh, you had to go in the opposite direction." The big word was always used to describe something that the child had just that moment done. After a few days the children would start using the probe word. We made a special effort to whip out our hipbooks whenever we heard a child use one.

Of course, the children would often use the probe word incorrectly (by adult conventions). But a child's use of the word was an expression of his or her understanding of what the concept meant. For example, one child said "Now stop it. Go opposite," pointing to a spot across the room. To this child, *opposite* probably meant any place that he was not. So we learned something about this child and, eventually, most of the children. Other probe words we used were *balance, middle,* and *almost*. These all gave us a lot of in-process information about our children. The semester ended before we could try words such as *sympathy, cooperate,* and *vertical*. Any word that the child can pronounce is suitable.

We had no fear in speaking words that were very complex in their meaning. Nor should you. What we should all avoid, however, is any attempt to directly teach the child what these words mean. We might stage the environment so that the child does something cooperative, so that we can say "cooperate" in a sentence. That's it. The child makes of the word what she will. We were not trying to direct the child by using these probe words. We were only trying to give ourselves a means to understand the child's view of the social and physical world.

Break Mental Sets

Start with an idea in mind, not with particular material in mind. Ask yourself, How can I stage a learning encounter with balance? rather than, How can I use this balance beam? The latter question is bound to yield fewer creative suggestions than the former. The physical balance beam itself sets too many constraints on your thinking. First of all, you will probably begin with the assumption that this thing before you is a balance beam. That is a mistake. It is actually two pieces of wood joined together at a central point. If you start with an idea, such as How can I stage encounters with functional relations, then this thing before you becomes subsumed under that general objective. The two pieces of wood joined together might function as an incline. This is exactly how we came to use a seesaw in the Teeter-Totter. We needed something to stage encounters with functional relations, and the seesaw fit that general objective, not as a seesaw but as a *transformable incline*.

Not only should you break mental sets, you should break furniture and toys and walls. Once we decided to cut a hole in a "good maple table" (essential for Cones in the Hole and the Shell Game), a whole world opened up. Everything in the classroom was stripped of its conventional meaning. The chair was a potential wall, the ceiling was a potential floor. One day we had the children dab the top of helium balloons with paint. We had papered the ceiling with butcher paper in advance. The children then proceeded to make "footprints" on the ceiling with the balloons. For the first time we heard several children use the word *under* in reference to the ceiling. Previously, they had always described the ceiling as being *over* them, rather than their being *under* the ceiling. This activity resulted from one teacher's thinking of the ceiling as a surface to "walk" on.

Use what you have in a variety of ways. As you have seen, Tinker Toys and blocks were used in many different ways. The Slatted Rollway used blocks duct-taped together. The Tinker Toy pieces served us well when we needed a better pizza cutter for unitizing motion in the rolled-out play dough. Do not throw anything out. Catalog it according to its physical description, not its function. Jigsaw pieces long since separated from the rest of the puzzle are "assorted shapes with parts of pictures." Who knows? You might need them to make some activity that requires the child to imagine the completion of the picture. Broken beads can be cataloged under "wooden hemispheres." Who knows? You might want to glue one each under a dozen unit blocks just to see how the children accommodate to the wobble factor. Recycle materials are very handy for solving creative problems. By their very nature they encourage the use of an object in some way for which it was not designed.

Make creative substitutions for materials and equipment that you have read about in this handbook. Instead of a Plexiglas easel for shadow play, a tightly stretched sheet could do as well. A slide projector could do as well as the Super-8 projector. Use what you have. Any pasteboard box can be made into a Silhouette Sorter; the Huge Hanging Hoop could be square; a Plexiglas sheet over a flashlight can be used instead of the overhead projector. You will lose some of the advantages of the harder-to-find materials, but you will still be able to do a lot.

Of course, there are limitations to substituting equipment. Video equipment really has no counterpart in the world of less expensive and more readily available equipment. It is fun for the children and has virtually unlimited educational potential. You are fortunate if you have access to video recording and playback equipment. Plexiglas also has no real substitute, at least for hard-surface games. It is the only surface that is both transparent and safe and hard enough on which to write and paint. Glass is too dangerous. Plexiglas itself is not expensive, and there are creative ways to make a Plexiglas easel that is cheaper than the one in the School for Constructive Play. Just cut a slit lengthwise in two cardboard carpet-roll cores about 12 inches in diameter. Stand the two tubes upright, like bookends, and insert a thick sheet of Plexiglas in the slits. This makes a fine easel.

Brainstorm

Bring your ideas in from anyplace. One day we were thinking about how to unitize and freeze motion. Someone said something about footprints, and I (GF) thought about a game my sister and I used to play with ice cream cones. Despite admonitions from our parents about making a mess in the back seat of the car, she and I would make imprints in the ice cream. First I would close my eyes, and she would make a mark in the ice cream. She would use her teeth, tongue, chin, nose, finger, or ear lobe. On "ready" I would look at the mark and try to guess what she had used to make it. Teeth marks were easy to identify, but tongue marks were her specialty. I could never imagine how she might have used her tongue to make a distinctive C in the ice cream. But little brothers have their way of frustrating older sisters. She never guessed my window-handle mark.

So this recollection of a childhood game led to the imprint game in the rolled-out play dough. Our children, like my sister and me, were delighted each time they correctly guessed what part of an object or what object in motion had made a particular impression. Ideas can come from anywhere.

CHILDREN AT HOME

Children do not leave their curiosity at their school or play group. A major part of life's learning occurs at home for children, among the family members and family pets. The home is generally the most comfortable setting for children and therefore allows freer reign to their curiosity and experimentation, given that parents desire these possibilities. The home is also the setting for strong emotional bonds, therefore the events that happen at home and the knowledge that is acquired there is often vested with an emotional significance that is not duplicated elsewhere. A little boy remembers the occasion when his dresser drawer got stuck and his older sister showed him how to lift up on it each time to get it to work. The reflection on this physical event was vested with the love and care the young boy felt from that significant other in his life, his older sister. The little girl vividly remembers how to make the soap bubbles drain down the tub by herding them down with the flat of her palm, because Mom was there smiling. It is only natural that we include the home setting in our discussions of the young child's conceptual development.

The home necessarily places restrictions on play that are not as true for a classroom designed specifically for children. The home is a multi-purpose space and serves children and adults alike. Therefore parents will find themselves in the role of the disciplinarian and admonisher more often than even they themselves wish. But with some planning parents can discover that they can spend quiet times with the children, observing them explore and experiment, and at those times enter the child's world as a partner in discovery and invention. Toward this end we have a few comments to make.

To enter the child's world, dispense with your thoughts about warning or directing the child. Prepare the environment as much as possible beforehand so that the fragile items or areas that have to stay clean are not a continual obstruction to the child's play. Now spend the first five minutes or so carefully observing what your child is doing, what goal she sets for herself, what means she uses to obtain these goals. Do not expect to recognize the goal right away. Sometimes the goal is just to test the limits of the material or the medium. How much can I wind the toy up? Can I color over the entire page? Does this lid come all the way off? Objectives for the 2- and 3-year-olds stay very close to the physical materials themselves, while objectives for 4- and 5-year-olds become more thematic, such as setting up a sequence of cause and effect or trying to make particular patterns with the Water Pencil.

Once you feel the rhythm of the child's play and have a budding sense of the child's objectives, then you should imitate the child's play somewhat. Do this in a casual manner as if your actions were your own idea. In this way you will both get a better sense of what the child is doing and at the same time prepare the child to notice you without feeling pressured to perform. After all, your play is not a direct request for the child to do something that deflects him from his self-set goals. Indeed, the fact that you begin your entry with an imitation of the child's play serves to amplify the child's self-set objectives. Of course you cannot imitate the child if she is playing with the only Scaled Down Floorplan in the house, but you might ask the child if you can play with a portion of the toy set.

Once you have been accepted in the child's space you will no doubt receive glances from her. She is interested in what you are doing. At first she sees that you are just having fun as she is. Then after a while you begin to introduce new ideas into your play, not into the child's play. The child witnesses your variations on her play and either sees possibilities for her own play or does not. Either way this is all right. If the child picks up the cleverness of your variation, then the child is ready to assimilate that variation into her own play to make it her own. If the child does not see the cleverness of your idea, telling her will probably not lead the child to assimilate its meaning.

For example, say you have decided, after a period of jumping your doll from room to room over the walls as did your child, that you now will only move from room to room by walking through the doors cut in the walls. This adds an element of realism to the symbolic play. The child may look on your actions as cumbersome and unnecessary or she may pick up on its symbolism and then make it her own by generalizing this constraint to other situations, i.e., toy cars that now are not allowed to drive on the grass, but only on the painted roads. The door is left open for the child to decide.

In the course of this type of parallel play you may find an occasion to add a slight challenge. You may remember how the teacher, Lisa, added a slight challenge in the Wheels and Wedges by moving one of the wedges inward, thereby making it necessary for the child to make some adjustment, either in the wheels or the wedges. This type of challenge is effective when the adult has a very good sense of the child's tolerance for "friendly disruptions." A parent is in a good position to know the child's reactions in advance. Yet reactions change with a change in mood and with the quality of the interaction at that particular encounter. One must assess both the general frustration tolerance for the individual child, and also the range of this tolerance as the rapport between parent and child fluctuates.

Given that the play has been unhalting and creative, and given that the child has had sufficient experience with the material to make its use familiar, the parent can introduce the challenge in a casual manner. A car won't roll because it picked up a piece of gum on the wheel's rim. The spoon is lost in the sand and now we need to invent a new shovel. My string has a knot in it and I can't get it through the pulley. My water pencil is clogged with sand and it does not drip. The incline on the Hot Wheel is steeper now and the car will not shoot off the end. Will the child lower the incline some or build up the start-up shoot more? This type of challenge, or "conflict inducement," as we have called it elsewhere (Forman and Kuschner, 1977), can be a useful way to extend a home-based or school-based learning encounter to concepts beyond those spontaneously considered by the child.

Yet we once again caution the reader to realize that there is no pressure associated with the introduction of these small challenges. If the child is amused by them and takes them on as a game to be played, an interesting problem to solve, that's great. If the child wants no more than to ignore the variation or ask that you put things back as before, that too is fine. In fact, if the child does not sense cleverness of your variation or sense the implicit request for him to reverse your modification, that should be seen as a sort of diagnostic about the child's understanding of this particular system of relations. Such interactions with the child are all part of fostering constructive play, through fostering the child's understanding of events and our understanding of the child.

CHILDREN AS A WHOLE

The activities mentioned in this book have centered on children's encounters with the physical world of objects, such as balls, balances, paint, sand, and water. Even the social activities, such as the Sharing Chariot, Tote Together, and the Co-op Board, involved physical objects. We did not include role play, story telling, and other activities that have traditionally been used to foster the expression of feelings. We could have, and perhaps we will in a future book. But before you conclude that we have omitted one-half of a whole child, let us make a few comments.

First, there is no way that any set of activities, no matter how designed, can "omit" the emotional and social parts of a child. A child playing in the block corner does not leave her emotions in the role-play corner. Second, the same intelligence that decides whether a block will stand or fall also decides whether a peer will be kind or mean. The child's intelligence is unitary and does not shift to a completely different mode of functioning when dealing with her feelings and with other persons' feelings. This last section will elaborate these two comments.

The Whole Child

The distinction that educators make between the social world and the physical world is a surface distinction. Given that children use one intelligence to make both types of events coherent, they no doubt must use their knowledge of objects to increase their understanding of people and must use knowledge of people to understand objects. "I'm feeling jerky," the nervous child says. "That play dough [too limp to work with] is lazy," says the same child on another occasion. If we teachers move in quickly with our corrections that "help" the child make the social world/object world distinction, are we truly helping? Might not our corrections cause a split in the way that the child thinks about the world? We could maintain that any such split is inherently bad pedagogy and works against the whole-child principle—to wit, help the child make coherence of the world.

Certainly, it could be argued, we do not want children to treat people as objects or objects as people. Think of the indifference children might develop toward the intentions and feelings of people. Think of the mistakes they will make if they assume that inanimate objects can will their own movements and the guilt they might feel if they attribute feelings to a broken toy. We would agree that these types of confusion should be dispelled, but to focus on the absolute difference between the social world and the physical world is probably not the best means toward this end.

Instead of fighting the child's attempts to personify objects and objectify persons, we should try to understand these attempts. These are not "errors" in any absolute sense. They come from somewhere. The child is trying to apply the same rules of understanding to both objects and people. Yet it could be that the adult culture with its ready-made vocabulary, one for objects and one for people, diverts the child away from rules that could commonly apply to objects and people. Children are socialized and taught by rote that a doll is not a person and little brother is not an object. What they could dearly use, however, is an awareness of themselves and the world that applies to both objects and people. We call this awareness *interactive consciousness*.

The Aware Child

Help children become more aware of their own role in creating social and physical events. The child who has become aware of the role she plays in what is happening has increased her interactive consciousness. She has discovered that what happens is an interaction between herself and her surroundings. Whether the event is a rotating easel or a crying playmate, the child who has the means to reflect on her role in the production of these events will increase the coherency of her world. The more coherent the world, the more "together" the child feels.

Interactive consciousness can develop equally well in reference to objects or people. Consider a child trying to push a ball down an incline, when a simple release would improve his success rate. This child is failing to use the natural movement that "resides" in the objects—that is, what we call gravity. The child is being egocentric in the way he treats the ball. He assumes that motion derives its power from the self—that is, the push. So he is overdetermining the movement of the ball.

But if this child developed greater interactive consciousness, the role of the self would not be overgeneralized. The child with a greater interactive consciousness would know that, in a push down an incline, part of the motion is determined by the action of the hand and part by the natural motion (gravity) inherent in the ball. This awareness is what we call *savoir faire*. Savoir faire is doing just what is necessary to get a rather precise result to occur, a delicate touch and subtle move. Savoir faire requires a concentration on the present and an intimate familiarity with the medium. It is one result of interactive consciousness.

What about examples of interactive consciousness in reference to people? Consider a child who is trying to carry the play stretcher with another child. Bobby, in the rear, pushes forward a little faster than Nauman is walking. Bobby, feeling the resistance of Nauman, pushes harder. Nauman, feeling the pressure from behind, balks, drops his end of the stretcher, and walks away. Bobby asks Nauman to return, but Nauman does not. Is Bobby aware of his role in Nauman's decision to leave? Bobby could think that Nauman was too slow, tired, distracted, or anything else that externalizes the source of Nauman's behavior—that is, makes it independent of Bobby's own behavior. In other words, Bobby could have underdetermined the role of himself as a source of Nauman's behavior.

Alternatively, Bobby could reason that Nauman has his natural motion (preferred rate of walking) and felt rushed by the pushes from behind. The latter demonstrates better interactive consciousness. Bobby, in this latter case, is both respecting the attributes of the other person and acknowledging his own role in determining what happens around him.

The point we are making here is that the whole-child approach to education sets interactive consciousness as its goal. The pursuit of this goal need not fragment early-childhood curriculum into art, reading, group games, physical-knowledge games, or movement education. If we had to use any one category to denote this pursuit, we would do well to choose *spiritual education*. We realize the risk in using the term *spiritual*, because it evokes images of Bible school and religious training. But we define *spiritual* in the secular sense of an openness to ourselves and the world around us.

The Open Child

To open, we must find gates through barriers. Gates are nothing more than a means of easy access to different regions. This access results from an awareness of the limits and resources of the self—which is attempting to negotiate from one region to the next—combined with an awareness of the limits and resources of the terrain through which one is moving. The combination of these two forms of awareness is interactive consciousness.

The concept of the *spiritual* takes the notion of permeable boundaries as its essence. The concept of the *whole* also takes the notion of complete access to all regions as its essence. A whole divided into two parts inaccessible to each other is two wholes. A child who constructs barriers to parts of his world is deprived spiritually, less than whole, and less than open to the world around him. The barriers that a child constructs are usually some form of egocentric thinking, either overdetermining or underdetermining his role. Teachers and parents of young children can do a great deal to facilitate interactive consciousness and thereby improve the spiritual quality of the child's life. This openness to the world can be found in people who have made friends with objects and respect the natural motion of friends.

The Growing Child

As children continue to grow, they become more aware of the bias they inject in the events they see. There is a profound continuity between childhood and adulthood, in the sense that interactive consciousness continues to be a goal of self-development. As adults we rework the same problems that we had as children, only in different forms. To illustrate this point we will take the case of Alex, tugging steadily on the pendulum ball.

Alex has pulled the ball all the way up to the pulley hanging from the ceiling. He wants the ball to come down. After a slight tug he notices that it does not come down; so he tugs harder. He should release the ball to let it come down of its own accord. But he tugs as if the ball is disobedient. He has overdetermined his role in regard to the behavior of the ball. Eventually Alex, like his older friend Loren, will learn to consider the role of the object as well as his own role. Now, what analogous situations do we find across the span from childhood to adulthood?

Assume that Alex learns not to make futile attempts when tugging ropes. But before he learns this savoir faire with ropes, he has probably assimilated other things to this scheme. Call the scheme this: when an action meets resistance, increase the force of that action. So, even if Alex learns savoir faire with ropes, his initial scheme has already generalized to analogous situations. For example, when a jigsaw piece does not fit, he will press it harder. When a block falls off the tower, he will put it back on and press harder. Even after he learns not to pull the rope harder, he still has assimilated this scheme to more advanced situations. He never quite gets away from the application of this scheme and thus never quite gets away from his need to increase his interactive consciousness.

In adulthood this scheme—when an action meets resistance, increase the force of the action—can take even more advanced forms. For example, when my friends do not like me, I try harder to be popular. Or when a Frenchman doesn't understand my high school French, I speak louder. These inappropriate schemes that we used as children are always with us. The continuity between childhood and adulthood is two-fold—(1) in terms of the analogous problems that we face across our life span and (2) in terms of our need to be more aware of our own contribution to our interpretation of the "facts."

Early-childhood educators need to understand more fully the nature of the continuity that defines the growing child. If we can develop means by which to heighten the child's awareness of *procedures*, as we have been emphasizing in this book, this might also be a means to increase interactive consciousness. And because interactive consciousness is a recurrent theme throughout life, we are probably helping children in a very significant way.

APPENDIX

The following items are commercially available materials that were useful for many learning encounters in the School for Constructive Play. We did not specifically select and purchase these materials. Rather, we found them as part of the laboratory school's equipment and adapted them for our use. We realize that many programs do not have the resources required to purchase these items. Nor do we feel that they are necessary in order to carry out a Piagetian preschool curriculum. For those who can consider the purchase of these materials, here is the necessary information:

From New England School Supply, P.O. Box 1581, Springfield, Mass. 01101, came the following (page numbers and prices are from the 1978 catalog):

1. Nok-Out Bench, Playskool, p. 22, #PS 101, $7. Peg-pounder bench with inner channel.
2. Roll-a-sphere (called the Blue Bubble at the School for Constructive Play), p. 37, #7040, $34. Hollow ball 30 inches in diameter.
3. Tike Wagon, Little Tikes, p. 38, #4840, $12. Small plastic wagon.

From the 1977–1978 catalog of the Childcraft Education Corporation, 20 Kilmer Road, Edison, N. J. 08817, the following are available:

1. Moon Buggy, p. 41, #7A 527, $49.95. Large four-person vehicle of steel tubing.
2. Pipe Put Together, p. 58, #7M 575, $49.95. Pipe pieces and joints.
3. Connector, p. 62, #7M 118, $24.95. Wooden set similar to Tinker Toy but larger.
4. Girders, by Asmeca, p. 64, #7M 502, $39.95. Plastic construction set with wheels and bolts.

Available generally in toy departments:

Wonderful Waterful, by TOMY, approximately $5. Water-powered ring game.

INDEX